'Tim Farron offers a stark alternative to the self-help guidebooks that promote narratives of success and acquisition. Instead of living the dream, he speaks of personal failure; in place of self-aggrandizing spin, he is transparent and self-critical; and rather than blaming others, he takes responsibility. In the process, he presents a compelling case for the upside-down economics of the Christian gospel: that the first shall be last, and that we can live for a better ambition.'

Martin Bashir, Religion Editor, BBC

'This book is a challenge to the religious illiterate and liberal illiterate. If you are either, read this book at your peril but, whoever you are, you will find it refreshingly (at least for a politician) frank, humble, faithful and full of grace.'

David Burrowes, former Conservative MP for
Enfield Southgate

'Tim Farron knows better than anyone the stresses and challenges of leading a party in the febrile politics of our time. But this is not a conventional political biography. It reveals, in frank and courageous detail, the acute conflict between political loyalty and religious commitment.'

Sir Menzies Campbell, former Leader of the
Liberal Democrats

'Those who know Tim Farron personally will not be surprised by this book. They know his anger at injustice and his generosity of spirit first-hand. I would recommend this book to anyone who knows him only from headlines. You may not end up agreeing with everything he says, but you will be inspired, be a whole lot wiser and perhaps even be ready to follow his lead into public service.'

Andy Flannagan, Executive Director, Christians in Politics

'A provocative read for many in politics who would rather all politicians thought the same. You might not agree with everything Tim Farron says here, but it deserves to be heard.'

Isabel Hardman, Assistant Editor, The Spectator

'Tim tells a fascinating story of family, football, faith, music and politics. It is a story about private and public, highs and lows, passion, pressure and pain. As a friend of Tim – with a parallel commitment to equality and social justice, and to advancing both our shared liberalism and Christian faith – I watched, encouraged and supported him for years as his star rose in the British liberal sky. He became the most decent, skilled and valued campaigner and colleague. And one of the best communicators in British politics. Yet in leadership, very publicly and surprisingly, Tim was seen to struggle with communication. So it is to Tim's great credit that he now is willing to share not just the story of his journey, but also his considered reflections and questions and answers. Many of us can learn from this book. I am certain that, with gratitude, many will.'

Sir Simon Hughes, former Deputy Leader of the Liberal Democrats and Minister of State for Justice and Civil Liberties, 2013–15

TIM FARRON

A Better Ambition

Confessions of a Faithful Liberal

First published in Great Britain in 2019

Society for Promoting Christian Knowledge
36 Causton Street
London SW1P 4ST
www.spck.org.uk

British Library Cataloguing-in-Publication Data
A catalogue record for this book is available from the British Library

ISBN 978–0–281–08358–9
eBook ISBN 978–0–281–08360–2

Typeset by Fakenham Prepress Solutions, Fakenham, Norfolk, NR21 8NL
First printed in Great Britain by TJ International
Subsequently digitally printed in Great Britain

eBook by Fakenham Prepress Solutions

Produced on paper from sustainable forests

Contents

1

Take-off

I was above the clouds when it all happened. Blue sky above, rolling seas of cotton wool beneath, and the Midlands beneath that. An 11 a.m. flight from Manchester to Newquay was the first step in my tour of the West Country and Wales in the run-up to the May 2017 local elections.

While I was in the airport lounge, I'd heard that the Prime Minister was making a statement at 11 a.m. I had also seen the lectern standing ominously outside Number 10 and my heart fluttered when I noticed that the lectern did not carry the government crest – a hint that this might be a statement she would make as a party leader rather than Prime Minister? But we boarded the plane and took off before we knew anything.

Fifty minutes in the air, guessing. Guessing and listening to *The Race for Space* by Public Service Broadcasting. While epic things were going on beyond my knowledge down below, why not listen to something even more epic – the triumphs and disasters of the US and Soviet space programmes set to music? It almost took my mind off things. Almost. In that sterile state, out of range of the developing news from Number 10, I took the chance to compose myself, to work out how I felt. Was I dreading an early election? Was I excited? The answer was that this was surely what I'd been aiming for all these years, ever since I'd joined the Liberal Party at 16. To lead your party is the political equivalent of playing football for your country. And to lead the Liberal Democrats through a general election – up against the Prime Minister and the Leader of the Opposition – is the political equivalent of qualifying for the World Cup and playing against Germany and Brazil.

Christians pray. That really shouldn't come as a surprise. It's like asking newsreaders whether they read the news. Nevertheless, the questions I have been asked by journalists most often are 'Do you pray?', 'Do you pray for Theresa May?' and 'Did you ask God's will before you did X?' Having sometimes answered these questions with an innocent response – which is usually some version or other of 'Yes' – it became clear that these questions are often asked for a sensational write-up, which inevitably ends with my being made to look like some kind of pious, otherworldly weirdo. So, I learned to say that my faith was a private matter to avoid that line of questioning. However, on that flight I prayed. I prayed for wisdom and a right response to the tumult that was, in all likelihood, going to be unleashed when I landed. I prayed that the election wouldn't be called after all – not least because I had a holiday booked with Rosie and the children in the Hebrides in May and I really didn't want to have to cancel that . . .

On that latter matter, my prayer was answered. With a no.

I landed at Newquay. Airplane mode was switched off. I waited for a signal . . . I rushed to Twitter to see what had happened . . . and cursed. No Hebridean holiday for me. Theresa May had called a general election.

I emerged from the small terminal building to be greeted by Jon Aylwin, one of the party's finest organizers and agents who had that 'nothing surprises me any more' look on his face. We drove to Truro where a hastily arranged rally had been called outside the city's beautiful cathedral. There, standing among the placards of orange diamonds, the excited and slightly shell-shocked Liberal Democrat activists cheered as I walked towards the square. I began with a short speech – 'This is the chance for the British people to change Britain's future', a deliberate allusion to the opportunity that the election afforded to voters who wanted to reject the direction Theresa May had chosen towards a 'hard' Brexit, with the UK leaving not just the EU but also the Customs Union and the Single Market. I also pointed out that the Prime Minister had clearly looked across the Commons' despatch box, seen a divided and apparently unpopular Labour Party led by Jeremy Corbyn, and been unable to resist the temptation to dash to the polls. This was a Prime Minister expecting a coronation, who was taking the country for granted, and whose party was in dire need of an opposition. If Labour had opted for Trotskyist fantasyland, then the Liberal Democrats could be that opposition instead. It didn't quite turn out that way in the end, but it sounded plausible enough – and who is to say that we won't end up somewhere like that in the not-too-distant future?

It seemed serendipitous that an election campaign we weren't expecting was to be launched in the epicentre of Cornish liberalism. Truro – the seat of the late David Penhaligon, the man who more than any other had painted a picture to me, then 16 years old, of a politics I wanted a part of: idealistic but earthy, internationalist but community-focused. His death in December 1986 came just three months after I'd joined the Liberals. Since that time, the party had grown from one MP in the Duchy, to winning a clean sweep of all five in 2005, only to be fully wiped out to zero in 2015. Cornwall may not always elect Liberals, but it *is* liberal: non-conformist, independent-minded and unaffected. It reminds me of my own Cumbria in that respect. I wanted to be the leader who got Liberal MPs from the land of Penhaligon back into Parliament. I failed, by just 350 votes. But on that sunny April lunchtime, in the first few hours of the campaign, it seemed as though things were moving our way. A text from the party's chief executive, Tim Gordon, told me that we were having another membership surge triggered by my call to pro-EU voters across the country to grasp the opportunity that this snap election presented.

The diary was torn up. I was to return to London that night, instead of heading to Cardiff and Brecon for what was to have been my next local election visit. Nevertheless, we stuck to our plan for me to speak at the rally in Bristol, in aid of Stephen Williams, the Liberal Democrat candidate for West-of-England metro mayor. Stephen had been an outstanding MP for Bristol West from 2005 to 2015 and a remarkably bright and capable minister for local government during the coalition. I'd known Stephen for about 17 years, since the time we'd both been first selected as candidates for our constituencies in the late 1990s.

Stephen was one of the many casualties of the Liberal Democrats' electoral annihilation in May 2015 when 56 Liberal Democrats in Parliament were reduced to just 8. The rally went well, but it was turned on its head – rather than me being the warm-up for Stephen, Stephen became the warm-up for me. The cameras were there, and our message was clear – we're the only opposition party ready for this election, the official opposition is hopeless, Theresa May is taking you for granted, Brexit will be a disaster . . . the Liberal Democrats are the answer.

There is no doubt that we were having the best start of any party. The early evening news bulletins had a self-crowning Prime Minister standing alone in Downing Street, a startled Jeremy Corbyn standing alone in front of a camera, and pictures of me in front of excited activists, meeting voters and sounding up for the fight. We were lucky that my local election itinerary for that day had helped to set up those images. The result was that over the coming days our membership kept going up, heading towards 100,000 and indeed past the 101,000 which had been our record high under Charles Kennedy during the Iraq War. The polls were moving for us too – from a starting point of around 6 per cent we started clocking up 12, 13 and 14 per cent. After the rally in Bristol, I went out to speak to the cameras . . .

The next 50 days were a colossal challenge. I'd set out two years earlier to save the Liberal Democrats and the project was going very well. Our membership was soaring, our local by-election results were at an all-time high. In the 2016 local elections, we'd had our first net gains since

2008 – we'd taken votes away from the Scottish Nationalist Party (SNP) in the Scottish parliamentary elections, we'd had the great result in the Witney by-election (moving up from fourth to second place) and the immense win by Sarah Olney over Zac Goldsmith in Richmond Park. My choice, to focus our revival on the twin track of liberal community politics at the grassroots and standing proud as the pro-European party on a national level, was reaping rewards. If the general election was to be in 2020, we were set to make a serious comeback. All was going well.

The calling of the 2017 snap election risked all that. It was at the very moment when the Brexit issue was at its most emotional. Most who had voted to leave saw no reason to change their mind, and most who had voted to remain had moved into a state of mind that said, 'Well, it's just not cricket to complain when you've lost,' leaving a relatively small proportion of voters who felt strongly enough that our place in Europe was worth fighting for. The problem of course was that those people tended to live in metropolitan areas and had strong liberal values across the spectrum so they were easily put off by the sight of this weird northern bloke who couldn't give a straight answer (no pun intended) to a question about whether gay sex was a sin. It was not the best of circumstances to take advantage of this snap election.

Our other problem was that Theresa May seemed popular. It's easy to forget now, but at the beginning of the election campaign, the Prime Minister's 'strong and stable' brand was sweeping all before it. A party knows that it's doing well when people start repeating its main strapline, unsolicited

– and that's what was happening. 'Strong and stable' poured from the lips of the voters, and strong and stable seemed to sum her up. By implication, of course, it bracketed her opponents as the opposite. We were the coalition of chaos. 'Strong and stable' was a load of vacuous rubbish, but for the first part of the 2017 election campaign, it was effective.

2

Spaniels, buses and tricky questions

I returned to my patch on the Thursday and went canvassing in beautiful Sedbergh, the largest town in the Yorkshire Dales, yet now – technically – in Cumbria. It was obvious that the mood had changed dramatically in the two days since the general election had been called. People who had been inclined to support us in the local election were very much affected by the fact that we were now also facing a general election. Many of them were considering voting for the Tories, and those voters who were already supporting the Tories were emboldened by Theresa May's decision to go to the polls.

I'm pretty convinced that the Liberal Democrats would have made in the region of 200 gains in the local elections had we not been landed with the general election. With a general election now on the horizon, the local elections became a very different beast. The increased party tribalism that a general election brings, and the intrusion of the Brexit issue into what would otherwise have been local contests, cost us. Having said that, we increased our share of the vote by 7 per cent nationally although we lost council seats overall. Our performance was much better than Labour's or UKIP's, but UKIP's obliteration was largely to the benefit of the Conservatives, and so Theresa

May's party had the best local election night of any party for many years.

I spent 4 May, the day of local elections, in Cartmel helping our local councillor Sue Sanderson. Once the polls had closed, I headed south through the night to London as I kept up to date with the results coming in from my own area and from around the country.

Two crucial developments unfolded that night but I wasn't conscious of the second one at the time. The first was that in Westmorland and Lonsdale we had won the popular vote, but by only 1,000 votes. As the news was fed to me at 2 a.m. by my agent Paul Trollope, I felt sick. I had sensed that the Westmorland contest was far closer than people thought, and now I knew it for certain. I now had to lead my party and fight to save my seat at the same time.

The second major change was unexpected and didn't become apparent for several days. The Tories' huge success and Labour's failure in the local elections changed the terms of the general election. It meant that attempts by Australian political strategist Lynton Crosby to portray the election as a battle for Number 10 between 'strong and stable Theresa' and 'Jeremy the raving Trot', just didn't seem plausible any more.

The local election results turned the general election into a foregone conclusion, a coronation. From then on, people didn't feel compelled to 'cling on to nurse for fear of something worse'. Theresa May was going to win a landslide and so people were free to look elsewhere and cast a vote for a party that could provide an alternative.

Jeremy Corbyn has always struck me as a nice person. Genuinely principled, hard-working and good-natured. Of course, during the years of the Blair-led Labour government, he was always in the Lib Dem lobby, rebelling against his own party, so we saw a lot of him.

Soon after Jeremy became Labour Leader, I was in a taxi with the right-wing columnist Melanie Philips (the print version of a shock jock) on our way to appear on BBC *Question Time*. We discussed the rise of Jeremy and agreed that while we thought that his victory meant utter disaster for the Labour Party, there was a 10 per cent chance that his unspun, authentic and optimistic appeal could actually be hugely successful – which means that I was 10 per cent right.

Maybe Jeremy wasn't a plausible prime minister, but that didn't matter if the local elections had proved that Theresa May was a shoo-in anyway. That meant that people could feel safe voting for his values without having to worry about the possibility of his ending up in Number 10. The Conservatives had banked on their landslide partly on the basis that they assumed that Labour was fatally damaged by having a leader who was pro-CND, who had shared a platform with Hamas and the IRA, who was a Marxist and supported mass nationalization. But these were extremely flawed assumptions because, if you are under 40, most of this stuff is ancient history and has zero resonance, and whatever age you are, being warned off voting for someone in the hysterical political language of the 1980s just sounds unconvincing, and even off-putting.

Jeremy Corbyn's stock began to rise, so why didn't the Lib Dems rise with him? There are two reasons, the main one being that our hammering in 2015 meant that for the first time ever, the Liberal Democrats weren't even the third party, so our access to media coverage was extremely limited and, because of our greatly reduced size, we just didn't look sufficiently credible. Millions of people agreed with us on Brexit, and on our honest approach to funding the NHS by an increase in income tax, but with just nine MPs, we simply didn't have the mass to draw people into our orbit. You can agree with a party, but if you don't think it is big enough to be credible, you may decide to place your vote somewhere else. That's why my job as Leader was always to save the party from oblivion first before I could move on to the business of building us into a party that could aspire to being in government.

The second reason we didn't rise is painful to admit, but it needs to be said. It was because of me. As Leader of the party I was failing to get our message across because the brief airtime I did have each day was being eaten up with more and more ludicrous questions to do with my faith.

BBC Radio 5 Live's Nicky Campbell is one of my favourite broadcasters, and there was an apologetic tone when he asked me what I thought about the Bible's teaching in the Book of Leviticus on the consumption of shellfish . . . but he still asked it.

The focus on what my Christian faith did or did not teach on various matters meant that I was like a vandalized advertising hoarding: the intended message obscured by whatever someone else had daubed across it.

All this added up to the Lib Dems stalling, the Tories falling and . . . Oh, Jeremy Corbyn!

11

The leader's battle bus is a familiar sight during an election campaign. We had secured the Crystal Palace team bus, re-liveried for the Liberal Democrats' campaign tour. Custard yellow replaced the red and blue of Palace. Now, the Lib Dem bus used for the 2016 EU referendum had previously been Charlton Athletic's team transport. Charlton had at that stage been relegated from the Championship to League One, so the bus had the smell of utter disappointment about it. But Crystal Palace had just managed a hugely impressive escape from the relegation zone to remain in the Premier League, so we expected better things . . . and it was certainly a better bus. The back quarter of the bus was an enclosed space with a meeting table and soft leather seating. I dubbed this area the 'Pardew Boudoir' (after Palace's former manager, Alan Pardew) and it served as my home for much of the campaign. On the penultimate night of the campaign, it also served as a karaoke venue for both the Lib Dem team and the press organizations. That the papers have chosen not to make anything of the karaoke in the Pardew Boudoir™ may prove that there is honour among fellow travellers, that what goes on the bus, stays on the bus. Maybe. Of course, this rule does not apply to you if you are Shaun Connolly from the Press Association.

Shaun's main job seemed to be to inveigle himself into anything and everything and make a story out of it. My favourite Shaun moment happened at a service station near Oxford. I'd got myself a can of drink, a chocolate bar and – out of my love for all things Geordie – the latest copy of *Viz*. Shaun's eyes lit up as he sneaked along the outside of the queue and, with no shame, pushed in front of the chap behind me with his camera phone in an attempt to photograph me in the act of purchasing the UK's sweariest comic. I noticed him just in time and managed to turn the comic over so he couldn't snap the front cover, only to realize that the back cover was given over to an immensely rude advert for gentlemen's underwear . . .

The leader's battle bus is one of the clichés of general elections. Everyone has one, but what is the point? With around a dozen journalists from broadcasting and print media outlets joining us on our journeys, the point was to get me in a position where I had the best chance of influencing what was reported in the TV and radio bulletins as well as in the papers and online. The other key point was to give impetus to our campaigns in the places that we visited. Our visits were about adding to our media profile and giving a boost to our candidates in our most winnable seats. Starting with just eight MPs elected in 2015, and then adding Sarah Olney to our ranks after she won the Richmond Park by-election the previous December, we knew that our very survival depended not so much on the national air war, but on-the-ground campaigns in a couple of dozen constituencies.

The bus was commissioned quickly, and it first took us to Withington and Gorton in Manchester. We had high hopes of winning these two seats at the beginning of the campaign, one of which, in a parallel universe, now has a Lib Dem MP. I will explain . . .

Manchester Gorton was due to hold a parliamentary by-election on the same day as the local elections following the sad death of veteran Labour MP Gerald Kaufman. Our candidate Jackie Pearcey was a former local councillor, an academic, an incredibly bright and immensely well-liked member of the local community, and – for what it's worth – someone I had known since I was 16.

The Labour Party was in a desperate position with Jeremy Corbyn's leadership under so much pressure. Even the *Guardian* columnist Owen Jones was writing him off and calling for change at the top. The weekend before the general election was called, Liberal Democrat internal polls showed us heading for a sensational by-election gain. The morning that the election was called, we were planning to go for broke and release our figures in order to build up our credibility as the by-election campaign entered its final fortnight. Gaining a seat off the official opposition in a parliamentary by-election would have changed everything – we'd already taken Richmond Park in a Tory remain area, we'd increased our vote in leave-leaning places like Stoke and Sleaford, and now we were set to gain a seat in a remain-leaning Labour place where we'd previously come fourth. And in that parallel universe Jackie Pearcey is serving Manchester Gorton well as an excellent MP. But in this dimension, Theresa May's snap election plans meant that the by-election was cancelled. We will never know whether that polling was accurate or not. I wonder what would have happened if we had gone on to win that by-election? I suspect the pressure on Jeremy Corbyn to step down as Labour Leader would have become immense, coupled as it was with terrible local election results for Labour. And what then? I suspect that a major factor in the Conservatives' decision to hold that surprise early election was a desire to make sure that they took the chance to face up against the apparently weak, extreme and unelectable Jeremy Corbyn. If they had waited, then Labour might have got rid of Corbyn, chosen an electable moderate and then the Conservatives would have missed their best opportunity.

As Jeremy Corbyn's standing was reappraised in subsequent months, and his electoral appeal somewhat upgraded, it is easy to forget how tempting an opponent he appeared to be at the beginning of that unexpected election campaign. The Conservatives surely wanted to do all in their power to ensure that it was Jeremy leading the Labour Party at the time of the election, even if that meant bringing forward the date of the election to make certain that he was still in place. One way of looking at this is that maybe Theresa May made a clever decision to call the election when she did, but then was anything but clever about the campaign itself.

One thing Theresa May certainly achieved, probably by accident, was to stop the Liberal Democrats' revival.

In the previous ten months, our membership had all but doubled, we'd been winning council by-elections at a rate we hadn't achieved for 30 years, we'd had those great by-election results in Witney and Richmond Park and encouraging results in Sleaford and Stoke-on-Trent. The polls had us up into double figures and overtaking UKIP for the first time in five years. We had a USP. It was Marmite-ish but it was effective. We were increasingly confident of winning the Manchester Gorton by-election from Labour and were facing local elections on the same day where we expected to make more than a hundred gains . . . but then with just over two weeks to local election day, the general election was called.

With postal votes landing just 72 hours after the Prime Minister had made her announcement, we faced a local election campaign that had been turned completely on its head. People's minds were on 'strong and stable Theresa' versus the 'coalition of chaos', and their thinking was taken away from picking the best team for your local community and towards picking the best prime minister to see us through Brexit. For the two weeks up to local election polling day, this meant that the Liberal Democrat revival was stopped in its tracks while Theresa May hoovered up the votes. Our local election results saw an increase in our share of the vote by 7 per cent but it was washed over by a bigger increase in the Conservatives' share, and so those expected Liberal Democrat gains turned into losses – not as bad as Labour's losses, but still bad. And so our revival juddered to a halt in the early hours of Friday 3 May.

The first two weeks of the campaign gave us the veneer of a continued revival. We had energy, we had a message, we were edging up in the polls, even getting into the teens for the first time since the tuition fees debacle in 2010. Looking back though, it was clear that the wheels were coming off the bandwagon. My travails with the media over questions to do with my faith didn't help, but it was the transformation of the local elections into a prime minis-terial plebiscite that knocked the stuffing out of us. The results were clear. We'd lost seats, the Tories had gained and our claim to be a better, more interesting opposition than Labour just lost all credibility. After that, we didn't seem to get the chance to restore our momentum. We'd had a great ten months, but the revival had hit a wall.

Whatever we say now, at that point it really looked as if Theresa May had pulled off a stroke of genius in calling the early election. So what went wrong for her? Well, when you are the prime minister and you call a general election, you have the advantage of the element of surprise. The problem was that Theresa seemed to have surprised herself and her own party. If she had planned for this snap election, it certainly did not look like it.

At the Liberal Democrats' HQ we had a plan. Following Theresa May's elevation to Prime Minister in July 2016, there were many circulating rumours that she would go for a mandate-securing early election that autumn, to avoid Gordon Brown's fate of being afflicted by the whiff of illegitimacy for having no mandate of his own. That possibility of an Autumn 2016 general election led me to commission work on a manifesto and the outline of a campaign, including a leader's tour. With the calling of the election in April 2017, we were able to take those plans out of the drawer and put them into practice – we were out there in our big yellow bus before the other leaders mounted the steps to theirs.

The visits were exhilarating. The people I met were inspiring. The format was peculiar. I'd arrive at Manchester, or Edinburgh, or St Albans, or Oxford, or Twickenham, and there'd be a great crowd of people waving orange diamond-shaped posters, gathered to listen to me. I'd come down the steps of the bus, wade into a mass of handshakes and hugs, then speak some words of encouragement and inspiration to this crowd – with my back to them. Indie legends of the 1980s, the Jesus and Mary Chain, were famed for playing gigs with their backs to the audience, and I referred to this on my first couple of stops until it occurred to me that the chances of there being more than a couple of fellow nerds in the crowd who would understand what I was talking about were slim. Most would simply think I was making some obscure religious reference – and in the circumstances, no one wanted that!

This was not the only time that I'd say something that meant one thing but was taken to mean another.

I arrived at Cambridge, gave another speech to the cameras alongside our candidate and former MP, the effervescent Julian Huppert, with my back to the crowd and then had a nice chat with some local party members. One person had brought his dog, a terrier or similar. The dog took well to my stroking it and was having a smell of my coat sleeve, to which I responded with the enquiry, 'Can you sniff my spaniel?'

I have a spaniel called Jasper, and there is a chance that a terrier would be able to smell the scent of Jasper upon my coat, so it would have been an acceptable enquiry had it not been for two reasons: one, dogs cannot talk or understand complex questions from humans; two, I had my lapel microphone on which simply picked up the phrase 'sniff my spaniel'. Social media and the news bulletins were full of it for 24 hours. I suppose it was better than being asked about faith and sexuality. A school friend of mine, who texted me often throughout the campaign to offer his thoughts, told me that he thought 'sniff my spaniel' sounded like something Happy Mondays' front man Shaun Ryder might have said. You know – 'twisting my melon'/'sniffing my spaniel'. I can now imagine lots of E'd-up Madchester-types at the Haçienda in 1988 shouting, 'Sorted! I'm sniffing my spaniel. Man'. No? Well, I used to go the Haçienda and it sounded plausible to me . . .

Looking back, I'm rather proud of the 'sniff my spaniel' incident. I mean if you're going to make a gaffe, make sure it's completely bizarre, off the wall and unintelligible.

I also managed to steal some headlines for my ability to do a Norman Wisdom impression by haplessly falling down the steps to the loo while walking down the aisle of the bus at the same time as Darren McCaffrey from Sky was doing a live piece. If you're going to make a prat of yourself, do it well. I did it well. It was 'comedy gold', the kind of clip that gets sent into *You've Been Framed*, only there's no need to send it in because everyone's watched it now. Move on, there's nothing to see . . .

Perhaps the best thing we did during the campaign also happened by accident. It happened in Kidlington, a town in the Oxford West and Abingdon constituency. I was doing TV interviews in the square with our candidate Layla Moran when a chap came up behind me and started heckling. He said I was denying the will of the people, that I should accept Brexit and get behind Theresa May. His name was Malcolm, it was his birthday, and he'd especially travelled from another village to come and have a go at me as his birthday treat. I broke off from my interview and I talked to him. I took him on but tried to do it graciously. The best advice Charles Kennedy ever gave me was, 'Just be yourself, they can't catch you out that way'. Well, if Malcolm had come and had a go at me at one of my outdoor surgeries in Kendal, I'd have enjoyed the banter, I'd have treated him with warmth and respect, I'd have robustly disagreed with him, and I'd have made certain that we parted on good terms. That's exactly what happened here. It was one of those moments during the campaign when I got to properly be myself. It wasn't scripted. I was in front of the cameras and I just did what came naturally. Seven weeks of that kind of thing and who knows what we might have achieved?

All of us perform better when we are going with the grain, rather than against it. Having banter with voters goes with the grain. I love it. I like people – they're wonderful, they're different, they're complex, and if you try hard enough you can find something that gives you a connection. The most fun I have is when there are people like Malcolm who are desperate to think badly of me, and so when I try to treat them with warmth, kindness and grace, it completely discombobulates them. I don't just do it as a tactic, I do it because it comes naturally and because kindness and understanding ought to be demonstrated to all I come across, not just those on my side.

Keeping myself sane as Leader during the election campaign was a challenge. Maybe sane isn't the right word. Maybe 'happy' or 'at peace' is better? I love my wife and children. I love being with them. Being away for days on end makes me miserable. I got home as much as I could, including at the weekend just after the local elections, and took part in the Colour Dash in Kendal to raise funds for Cancer Research. It was one of only three times I managed to get out for a run in the entire campaign. The other two runs I did were in Edinburgh West and Bath . . . which, given that we won them both (along with Westmorland of course), means that we have a 100 per cent record of winning all the seats in the places I went for a run during the campaign. I should have done more running . . .

The Colour Dash involves running an easy 5 km around Kendal Castle while various people throw coloured paint at you. It mostly comes off in the wash and in the shower, with the exception of the paint powder that got into my contact lenses. I'm not sure if anyone noticed my looking like Marilyn Manson as I spent the next day or so with pink lenses.

The Colour Dash took place in beautiful Lakeland sunshine. The colour, the weather and the scenery contrasted with my spirits. Following the local elections three days earlier, I now knew that my seat was in peril. The questions about my faith, my answers to those questions and the impact on our campaign were getting me down. Seriously down. There was another five weeks of this, and I just didn't know if I could sustain it. And then, that afternoon of 7 May, Blackburn Rovers were relegated. I got home after the Colour Dash, incongruously looking like some kind of jolly children's entertainer in my multicolour-stained kit, and wept. I was nine years old the last time Rovers had been in Division Three. It hit me like a kick in the guts.

I'm not going to let you believe I'm so shallow as to be thinking that Rovers' relegation was the low point of those seven weeks. It was a low point, but it was expected . . . and there's always next season (indeed, we won promotion the next season!). I mean, when I started following the Blues we were in Division Three, and in the years that followed we've spent almost 20 years in the Premier League, we've won the Premier League and we've won the League Cup. If you'd offered me that deal when I was a child, I'd have bitten your hand off and happily accepted our subsequent decline as part of the bargain.

But the real low point happened almost two weeks earlier on 25 April when I chose to give a simple answer to a question that was so much more complex than most people realize. I gave that answer just a week into the campaign, a week after it had first reared its head on the evening of day one of the election. That first week had begun so well in the hours following Theresa May's shock announcement. The Liberal Democrats' immediate response to that snap election was so much better than Labour's. Our message was clear, and our optimism and positivity was tangible. We were surprised by the calling of the election, but we were obviously up for it. Our body language was full of confidence and expectation. Within hours, however, we were derailed by *that* question. I'd been asked it before, but it made its general election debut in an interview at the end of that first day on 19 April as I faced the cameras in Bristol.

The question was carefully crafted. 'Is gay sex a sin?' Well, what's the answer? If you aren't a religious person, in today's culture you might have two answers to this. The first instinctively would be 'no' and the second would centre on the anachronistic nature of any question that contains the word 'sin'. Sin is an alien concept. It implies judgement and disapproval and to even deploy it without irony or jest in

2017 was just odd. Journalists knew this. That's why they deployed the word and it's why I never did.

I don't judge people for their sex lives. I don't judge people full stop. For a simple reason: I am in no position to judge. Jesus makes it clear to his disciples in the Sermon on the Mount that we should judge no one. It's one of the few commands that I find easy to follow. But what many struggle to grasp is why the concept of sin is not anachronistic to people of faith; it is live, real and crucial. To be a sinner is to be one who instinctively turns away from God. And that describes me. It describes us all, in fact. By this definition we are all instinctive sinners. My failure to give the easy and obvious answer to the question of whether something constituted a sin caused many subsequent problems – as did my later decision to give a much easier answer on 25 April. More on that later, but for now let me make it absolutely clear, in case anyone still has any doubt, that I don't spend half my life simmering with disapproval over what people do in their sex lives.

I still feel pain at the assumptions behind the repeated questions I was asked about gay sex – pain that people look at me and think I am uncomfortable with or dislike people because of their sexual orientation, and that I must see them differently or care for them less. But back in Spring 2017 I had no time for such self-pity or reflection. The snap election had brought the Lib Dem revival of the previous ten months to a shuddering halt. Now, with the local elections having changed the terms of the last five weeks of the general election campaign, the party began to look in serious danger.

The Corbyn revival meant that our hopes of winning seats from Labour in places like Cambridge, Bermondsey, Vauxhall, Manchester Withington and Cardiff Central were declining to almost nothing. Worse still, Labour's popularity threatened to take out Greg Mulholland in Leeds North West and Nick Clegg in Sheffield Hallam. It staggered me that people would enthusiastically rush to support a Labour Leader who had done so much to enable Theresa May's hard Brexit – after all, Jeremy Corbyn had ordered his MPs to vote for the triggering of Article 50. What I have noticed over the years, though, is that voters are often willing to project on to a candidate, the cut of whose jib they rather like, everything they want that person to be and to discount anything they'd rather they weren't. That's the only reason I can think why centre-left remainers were getting behind Jeremy.

But with Labour seats looking out of our reach, the Liberal Democrats faced another serious challenge. Namely, that the seats we could realistically win against the Conservatives were so small in number, and so obviously on the Tories' own radar, that to win them would mean overcoming the bottomless Tory coffers. In seats like Westmorland, Richmond Park, St Ives, Cheltenham, St Albans, Kingston and Cheadle, the Conservatives were buying up newspaper advertising, direct mail, phonebanks, social media advertising and everything else you could think of in order to defend or to gain those seats. We were attacking and defending on a narrow front, we had no element of surprise and the Tories had unlimited pots of boiling oil to pour over those seeking to scale their walls. We also faced the problem of Labour-inclined voters who were so caught up in the thrill of the Corbyn comeback that they were beginning to forget about the need to vote tactically in Lib Dem/Tory marginals.

In Scotland, our campaigns in East Dunbartonshire, Edinburgh West, North East Fife and Caithness and Sutherland were going well, but the SNP are almost as well funded as the Tories and so our chances of going forward north of the border were by no means certain.

All that added up to a serious existential crisis. Probably the worst for the party since 1970 when we held six seats, three of which had majorities of fewer than 500. I saw one projection that would see us with just three MPs after the election, and that I wouldn't be one of them.

It seemed to me that I could take two courses of action: first, make sure that the party doubled down hard on around 20 seats and throw the kitchen sink at those campaigns. Second, I had a series of TV set-pieces and I needed to do everything I could to make them work to my advantage.

As Leader of the Liberal Democrats in the 2017 election, I had a disadvantage that none of my predecessors had encountered. For the first time ever, we weren't even the third party. I wouldn't have the opportunity that Nick Clegg had, to appear alongside the Labour and Conservative leaders and to debate them directly – to be considered as the main alternative to the big two.

Following the 2010 debates, 'Cleggmania' was a wondrous phenomenon which had epic consequences. I was there in person, in the spin room in Manchester when Nick won that first debate hands down. He was awesome that night, and it changed that election overnight and created the first genuine three-horse race since the 1920s. I recall being in Kendal market place 36 hours after that debate, being mobbed by locals and tourists, all wanting Lib Dem posters and stickers. One chap waited patiently for his poster, handed me his business card and said to me, 'My Facebook has gone bananas since Thursday night, I've not seen anything like it!' I looked at his card. He was an estate agent from Bury. His name was Nick Clegg . . .

'Fazmania' would be somewhat harder to engineer if I was up against half a dozen others all seeking their five minutes of fame.

Nevertheless, those set-piece TV opportunities looked to me to be absolutely crucial. The Liberal Democrats could face complete wipe-out on 8 June, that much was becoming clear. I always feared that possibility, and the eight of us who survived the 2015 election disaster had no automatic right to see ourselves as the springboard to a recovery. We might simply be the eight desperate souls clinging on to one of the funnels of the Titanic as it sank, still above water but destined to join the rest of our friends in the icy depths before too long.

Those debates and one-on-one interviews seemed to me to be the only chance I had to cut through and influence our national position at all.

I had my one-to-ones with Julie Etchingham on ITV and Andrew Neil on BBC1. I was also scheduled to appear on BBC's *The One Show*, in ITV's five-way *Leaders' Debate*, the BBC's seven-way *Leaders' Debate*, and on BBC's *Question Time* with Nick Robinson and an audience in Edinburgh.

Preparing for those set-pieces was a priority. But we also sought opportunities to make the news, to set the agenda, to get people on to our territory. We made the decision then to set the agenda – by leaving the country!

Monday 22 May started in Manchester with a trip to a Didsbury surgery with John Leech, our candidate for Withington. We then took the campaign bus south to Twickenham and Richmond to support Vince Cable and Sara Olney, and then, after a town hall meeting in Vauxhall where I'd seen off a fairly sorry attempt at being ambushed by a few Kate Hoey supporters, we made our way to Gatwick ready to fly to Gibraltar first thing in the morning.

The impact of Brexit on Gibraltar was huge. Support for Gibraltar remaining a UK territory is extremely strong especially among those who voted to leave, and yet Gibraltar had voted almost unanimously to remain, and indeed had voted heavily for the Liberal Democrats at the previous European elections. A trip to Gibraltar might have been a complete waste of our time in the middle of a general election, but not much else was getting us noticed so we thought it was worth a try to get our case across.

At 11 p.m. that night, as we were finalizing the arrangements for our trip the following day, the news came through of an explosion at the Manchester Arena. Many were feared dead at an Ariana Grande concert and most of those affected were children. I cancelled our Gibraltar visit.

As the hours went on, it became clear that this was a terrorist attack, a lone wolf in all probability. Children had died in the blast, as well as parents who were waiting outside to collect their children, and staff – in total, 22 dead, dozens injured, some horrifically. All my children knew people who were at the concert. The wait for news on each of them was excruciating, all the time knowing that there were mums and dads now being confronted with the unbearable news that their child was not coming home. It's easy to say that tragedies like this put things into perspective, but they do – at least this one did for me.

As a lad from Lancashire, Manchester was always my capital city. It's where I went to see the bright lights – trips to the Haçienda and to Affleck's Palace in the 1980s, the Smiths, New Order, the Stone Roses, Anthony H. Wilson. A bomb in 1996 had transformed the city, and in defiant response Manchester had risen reborn as the great counter-point to London, the capital of northern Britain – with a soft-hearted, big-hearted arrogant swagger. The attack on Manchester felt personal to me.

Politics goes on. I should explain, of course, that the election campaign was then suspended – all parties agreed that as an act of respect to the victims, there would be no national campaigning for now. But politics went on because it became apparent that the Conservatives were seeking to prevent a return to campaigning until after the bank holiday weekend. The bombing had happened late on Monday 22 May and the Conservatives were seeking a delay in the campaign until the following Tuesday, 30 May. On the Wednesday, I spoke to Jeremy Corbyn and we agreed that to allow such a long hiatus was to play into the terrorists' hands – after all, what was it that the murderers of those children were trying to achieve? Surely it was to subvert our democracy, to commit an assault on our values and our way of life? That being so, wasn't it wrong to let the terrorists have what they wanted? In the midst of an unspeakable tragedy, you would hate to think that others are using it to their advantage, but it was now quite obvious that the Conservatives saw this as an opportunity to prevent further debate, and freeze the campaign at a point where they still apparently had a commanding lead.

On the night of 23 May, I joined Home Secretary Amber Rudd, Jeremy Corbyn, Manchester Mayor Andy Burnham and thousands of citizens in Albert Square in Manchester as we paid tribute to the victims of the attack and stood in defiance. Tony 'Longfella' Walsh, the Mancunian poet, read out 'This Is the Place', his stunning and inspiring ode to Manchester, its people and its heritage. The hairs on the back of my neck stood on end as the whole crowd held its breath, hanging on to every one of Tony's words, proud to be Manchester, and proud to be in Manchester. There is so much vanity expressed through the media and social media as politicians and others seek to express themselves at awful moments like this, but there was a sincerity and authenticity to that gathering, galvanized by the poetry, a hearty 'Up yours!' to the attack that had brought such heartbreak and tragedy just hours before.

Today, I cannot remember the terrorist's name, but I remember Tony 'Longfella' Walsh and I remember so many of the people I spoke to in the square and in the streets afterwards. I remember talking to an elderly couple, asking them, 'Have you come far?'

'Oh yes!' said the lady, quite earnestly. 'We're from Oldham'.

Lovely. I remember chatting with people queueing to go into a gig at the old Albert Hall, fewer than 24 hours after those murders at another gig just up the road at the Arena. That's defiance for you. I shook hands, exchanged a couple of hugs and wished them a great evening. As I walked away from the Albert Hall, I did a double-take. There was a poster on the side of the building that grabbed my attention – it was an advert for the Avalanches, in concert, two weeks after the election. I love the Avalanches. I really love the Avalanches. I count their first album, *Since I Left You*, as my second favourite album of all time (I'm afraid nothing quite competes with *Steve McQueen* by Prefab Sprout). There were so many competing emotions, the hideous tragedy of the previous night, the visceral grief and anger, the warmth of that long sunny May evening, the almost joyous defiant camaraderie on the streets, my own personal turmoil over the campaign and now this wonderful promise that Rosie and I were going – there was instantly no doubt that we were going – to see the Avalanches after the election (we did, and they were awesome).

Elections take place in time and space – they are linear and have a chronology but perhaps some things only make sense when you look back on them.

The manifesto launches were a case in point. Labour's manifesto was leaked several days early. At first glance this seemed symptomatic of a chaotic leadership caught off guard by the early election. That might have been an accurate assessment, but the consequence was that Labour got two bites at the cherry when it came to unveiling its policies. Its manifesto was of course an uncosted work of fantasy, but it contained plenty of good populist stuff which caught many an imagination: re-nationalization, increased spending on pretty much anything you fancied, scrapping tuition fees, and repaying existing student debt. The one thing worse than no hope is false hope, so Labour must be relieved that it didn't win because there is zero chance it could have delivered on much of this. The sense of betrayal directed at Jeremy Corbyn had this happened would have made the treatment dished out to Nick Clegg after 2010 look warm by comparison.

But the double exposure of its brand of left-wing populism helped the Labour Party enormously. It contrasted with the disaster of the Tory manifesto. Who remembers anything from the Conservatives' manifesto aside from their so-called Dementia Tax? The Dementia Tax was surely a political own goal. It was demonstrably unfair and hit at the Conservatives' core support among older voters and home-owners. However, I don't believe that this policy would have been fatal if Theresa May and her team had toughed it out and made the case for it. What killed the Prime Minister's reputation wasn't the Dementia Tax, it was the U-turn. As the Tory manifesto unravelled, I was sitting in the Pardew Boudoir™ at the back of the yellow bus and was about to tweet 'not strong and stable, but weak and wobbly' when Michael Crick beat me to it. No hard feelings! But the phrase stuck. The Prime Minister's USP, that she was solid, reliable, unflappable, grown-up and in control, just evaporated in the space of a morning. I don't claim to have known that at the time, but in retrospect that was clearly the moment that she plucked defeat from the jaws of victory.

What about our manifesto? Well, we pretty much had ours already written in readiness for the October 2016 election that never happened. But the Liberal Democrats have never lost an election because our manifesto wasn't worthy or long enough. We are famed for well-written, detailed, well-costed manifestos . . . that nobody takes any notice of. We chose to double down on our flagship policy of offering a referendum on the Brexit deal which would give people the option – as Vince Cable has put it – of 'an exit from Brexit'. On the domestic front, we majored on offering people the opportunity of paying 1p in the pound more in income tax in return for a significant boost in funding on health and social care. This was a strong policy chosen because the NHS and care are in crisis and matter to just about everyone, and also because politicians never tell the voters that they are going to increase taxes, so our decision to do this was attention-grabbing and carried with it an air of integrity, of telling voters something they sensed must be true.

Of course, though, if we insist on having a manifesto policy on the legalization of cannabis and regulating sex work (however justified and wise those policies are), don't be surprised if the media decides to talk about those issues instead. My key learning point on this is that if you've got key messages on the NHS and Brexit, don't get them lost in a fog of sex and drugs . . .

3

Rallies, debates and recounts

Our manifesto launch took place at Holland Park School in London – dubbed, to the school's distaste, the socialist Eton (mostly because Tony Benn's children went there). I was interviewed by BBC, ITN, Sky, Channel 4 and Channel 5. Every one of them, with the exception of the BBC, wanted to focus on my views on abortion. Great. We saw this coming. The previous day we had got wind that Labour had fed the media an interview I had done with the Salvation Army's newspaper *The War Cry* about ten years earlier. In that interview I hadn't called for abortion to be made illegal or for the law to be substantially changed, but I had referred to abortion as something that was a 'tragedy'. If I wasn't Leader, I'd have unpacked what I meant. I mean, of course each abortion is a tragedy. Isn't it an insult to women who have abortions to suggest that it's not, or that it's a trivial, benign or neutral event? Doesn't the denial that abortion is a tragedy just play into the hands of those who seek to judge and condemn women and who suggest that they make that choice lightly? I believe that in many situations it can be the least wrong or tragic of a set of appalling choices. But I was Leader, and so this approach would have just riled people and eaten up all the space I had to set out our messages on health and

Brexit, and so I felt I had to dismiss this latest challenge and move on.

My response under questioning then was that my language ten years earlier was poorly chosen and that I supported choice under the law. This was a true statement. *I do think abortion is wrong*, but I also think that it needs to be legal so that women aren't forced on to the backstreets. Given that the law exists, I accept women's ability to choose to access abortion in that safe and legal context. But what good are we doing when we assert a child unborn is not human and has no rights? We might try to use language to fool ourselves, but it remains a mystery to me that people who are liberals or of the left, and who are so motivated by a desire to stand by the vulnerable and the helpless, are able to perform mental gymnastics in order to ignore the plight of those human beings that are the most vulnerable and helpless.

My view that abortion should remain legal comes from a compassion for women in desperate situations, a pragmatic acceptance of social realities, but not out of a belief that this is about rights. It isn't liberal to airbrush out a human being's freedoms simply because it doesn't fit with a current world view.

Again, tough talk, but at the time I gave a weak, semi-apologetic answer that was just about true in order to get me – and more importantly the party – off the hook so that we could move on.

Our manifesto launch event was that evening in a Bethnal Green nightclub. The party's former Director of Communications, James Holt, was back on board for the duration of the campaign and had put together a slick, energetic set complete with a stage depicting the Union Jack and EU flags. The atmosphere was fantastic, and our pitch to the voters was clear – if you want to stop Brexit, we're your only hope!

Our position in the polls wasn't moving. We ran the risk of dropping out of the story altogether. I made a clear choice: ramp up our position on Brexit, better to be Marmite than irrelevant. I'm sure now that this decision saved the party. It gave us a reason to be.

The manifesto launch was on Wednesday 17 May, and the Manchester terrorist outrage happened on the night of Monday 22 May. In between, I had done a round of Sunday interviews, including one with Sophie Ridge on Sky where once again I was questioned on abortion and my views on a number of matters as a consequence of my faith. My recollection of that particular interview was that I lost my patience a little, and challenged Sophie that people had a right to a private faith. I went straight from the interview to my church in Kendal. It was good to see friends that I hadn't seen so much recently. While I was chatting with people after the service, it became apparent, though, that the media was investing quite a bit of energy in investigating our church. Several members had been contacted by journalists. Journalists had been to a number of services to collect intelligence of what weirdo Farron really believed!

One of our elders – our former, now retired, pastor – is Brian Maiden. He's the main reason we made the decision to go to Parr Street Evangelical Church about ten years ago. Listening to his sermons online was what persuaded

Rosie and me to move from our Anglican church to Parr Street, because the church's teaching was clear, biblical and inspiring. I remember walking into the Commons one morning years ago listening to Brian on my MP3 player, when my friend Greg Mulholland came up behind me and asked what I was listening to.

I replied, 'Brian Maiden.'

'Iron Maiden?' said Greg . . .

Now it turns out that there is an Iron Maiden tribute band called Brian Maiden – suffice to say that our Brian hasn't heard of either of them. Brian, it turned out, had given a fairly full and frank exposition of church teaching to a *Daily Mail* journalist. It was clear, then, that we were now just waiting for the moment when a several-page splash would appear, tearing into me and my beliefs.

After my wriggling on questions on previous matters, I had set my face firmly not to give in if the media came after my church. These were my friends and I wasn't going to throw them under a bus.

I assume that article was written. I don't know what favours my skilful former press advisor Paul Butters had to call in or debts he had to rack up in order to keep it from publication, but it never saw the light of day. A blunt assessment is that the terrorist attacks, especially the outrage on London Bridge and Borough Market on the weekend before polling day, just displaced second-order stuff like Farron and his whacky religious views. I almost wish that the article had been printed. I felt such a weakling having equivocated on previous questions relating to my faith, that I relished the chance to learn from that and to make a stand. We will never know whether I would have kept my bottle had the story come out.

The first set-piece came on 5 May, a one-to-one interview with Julie Etchingham for ITV. Again, the subject of my faith was a focus for Julie's questions, but by now I had begun to perfect the straight bat of 'my private faith is not up for discussion' before pivoting on to what we needed to talk about. Attached to my interview was a separate interview with one of my best friends, Ian Cuerden, tracked down by ITN researchers via the forensic wonder that is Facebook. 'Cuey' and I had been at school together and been really close friends since our mid-teens. Ian is gay. I remember his coming out to me when we were on holiday with my mum and sister in 1990. I'm aware of the danger of ever employing the 'some of my best friends are gay . . .' defence when accused of not being tolerant or liberal in such matters, but in my case it really is true. Ian was interrogated about me and my views, and how I had responded to his coming out. He was kindness personified. We'd often talked about sex and sexuality in the past. I mean it's the sort of thing you do talk about with your best mates. Ian knew what I consider to be the Bible's teaching on these matters. He also knew from experience that I judge no one and accept everyone as they are. Such nuances are irrelevant in an election, though, and typecasting me as a religious nutter was maintained . . .

Just a few days later, I was in front of Julie Etchingham again, this time in Manchester as she chaired the five-way *Leaders' Debate*. It would have been seven-ways but neither Theresa May nor Jeremy Corbyn came along. The debate was therefore between me, Nicola Sturgeon, Caroline Lucas, Paul Nuttall and Leanne Wood. So, we were a group of pro-European *Guardian*-reader types versus the Pub Landlord! It was always going to be hard to shine in that size and type of line-up but, according to most of the polls afterwards, I was judged to have come first or, at the worst, second. I was a bit ranty, and apt to turn just about every answer into a story about my personal family experiences. The line 'I grew up in Preston . . .' started getting groans in the spin room, apparently. Nevertheless, I made my points well, was fluent and didn't drop any clangers.

The next set-piece was a few weeks later and it turned out to be fairly emotional and cathartic. Unlike Theresa and Jeremy, I wasn't deemed significant enough to get my own on-the-couch interview for *The One Show*. Instead, it was decided that there should be a piece about me and my background filmed on location. The agreed venue was the Anchor pub in Lostock Hall, between Preston and Leyland. The Anchor Inn was our local when we were in our teens and 20s, right up until I moved to Cumbria when I was 28. The pub stands set back on Croston Road, close to the railway bridge on the east Lancashire line, opposite a row of about 20 terraces. In the midst of those terraces is the family home of another of my best childhood friends, David Smith. David's mum and late dad had hosted us on hundreds of evenings after closing time at the Anchor and also provided the venue for David, Robert Nickson and me to do our band practice sessions. We used to agree that David's home was the model for Caroline Aherne's *The Royle Family*. I was interviewed while sitting in the cosier part of the pub, the area that we used to sit in once we'd grown up and where older people used to gather. I don't recall all that I said in the interview, only that being in the Anchor opened the lid on a whole range of memories that must have been lurking at the back of my brain.

One in particular was that the very corner where we were sitting happened to be the same place where, in 1998, I had earnestly sought David's advice, as I was plucking up the courage to ask Rosie to marry me. (A few weeks later, on Christmas Eve, I asked her and she said yes.) After the interview was over, there was an amount of hanging around so I legged it over the road and knocked on David's mum's door on the off chance she was in. Linda's granddaughter Lianne (David's sister's daughter, born the night I went to university in 1988) answered the door. She and Linda were astonished to see me, and I was overwhelmed to see them. It was a beautiful moment of pure joy, proper friends, old friends, big hugs – for me, a brief oasis in what was becoming an emotional desert.

The campaign was into its last nine days when the rather unwieldy seven-way BBC1 *Leaders' Debate* took place in Cambridge. Mishal Husain did a good job chairing this odd and pretty awkward event. Unlike ITN, the BBC did permit parties to send whomsoever they wished to take part in the debate – the Conservatives sent Amber Rudd and Labour looked likely to send either Emily Thornberry or Barry Gardiner. The SNP sent their Westminster leader, Angus Robertson, rather than their leader Nicola Sturgeon. Greens, Plaid Cymru, UKIP and the Liberal Democrats all planned to send their leaders. That morning, it became apparent that Labour was likely to deploy Jeremy Corbyn after all. On arrival at University Senate House for the debate, there was a huge crowd of Corbynistas – and for the first time I got to hear the 'Oh, Jeremy Corbyn!' chant. I've seen the White Stripes live and seen them perform 'Seven Nation Army' from which the chant is borrowed, but even so, a crowd of a few hundred Cambridge Trots singing Jezza's name to the guitar riff is still pretty impressive. The Momentum crowd also seemed to have infiltrated the audience at the debate. There was no way that the crowd inside Senate House were in any way a balanced group. This wasn't a problem for me. They tended to clap along with me; they treated Amber Rudd and Paul Nuttall as the pantomime villains, and Jeremy got cheered to the rafters for what was actually an average performance. If you get cheered every time you clear your throat, you're going to come across OK. Jeremy's main and most significant achievement, though, was to turn up, which contrasted beautifully with Theresa May's absence. With barely a week to go, the impression of a weak Prime Minister hiding from the voters was being solidified, and Corbyn's star continued to rise.

Even so, most of the polls after the debate had me down as the winner, which isn't bad in a seven-way fight. My main contribution came down to a piece of luck. Before the debate had begun, we had drawn lots as to who spoke in which order. For the final closing remarks, I was drawn sixth of seven, and Amber Rudd came out seventh. This presented me with an opportunity to attempt to steal the show. I had 30 seconds, so I chose to use about 10 seconds restating my pitch, and for the remaining 20 seconds, I said:

> Amber Rudd is up next. She is not the Prime Minister. The Prime Minister couldn't be bothered to turn up. *Bake Off* starts on BBC2 in two minutes. Why not switch over now? Theresa May doesn't think you're worth her time, don't give her yours.

I was pleased with that, and grateful to my team for giving me the idea in the first place. In the months after the election, it's the line that I got quoted back at me on trains, in the street, in the pub – it's nice to know that I had a 'moment'!

But winning a seven-horse race wasn't enough to help me move our poll rating up more than by a point or so. I was running out of ways to improve our position. Maybe I am looking at this the wrong way? Maybe my performances in the set-pieces were part of what kept us in the picture, maintained our vote and helped us to win those 12 seats. Maybe without them we would have disappeared without trace?

We had come through that seven-way debate with flying colours, but my biggest test was fewer than 24 hours away.

The next day was 1 June – my date with Andrew Neil. Andrew Neil is a very tough interviewer and he has a particular style. With rare exceptions, his strategy is to destroy his interviewee and the chief tactic he uses is to ask a difficult question, then wait for you to get a sentence or so into answering it, before then firing a second, then a third, then a fourth. It's very effective, it knocks you off your guard, it opens you up to further lines of questioning, it puts him in control, and you can look as though you are on polished ice sliding all over the place. It normally works. I'd been done over by Andrew before and I thoroughly respect him for it, but I couldn't afford it this time. If my other set-piece TV appearances were a chance for me to put the ball in the back of the net and get three points, my Andrew Neil interview was a fixture where my task was to grind out an ugly nil–nil draw. And that is exactly what I did. Andrew came after me on the Brexit second referendum, that I was snubbing the will of the people, that I am not a democrat, that I was a bad Brexit loser, etc. . . . I answered the first question he asked me and I wouldn't let him draw me on to the second until I'd dealt with the first, so he attempted to talk over me to get me to answer number two before I'd got to the end of number one, so I spoke over him and he raised his voice and interrupted me, so I spoke slowly and firmly and interrupted him back. He'd asked me a question and so I was going to answer that question before he tried it on with his follow-up, or the follow-up to the follow-up.

It was like driving a car. When all is said and done, I was in the driving seat, I was going to go as slowly and steadily as I needed to in order to retain control of the vehicle. Andrew was the icy patch on the road, but if I kept my cool and trundled over him gently, I wasn't going to spin out of control. And then (back to football metaphors) the final whistle went. A tricky away point was in the bag. Off air, Andrew was unflattering about the interview and exasperated with my performance. Good. Job done.

The response I got from the public was mixed. I'd come across as a slippery politician in the eyes of some. But my job was to stand up to Andrew and defend my goal. As every football supporter knows, sometimes when you play the best teams, you just have to close up shop and have a game plan to keep out the other team. It is never pretty, but it is effective. I was proud of my day's work.

Maybe I was tired, or maybe I was feeling too pleased with myself after the previous two days. Whatever the reason, 2 June was a less successful day. I did the Nick Ferrari show on LBC – a phone-in discussion. Nick's a fair, effective and incisive interviewer. But it wasn't Nick who tripped me up. A listener rang in who angrily accused me of being a homophobe and I was angry back. No one likes being misunderstood, especially if you feel that the misunderstanding is deliberate, fabricated and contains with it an attack on your integrity. So, I ended up in a row with this caller. He spoke cleverly, as though I had expressed a view that his relationship with his partner was invalid, and as though I had judged him to be inferior. All of this was invented or imagined, but it was an effective tactic, whether he meant it as such or not. The cool calmness that I showed against Andrew Neil the previous day was lost in this particular contest. This all invited the 'Is gay sex a sin?' question again, which this time I refused to dignify with the cheap and simple answer. It wasn't a car crash, but it was a bit of a prang and it threw us off our step for another day.

On leaving LBC I did, however, get some good news. Our tracker poll for Westmorland and Lonsdale had me narrowly back in the lead. Well within the margin of error, but nevertheless it showed momentum swinging our way. The previous polls had showed us losing. In the end, I held my seat with a majority of 777. That poll on 2 June convinces me that, had the election been held two weeks earlier, I would have lost. We swung the campaign back in our direction in the last few days. Anecdotally, my TV set-pieces had an impact on bringing people back to us in Westmorland. However, the belief that I was safe coupled with a jubilee atmosphere around Jeremy Corbyn meant that hundreds of people voted Labour in our area, something that very nearly let the Conservatives in the back door.

But why did a man with a majority of 8,949, who had all the advantages of fighting an election as a national party leader, end up almost losing his seat? I can give you three reasons.

The Tories spent a fortune. They took out adverts, did direct mail, used paid phonebanks, brought in ministerial Special Advisors and did absolutely everything. They ran the kind of 'death star' campaign in Westmorland that had defeated dozens of my colleagues in 2015.

However, none of that would have helped them very much if it hadn't been for two main factors. I was Leader. People in Westmorland and Lonsdale rightly expect their MP to be immersed in their community, being attentive, involved, active and effective. As Leader, I continued to work just as hard locally but, when I was on TV every night from different corners of the country, jumping off the big yellow bus in Bath, Twickenham or Edinburgh, it was easy for the Tories to cast me as absent. I was accused of having lost my way, of going native, of not belonging to our community any more. In the eyes of some, I'd become one of those London politicians.

The third reason for my much-reduced majority is Brexit. As I said earlier, after the referendum I chose to fight for those whose hearts were broken and futures stolen by Brexit. I did it because I believed it and I felt it myself, but I also did it to save the party. I did it to give us a unique selling point, to create a sense of purpose and mission, to make us relevant, and to give us a reason to be. It worked. It saved the party. But I always knew that it was a position that might cost me my seat. Thousands of my most loyal supporters in Westmorland had voted to leave. Half of them forgave me and stuck with me. But half of them didn't. We were also at that point in the post-referendum era when more than half of those who voted to remain had decided that the only option was to go along with Brexit.

Looking back, given all that, it's a miracle that we won in Westmorland. I don't know what the future holds, but wherever I go now in the constituency, people tell me, 'We're so glad you're back.' This is a fascinating phrase. It tells you that people thought I'd gone away, but it also tells you that my return was welcomed, that my bridges aren't burned, that there is all to play for.

On 3 June I returned to Edinburgh ready for my *Question Time* appearance the following day. I had a campaign visit after which we prepared for my grilling by David Dimbleby and the studio audience. Then we went out for dinner. Throughout the campaign, being with the Lib Dem staff team kept me sane. Ben Williams, Christine Longworth,

Paul Butters, Sam Barratt, Phil Reilly, Fionna Tod, Vinous Ali, Daniel Callaghan, Meliz Ahmet, Simone Van Beek and many others joined us on the campaign bus during that time. All of them lifted my spirits, all of them demonstrated an awe-inspiring commitment to our campaign, a loyalty to me and an ability to make the whole experience seem fun and worthwhile. Despite the pressure that we were under, there was a real joy and release when we found time to socialize. Lovely though it was to have our fellow-travelling journalists join us, there was a special sense of freedom about being together unobserved in a restaurant talking about banalities and having a drink. That night out in a Lebanese restaurant in Edinburgh sticks in the mind for the fun we had, and for the horrific realization when we returned to the hotel that there had been a further terrorist attack, this time on London Bridge and at Borough Market. It was a different kind of attack from the one in Manchester, with more than one person, a vehicle and a knife as weapons, but the result was more death and injury – innocent people on a summer Saturday night out, caught up in horrific violence and tragedy.

We got up early the following day, still stunned by the attack and uncertain what the next few days would hold. It wasn't clear whether *Question Time* would go ahead that night or not. Jeremy Corbyn and Theresa May had done their slots the previous week, and tonight was Nicola Sturgeon's turn and mine, one after the other. If the programme was cancelled, we were running out of time to reschedule – but reschedule they did. Nicola and I got our chance the following night, but with Nick Robinson doing the honours rather than Sir David who was otherwise engaged.

So that Sunday was spent in a training room in our hotel, thinking through the issues that would come up at *Question Time* and considering the shifting landscape of the election in those final days of the campaign. During that day, Theresa May came out of Number 10 and made a statement. It was calculated, it was political, it wasn't statesmanlike, and it backfired. 'Enough is enough,' she said, as if there was a tolerable amount of terrorism that we could absorb but now we'd had too much. The language she used was of 'some' being apologists for terrorists, of those others not being tough enough, and so on. It was a clear pitch to seek electoral advantage from these terrorist outrages. I sat in the training room with Sam Barratt, Ben Williams, Christine Longworth and Phil Reilly, and we were stunned. I was appalled by Theresa's naked attempt to politicize the tragedy, but I confess I was also deeply worried that this bid would be successful. In the end, though, the Prime Minister's words sounded as grubby and calculated to the voters as they did to me.

Quickly, we responded – and so did others – that if we want to keep ourselves safe from terrorism, one key move would be to protect our police numbers. Who had been Home Secretary for six years and presided over the biggest reduction in police officers in British history? You guessed it. Theresa May's police cuts came back to haunt her and so a law-and-order Tory, playing the law-and-order card in the aftermath of a terrorist attack, was hoist by her own petard. How much this damaged the Conservatives, I can't say, but I can say that it meant that the debate in those last few days was on territory that robbed the Prime Minister of the chance to communicate her message. And something about that fairly transparent attempt to politicize this outrage made her look weak and desperate. 'Strong and stable' was a distant memory, and the more she fought to re-establish it, the frailer she looked.

Another night in Edinburgh, followed by flying breakfast visits to help Christine Jardine in Edinburgh West and Jo Swinson in East Dunbartonshire. We then headed south to Cumbria where I took part in my constituency hustings for Radio Cumbria. My Conservative opponent James Airey clearly believed that he was significantly ahead, which was alarming enough, but my impressive Labour opponent (Eli Aldridge, 18 years of age, in the midst of his A levels) was insistent throughout the debate that I was going to win anyway so people should feel free to vote for him. But the debate went well. I wished my opponents good luck and I legged it back to Edinburgh for the rearranged *Question Time*.

Eli may have been in the midst of his exams, but for me that *Question Time* appearance felt like my final paper. Sixty hours before the polls opened, I had my last big moment. The session went well, and in fact it flew by. I got the inevitable questions on sex and sexuality, 'Why haven't you answered those questions?' asked Nick. 'Because I'm not running to be Pope!' I replied, and the audience got it. It was probably too late to change the public perception of me, but my answer had been light but sharp, gracious but with a hint of irritation, and I sensed a huge amount of sympathy from the crowd. There had even been groans from a few when the question was asked, but my answer to all sides of that crowd felt right. Should I have deployed that approach from the beginning? Maybe, but we were too afraid of confrontation, too worried that we would look like we didn't respect the question or the questioner.

I walked out of that final exam and felt elation. I stood outside with Christine Longworth and Paul Butters, had a can of lager and a couple of Christine's expertly crafted rolled-up cigarettes and it felt great.

The end was in sight as I was picked up from my home in Cumbria at 5.30 a.m. on the Tuesday morning. Polls would be open in just over 48 hours. I kissed Rosie and the children goodbye – probably a selfish thing to do given they had another hour or so to go before they had to get up.

First stop was Radio Lancashire's studios in Blackburn where I did the *Today* programme without incident. My first campaign visit was to a care home in Southport for adults with learning difficulties, so I'm not sure why I had to go via Blackburn, several miles out of our way. But there was something reassuring, familiar and almost soothing about driving past Ewood Park, home of Blackburn Rovers and scene of so many formative experiences throughout my life during a week that – whatever happened – would surely also leave a deep impact upon me.

The visit to the care home in Southport was genuinely uplifting. There were the usual media interviews that seemed to go well, but the highlight was time spent talking with the residents about their artwork, the lovely garden at the home and, of course, football. I had landed in a nest of Evertonians who, with a mixture of pity and mischief, spent most of the visit reminding me of Rovers' recent relegation. I also observed Sue McGuire, our candidate for Southport, demonstrating the warmth and common touch that few of any party truly possess. She looked like she was enjoying being with people, not tolerating them. But the evidence on the ground in Southport was that we had fallen behind, and that defeat was likely.

We headed to a residential home in Cheadle next where our former MP, Mark Hunter, was bidding to win back his seat. As I came away, it felt like a tough call for us to win. If we couldn't win Cheadle, then our chances of getting into double figures were low, especially if I couldn't even count on holding my own seat.

The yellow bus took us next to Sheffield, to a factory in Sheffield Central with our candidate Shaffaq Mohammed. Nick Clegg came along to the visit too and was clearly immensely liked by the company management, but I confessed to being surprised that we didn't visit Nick's seat, Sheffield Hallam. The team on the ground told me that they were confident of holding on to Hallam, so they didn't want to make it look like we were overly concerned. A leader's visit would make it look as though we were concerned and – apparently – we weren't . . .

After Sheffield we made our way to Welshpool to visit Jane Dodds, our candidate in Montgomeryshire, the once-safe Liberal seat formerly held by Lembit Öpik, not a top target this time but a great prospect for us to build up for next time. On the way to Welshpool I made some phone calls for Westmorland from the back of the bus, with the curtain to the Pardew Boudoir™ drawn to prevent my being noticed by our travelling journalists. The last thing we wanted was for them to be alerted that I was worried about holding my seat. As I worked my way down the call list, the phone numbers of voters seemed randomly generated, at least not in any address order. So I was pleasantly surprised when the name and number of a stalwart supporter of mine came up.

'Hello Betty, it's Tim Farron,' I said.

'Pardon?' she said.

I repeated, and she repeated her confusion borne of being hard of hearing and so I repeated again as clearly as I could.

'Oh. Tim Farron! Yes, I'm voting for him. I'm a hundred years old and he's the only person I've ever voted for who actually won! I have a poster in my window, but please tell him I'm sorry I can't do any more this time. I'm a hundred now.'

'Thank you, Betty, but this is Tim. I'm Tim.' There was a silence.

'Oh Tim! Is it you?' And we both had a nice cry.

Having first voted Liberal in 1945, Betty Cain had always been so pleased to tell everyone she met that it took her until she was 88 to finally vote for a winner. As I put the phone down, I hoped that she'd be backing a winner again this time. I couldn't be certain.

We got to Welshpool to do a farm visit – my comfort zone. The journalists couldn't ask me anything about farming to which I wouldn't know the answer, and I gained perverse enjoyment from the blank looks on the press pack's faces as we discussed Pillar 1 and Pillar 2 of the Common

Agricultural Policy, the Upland Entry Level Stewardship Scheme, tariffs and other things alien to most people. I may not speak farmer as a native born, but I am nevertheless close to being fluent.

As we boarded the bus after the visit, Jane, a fellow Christian, promised to pray for me and I said I'd do the same. We pulled away from the farm and headed east. We had a quick stop for some selfies in the twilight with activists in Shrewsbury and then made our way to Solihull for our final overnight stop.

On leaving Shrewsbury, the mood on the bus changed . . . and out came the drink. For the first time in the campaign, I thought, 'Stuff this, I'm joining in!' So, along with our friends from the media I sat in the Pardew Boudoir™ drinking beer and taking part in the Lib Dem bus karaoke. I want it noting for the record that I sang every word of 'The Whole of the Moon' by the Waterboys entirely from memory.

We got to Solihull, to a fairly nice hotel. The party atmosphere continued, and I had a couple more beers and quite a few cigarettes before turning in. I checked my Twitter account and saw that I had a direct message from Wendy Smith from Prefab Sprout wishing me luck. Just in case you were wondering, this was a big deal. My teenage pin-up was mindful of me in those final stressful 36 hours. It was really thoughtful of her. I guess it's quite useful to have obscure tastes in pop culture. It means that your heroes aren't mega stars and they're a bit more accessible. I sent her a direct message back to thank her and then I texted a couple of my mates to make them jealous . . .

The eve of poll began at the crack of dawn in a café in Solihull. I had visited loads of different cafés and restaurants during the campaign and hadn't eaten so much as a crisp at any of them. My team were terrified of a 'Miliband moment', with my being caught on camera looking daft while eating something. Well, I had committed a pretty comprehensive list of mistakes, but among them was not a single food-related incident. Having served a 'café-ful' of activists and journalists for the last time in the campaign, I went into the kitchen, washed my hands, hung up my pinny and did a mini fist pump. I'd survived the election unscathed in one sense at least.

Throughout the campaign, though, my problem wasn't that I might get captured looking a bit silly. My problem was not getting captured at all. Maybe we spent too much time worrying about being careful when frankly I should have just been myself a bit more? You know – a bit of a prat, but at least authentic.

On leaving Solihull, we embarked on what turned out to be a glittering tour of seats that we would subsequently go on to win the following night. It was almost as if we'd planned it. We visited Twickenham first, had a quick rally in the high street with Vince where it seemed pretty obvious to me that he was going to regain his seat with a landslide. There was a tangible affection for Vince, but it was more than that. People were proud of him and were delighted to have the chance to 'right the wrong' done to him when he lost his seat in 2015.

We made the short hop to Carshalton to do a quick visit with the ever-energetic Tom Brake before heading to the

South West. Our scheduled stop was Bath. It had been noted, especially by the regional media, that my presence in the South West had been relatively limited in the last four weeks of the campaign. The reality is that while our pro-remain position on Brexit was challenging in the broadly pro-leave South West, it was also the source of our momentum. We had been heading for strong local election results in May, especially in Cornwall where we were hoping to take majority control, but with the arrival of the snap election, the political landscape changed overnight and, in the last two weeks of April, our surge was halted most visibly in the West Country by the appeal of 'strong and stable Theresa'. There remained some good prospects all the same. The city of Bath had been held by Don Foster for 23 years when he stepped down in 2015. We had lost the seat with a new candidate but with the city's strong opposition to Brexit at the referendum, the mood had changed in our direction. The candidate we selected in the days following the call of the snap election was Wera Hobhouse, who had taken on Jacob Rees-Mogg in the neighbouring constituency in the 2015 election. My last round of interviews was held in the rain outside Wera's HQ before heading inside for pizza with the activists.

We got back on the bus one last time to head for Oxford for the final rally in support of Layla Moran, our candidate for Oxford West and Abingdon. The rally took place at the Kassam Stadium, home of Oxford United FC. My green room was one of the hospitality boxes looking down on to the ground. All the boxes were named after famous players and managers of the club – mine was the Jim Smith Suite. It was fitting because Jim Smith had managed

Blackburn Rovers as well as Oxford United and had done pretty well with both clubs. The first game I ever saw was Blackburn Rovers against Oxford. It was a 1–1 draw with John Aldridge scoring for Oxford before Simon Garner equalized for the Rovers. Bored? So were the local party activists I chatted to about this outside . . .

There were no TV interviews at this one, but it was fed into all the main TV news packages. The message was that if you live in a place that the Liberal Democrats can win, then lend us your vote to change the future of our country and stop Theresa May taking you for granted. I looked into the camera and I didn't mention Brexit by name, but I did in reality when I said:

> You want to know why I am doing this? Why I am determined to change our country's future? It is this. In 20 years' time I want to be able to look my children in the eye and say that I did everything, everything I could to keep this country open, tolerant and united.

The crowd loved it, but it would have been had odd if they hadn't. Layla Moran gave a phenomenal speech before I came on. She showed no signs of the tiredness she too must have felt. She had been one of the stand-out candidates of the election, and it turned out that she would win a stand-out result the following night.

I left the Kassam Stadium at about 10 p.m. and was driven by car now that the bus was no longer required to my home in Milnthorpe. Everyone was asleep. Well, everyone but the dog. I sat outside on the wall with Jasper for a few minutes then I put him to bed and went upstairs. I got into bed about 2.30 a.m. I was too tired to worry so I fell asleep pretty promptly.

I was up in time to see the children off to school. It was clear from their expressions and their demeanour that the campaign was taking its toll. I think they knew that I had been under pressure, that this had hit their mum too and that there was a real risk that Daddy would lose his seat and lose his job. We aren't rich people so we couldn't take that easily in our stride. I mean we'd find a way to cope and we'd trust God to provide, but that morning I could sense feelings of real fear and uncertainty from the kids. I hated that. We'd tried to protect them from it all but at breakfast on 8 June, I felt that I'd failed to protect them enough. Whatever happened, I was determined not to put them through this again.

At 8 a.m. I was collected by my friend Giles Archibald, the leader of the local district council, and we drove from my village of Milnthorpe to Kendal, our main town. I spent the day in familiar surroundings. I don't just mean the familiarity of being in the South Lakes, but the familiarity of an election day in the surroundings that I had been used to for almost 20 years. We tend to have up to ten 'committee rooms' (informal mini-HQs) around the constituency on polling day. I was allotted to the committee room held at the home of Councillor Sylvia Emmott – known to us all as Auntie Sylv. Auntie Sylv greeted us with a warm smile . . . and a pile of leaflets. We were off to go and knock on doors on the Heron Hill estate in Kendal. Later though, we had to comply with the national media as I did my contrived 'voting shot'. It's the done thing for all party leaders to be filmed and photographed going into 'their' polling station on polling day. This was a sham, however, given that I had already cast my vote by post a fortnight earlier, and the polling station I was to visit that morning wasn't my polling station. My local polling station is in Milnthorpe but the polling station that the TV cameras and the press photographers had chosen was at the Stonecross Manor Hotel in Kendal. The sham soon became chaos though. Auntie Sylv came with me as I went into the polling station and had a quick chat with the polling clerks, both of whom I knew and who were highly amused by the charade outside. I shook hands with them both, told them I was looking forward to seeing them at the count later on and headed off to allow the media to get their exit shot. All was proceeding well, until I made my way down the ramp coming out of the hotel, when two cameramen who were pushing each other in the scrum came to actual blows, I mean rather serious, proper fisticuffs. The fight made the TV news, with me out of shot but Auntie Sylv looking suitably horrified in the centre of the frame. Goodness knows what the genuine voters thought of all this as they were coming in and out of the polling station!

The rest of the day proceeded more peacefully. I continued to knock on doors in Kendal, hour after hour until 8.30 p.m. when we decided that I would go to the Hallgarth estate at the north end of Kendal, off the Windermere Road. Hallgarth has a polling station right in the middle of it, at the community centre. I would spend the last hour and a half campaigning in a place that had loyally supported me for more than a decade. It might be my last hour and a half as an MP. I knew that we could lose. I could feel that it was close. One of my staff members, the epically named Sapphire Bleach, was busy running one of the committee rooms but her extremely positive and energetic mum, Debbie, was part of my team of volunteers as we rushed around the streets of Hallgarth reminding Lib Dem-inclined voters to vote. By 9.45 p.m., only Debbie and I were left. The light was fading. My Chief of Staff Ben and our volunteer driver Marcus were sitting in the car park by the community centre, but Debbie and I were going to continue until 10 p.m. If I lost by one vote, I didn't want to be in a position where I had packed up campaigning at 9.55 p.m. I was going to knock on doors until the final whistle went. I always do, but this time I felt that it really mattered.

We got one lady over the road to vote in her dressing gown at 9.50 p.m. I'm not sure who was the most apologetic. But then 10 o'clock arrived. The election was over. There was nothing more I could do now. As Debbie and I walked to the car, exhilarated that we had played to the very end, we got chatting about what would happen next. What would happen next of course is that I would go home, and that I would need to face the cameras parked outside our house. Rosie and the children had rung to tell me that there was no way into our home without going past them. Our back door only leads to a small garden, and behind us are the houses that front on to the A6 road. I was perfectly capable of talking to the media as I went into my home. Perfectly capable, but unwilling. The end of the election prompted a sudden sense of mischief. I knew what I would do.

Having dropped Debbie off in Kendal, Marcus drove Ben and me the eight miles south to Milnthorpe. As we entered Milnthorpe on the A6 road, I asked Marcus to drop me about 150 yards from the turn-off to our estate.

I then slipped up the driveway of our friends, Rick and Sheila Crawley (who were away on holiday), and into their garden. At the bottom of their garden was an old black, tin-roofed garage. I clambered round the back of this and over the fence behind it, then crawled up the bank, through the trees and brambles that led to the fence at the back of our garden. A few scratches later, I climbed stealthily over our wire fence, through our trees and tip-toed into the garden. I could see the arc lights in the street outside our house at the front, and I could hear the journalists talking. I made my way to our back door and rang Rosie, whispering that she should come down and let me in without causing a stir. Meanwhile, Marcus dropped Ben off at our front door and of course the media assumed that the car must have included me. This meant that there was sufficient distraction for me to quietly get into our house. Ben, Rosie and I were joined by Phil Reilly and Paul Butters, and the five of us were highly amused by seeing the reports on TV from outside our house saying, 'Tim Farron has yet to return home.' I would like to take this opportunity to apologize to those journalists and camera people. It was absolutely nothing personal.

The reports we were getting from the count in Kendal were mixed. It was going to be close. The Tories strongly believed that they had won. Labour's vote, though small, was up. It was going to be touch and go. Elsewhere, it became clear that we had lost two of my closest friends in Parliament – Mark Williams in Ceredigion and Greg Mulholland in Leeds North West – and that Nick Clegg was in real danger in Sheffield Hallam. Sue McGuire, our new candidate in Southport, looked increasingly unlikely to hold on to the seat in what had become a three-way scrap.

Of course, these weren't the matters that were exercising the minds of the commentators. Their focus was solely on the emerging drama that was the exit poll – the coronation that Theresa May had banked on when she had called the election had not materialized. There was to be no Conservative landslide. It looked as though there wouldn't even be a Conservative majority. This would be a humiliation for Theresa May, for her advisors and strategists. The election that was meant to provide stability and a mandate had delivered chaos and uncertainty. For the second time in 12 months, a Conservative leader had gone to the polls for selfish reasons and ended up brutally damaging the country in the process. The referendum was called by David Cameron after he made a manifesto promise to do so, only to provide a sticking plaster over the gaping wound over Europe that divided his party. The UK paid the price for his piece of temporary internal party management. Now the UK would pay the price for Theresa May's ill-judged power grab. It is often said that the electorate doesn't 'do' gratitude – how else could you explain Churchill losing the 1945 election? I wonder whether the electorate 'does' retribution? It felt like it for the Liberal Democrats in 2015. But the damage done to the UK by these two self-interested Conservative prime ministers far outweighs that done by any government I can remember. If there is any justice, the Conservatives should surely pay for this wretchedness for generations to come.

As the talking heads on TV became more and more excitable, and more and more interested in the Democratic

Unionist Party, I became aware that, despite our losses, the Liberal Democrats might quietly be making some interesting gains. Twickenham wasn't unexpected, but the scale of Vince's win was – he regained his seat with a 10,000 majority. Kingston came next, then Bath, East Dunbartonshire, Edinburgh West . . . A recount in North East Fife saw us miss out by just 2 votes, and then a recount in Richmond Park resulted in Sarah Olney missing out by just 45 votes to Zac Goldsmith. We had a near miss in St Ives, just 350 behind, and came agonizingly close to hanging on to Ceredigion after all, losing by just over 100 votes. North Norfolk returned Norman Lamb handsomely, as did Carshalton and Wallington for Tom Brake. Orkney and Shetland was a personal vindication for Alistair Carmichael. His huge majority was a defiant rebuke to the nationalists who had hounded him and his family mercilessly, seeking to ruin them, following Alistair's leaking of a memo in 2015. No one deserved victory more than Alistair. Victory in Eastbourne saw Stephen Lloyd returned after a two-year absence. Caithness and Sutherland came back into the Liberal Democrat fold as Jamie Stone ousted the nationalists. Oxford West and Abingdon was the icing on the cake. Along with Jo Swinson in East Dunbartonshire, Oxford's Layla Moran had something of 'being the future' about her . . .

I don't remember the order of all the above. I just remember being told at around 2.30 a.m. that it was time to head into Kendal Leisure Centre for the Westmorland and Lonsdale result. It was the first time in 12 years that I had approached the count without having a reasonably good idea of what the result was going to be. Ben, Rosie and I left the house, waved to the slightly bemused journalists outside who couldn't work out quite how I'd managed to get into the house, and got into the car. We waited for news in the Asda car park, about three minutes' drive away from the count. We had won and the Conservatives had asked for a recount. I was relieved and nervous in equal measure. I'd assumed that we were losing, but of course a recount could easily result in that majority being reversed.

Somewhat stunned, Rosie and I walked into the count to huge cheers from relieved activists and silence from the Tories who had apparently already briefed the media that they had won by 2,000. I shook hands with my opponents including, for the first time, Mr Fishfinger who, dressed as his name suggests, had decided to run for the election to make a point. I just can't remember what the point was . . .

Normally I spend a decent amount of time at the count. I get there early enough to chat with activists of all sides, to see the votes pile up, and to share the changing mood of the night with all the others in the room. This time, I'd come in only when we were fairly sure of the result. Ben, Paul and Phil were keen to keep me from the media. Maybe that was wise, but it meant that I hadn't experienced the ups and downs of the count with my team of volunteers who had clearly had a nerve-wracking time. I felt so grateful to them, not just for their hard, physical work, but for placing themselves on the emotional roller-coaster. This result was down to them far more than it was to me.

The majority was small, but significant. I won by precisely 777 votes. I didn't work that out until I'd finished a small number of media interviews, left the count and got back home.

At home, daylight had arrived with us and the children were stirring. Delighted and relieved and, in some cases, tearful at the result, we exchanged lots of hugs. After some breakfast Phil, Paul, Ben and I got in a car to be driven south from Milnthorpe to London. I slept much of the way and was taken to a rather posh hotel where a room was ready for us to prepare for my big speech at lunchtime. Phil drafted a good speech which I then tinkered with a bit.

I delivered the speech to an audience of supporters at the National Liberal Club where I was introduced for the second time in three days by Layla Moran, only this time Layla was speaking as the new MP for Oxford West and Abingdon.

Layla's excitement at having won her seat was infectious. It made me rethink my assessment of the overall result. Twelve seats. Put bluntly, out of the past three elections, this was the first in which the Liberal Democrats had gained seats. We'd been dead and buried two years earlier and now we'd survived and begun to grow. I looked around the audience at the National Liberal Club and I recognized dozens of members who had only joined us since we'd taken our bold pro-EU stance in the aftermath of the referendum fewer than 12 months earlier. From Layla, and from that crowd of new members I drew an overwhelming sense of achievement – between us, we had actually saved the Liberal Democrats and given us something elusive and special: a sense of unifying purpose. You know what? This had been a good result. That point seemed clearer when we considered the other parties' performances. Labour had outperformed its low expectations, but the others in the field had failed to meet their objectives. UKIP had been decimated, the SNP had suffered big losses and the Conservatives had lost their majority in an election that they had called for their own advantage. Our objectives were to survive and grow. While our performance wasn't as impressive as Labour's, out of the five main players we had done next best in terms of making progress.

No one (at least no one sane) is going to describe me as one of the great party leaders in British history. However, I am one of the few leaders who can honestly say that they achieved their major objective because, at the time of writing at least, the Liberal Democrats still exist!

4

Picking sides

In late May 1970, the England team were about to begin their defence of the FIFA World Cup, Harold Wilson was set to defend his parliamentary majority in the June general election, and a 20-year-old Susan Farron was rushed to Sharoe Green Hospital in Preston with her panic-stricken 21-year-old husband Chris. There, she gave birth to a fairly hefty ginger baby who promptly then pooped on his youthful father.

This means that I can claim to have been born while England were still World Champions (just), as Harold Wilson's new hope for the 1960s shuddered into the drudgery and decline of the 1970s and, to add to the sense of malaise, with the Beatles limping on in the final three months of their time together.

I was born at just the time when everything started going wrong!

My mum and dad had married the previous autumn and spent their honeymoon in Grasmere. I've got a lovely picture of my mum sitting by Rydal Water looking every bit the sixties starlet with her arms folded across her middle, concealing the first signs of being pregnant. This was probably a family scandal, but no one has ever spoken to me of it being so, and as a result I have never really enquired.

Chris Farron married Susan Trenchard when they were both just 20 years of age. Too young? I don't think so. I think it's good to have your children young. Rosie and I had three of our four children in our thirties, and my main concern is that I'll become too old and knackered to keep up with them as they get older. That's why I go running.

Nevertheless, my parents split up just before my fifth birthday. It's amazing to me how two incredibly young people could be so grown-up about something so traumatic. My sister Jo and I left our family home in Hoghton (midway between Preston and Blackburn) with our mum one Friday night to stay with our grandparents about five miles away. This wasn't unusual, but on this occasion, we stayed for more than a weekend. We stayed about 18 months. My mum spent every night in a sleeping bag on a Z-bed in the dining room. We were sad to leave home but too young to really understand. My sister was three and she barely remembers any of this. But from then on, Saturdays were special. Dad would come and pick us up late morning and take us out for the day. We'd go swimming sometimes at Brinscall's Victorian Baths or go on walks in the Trough of Bowland (Lancashire's version of the Dales), visit cousins, play football in the park and – more often than not – accompany Dad on his visits to the record shop. You see, my dad worked by day as a sales rep and later as a manager in the building trade. By night, though, he was a DJ at a nightclub north of Preston known as the Orchard Barn. I am proud of my dad for so many reasons, but as a child, I was proudest of all that my dad spun those wheels of steel and had his very own account at Mrs Allen's House of Records in Preston's Covered Market. I remember being intrigued, horrified and excited at the same time by the punk teenagers who hung around the record shop with spiky green hair, bondage clothes and safety-pin piercings – nothing this exotic had ever happened in Preston!

In the autumn of 1976, Mum, Jo and I moved out of my grandparents' house and into a two-up two-down cottage in Penwortham near Preston. The house was 200 years old, freezing cold, allegedly haunted and looked out on to Lostock Hall Gasworks. I loved that house. For the next 16 years it would be my home.

There was no privacy though, as it had once been a farm building and was very open plan. Mum's friends were, like her, children of the sixties. We often had those friends around. There were some in bands doing jamming sessions, people were smoking, the conversations were exciting, and everyone seemed to talk about 'big stuff'. After I'd gone to bed, I so often heard conversations that were either intriguing or just made no sense – a lot of weird hippy philosophy, astrology, re-hashed Nostradamus predictions, politics and the sexual revolution. I would lie in bed hearing all this. Mostly it was just noise, a comforting noise downstairs that helped me to feel secure as I drifted off to sleep.

One night I was in bed but in no mood to sleep while my mum had a couple of friends over. One of the voices was new to me, and one of them – my mum's great friend Yvonne – was familiar. The new voice belonged to a man I have never met and never even seen, but I heard him all right. He was a Christian. I don't know the context, but I recall him plaintively encouraging Mum and Yvonne to 'ask Jesus into your heart . . .' I was nine and his urgent-sounding request seemed to be directed at me. I have no idea what Mum and Yvonne said back to him, but I know that I screwed my eyes up and did exactly what the man had said – I asked Jesus to come and live in my heart. I hadn't the foggiest idea what this really meant. I didn't consciously follow it up, and I don't recall discussing it with Mum afterwards. Nine years later, as an 18-year-old, I would consciously 'become a Christian' but sometimes I ask myself whether that night as a nine-year-old might in reality have been my 'conversion moment'.

Born in Preston, and obsessed with football, I should naturally have turned out to be a Preston North End fan. Of course, most children at school followed the mighty Liverpool or Manchester United, but none of them actually went to games. They were football enthusiasts, not fans, and I was probably the same. But we had family in Darwen near Blackburn, and my Auntie Keva and Uncle Derek were dedicated Blackburn Rovers fans. Derek died suddenly when I was seven, but he had already fully indoctrinated his two teenage sons, my cousins Simon and Michael, in the ways of the Rovers. On Boxing Day every year, these two glamorous young men with Bay City Rollers haircuts, blue-and-white scarves and their dad's old rattle would leave the festivities and then return later on, hugely affected by what they had just seen at Ewood Park. I wanted a piece of that! There was something beguiling too about that unique blue-and-white shirt of two halves. There were teams in blue, teams in red, teams in white, teams who wore horizontal stripes, teams who wore vertical stripes, but no one wore different-coloured halves, at least not that I knew of. Glamorous cousins and a stand-out strip – that was more than enough to hook any ten-year-old back then.

Those were the days of football hooliganism, when violence and the English game seemed to be synonymous. My mum and grandparents were happy to let me have posters of Howard Kendal, Derek Fazackerley and Simon Garner on my wall, but I was 14 before my cousin Simon could persuade my mum to let me go with him to Ewood Park to watch a game. The result was a 1–1 draw with Oxford United. John Aldridge (later a League winner with Liverpool and a World Cup star for Ireland) scored first for the visitors before Simon Garner replied with an equalizer for Rovers. My first game was a love affair consummated followed by a lifetime of faithful devotion. You don't really pick your team. They pick you. I am not a Blackburn lad, but I am Rovers to the core.

At that time, I was more interested in politics than your average 14-year-old. But I didn't really have a passion for it. Like football, I saw it as something colourful and a source of entertainment. Margaret Thatcher (Conservative Prime Minister), Neil Kinnock (Labour Leader), David Steel (Liberal Leader) and David Owen (Leader of the Social Democrats or the SDP) were all household names to my generation, mostly because they were depicted every Sunday night in the satirical puppet show *Spitting Image*. The show's grotesque caricatures captured our attention. In those days there seemed to be two unifying televisual events every week – the music show *Top of the Pops* on Thursday night and *Spitting Image* on Sunday. The following day at school, we'd be full of 'Did you see . . .?' Then on Friday morning we would fixate on the bands we'd seen the night before, and on Monday morning there would be plenty of us doing bad impressions of the impressionists who did the politicians' voices on *Spitting Image*. Politics was an interesting spectacle, but I hadn't picked a side.

In Lancashire in the 1980s, with unemployment rife and poor housing and poverty alongside, it was rare to find fans of Margaret Thatcher. I've always been a contrary sort of person, as my choice of music and football team will testify. In my politics too, I rather enjoyed winding up my friends by saying that I liked Mrs Thatcher. But I had no idea of what she stood for. And as I became aware of the suffering of people I knew and loved as the recession bit harder, I understood that I didn't really agree with her, much as I admired her for being unpopular and apparently unaffected by this.

In the UK at that time there were just four channels: BBC1, BBC2, ITV and the new and exciting Channel 4. One evening I was sitting on my own watching the box when a film came on. We didn't have a remote control, and I couldn't be bothered to get up and turn over, so I acquiesced and continued to watch. The film was a repeat of Ken Loach's *Cathy Come Home*, made originally in 1966. The story focuses on the plight of Cathy and her husband Reg, a working-class couple whose lives slowly unravel. Reg's ill health and resulting unemployment leads to the family losing their home, and the couple separate under the pressure. In the end, Cathy loses her home and finds herself on the street where the authorities catch up with her and take away her children. The film ends with a distraught Cathy clutching her baby screaming 'You're not having my kids!' as Social Services remove both children from her.

Stunned, I sat there and read the caption stating that while this had been a drama, everything in the film was based on a real occurrence in England in the previous year. I broke down in tears and was brought out of my distress by an advert at the end of the programme for Shelter, the campaign for the homeless. I scribbled down the address for Shelter (this was a good decade before the Internet) and the following day I gathered together what I had saved from my previous three weeks' pocket money and went to the post office, where I bought a postal order for £1.50 and sent off for my membership of Shelter. Why had I been so affected? Well, I don't have a heart of stone. Anyone would have been moved. But I think I was especially moved for three reasons. First, Cathy looked like my mum and I knew that my mum didn't have that much money and had been out of work from time to time. Second, we knew people who had been homeless – a few years earlier a friend of Mum's and her two daughters had moved in with us in our tiny house for almost a year after the breakdown of her marriage. At the time it seemed like fun to us children, but *Cathy Come Home* made me understand something of the reality. Third, the thing that moved me was Cathy's plight, but the thing that angered me was the indifference of those in authority. Cathy was powerless and no one stepped up to help her. The weak need strength, the powerless need power and I wanted to be someone who would meet those needs. I didn't realize it at the time, but I had just become a liberal.

Televisual events are powerful. About a year later, the musicians Bob Geldof, Midge Ure and others organized the *Live Aid* concerts to raise money to relieve the appalling famine in Ethiopia. It was July 1985. My Dad was playing cricket that day, so I went to watch him at the Vernon Carus sports ground in Penwortham. It was a scorching hot summer's day, but I left my sister sitting by the pitch and sneaked inside to watch the concert. I remember some of the bands, but I remember more clearly the video footage from Ethiopia that punctuated the performances. The BBC journalist Michael Buerk and others brought the horror of the tragedy to life. We were a generation brought up on *Blue Peter* appeals. *Blue Peter*, the BBC's flagship after-school children's TV show, held an annual appeal. The children were invited to help raise money, often by collecting bottle-tops or similar for sending in to the BBC to reach a target amount. The funds would then go to help disadvantaged groups. These might include a group overseas, maybe even the victims of famine, but *Blue Peter* presented those crises in a sanitized way. We never got to see the true horror, and what's more no one was ever held to blame for their plight. These people were poor, unfortunate people who had become victims of something that was just, well, unfortunate. Then, while sitting in the cricket club watching the footage from Ethiopia during *Live Aid*, it occurred to me that famine, poverty and need are never just accidents, but rather the result of political failure or downright wickedness.

Picking sides

I was extremely lucky that my comprehensive school, Lostock Hall High School, had a teacher who offered the unusual option of an O level in economics (for the more youthful among you, GCE O levels were what we used to call GCSEs). Mr Hubbersty was, I suspect, a Labour supporter but he was always fair and encouraged us to hold opinions so long as we were able to back them up. My opinion of Mrs Thatcher and the Conservatives was sealed as I wrote an essay on inflation and unemployment in early 1986. The penny dropped that the Conservatives' strategy to keep down inflation was essentially based on artificially keeping unemployment high. People don't tend to spend that much money when they are out of work, so you can see that this would be an effective approach. Only, I knew people who were unemployed, and lots of them at that. My blood boiled.

The North of England was largely, if not entirely, Labour. Labour seemed to me to be part of the establishment and interested mostly in standing up for organized labour, not for the individual. As I paid more and more attention to politics, it was the Liberals I heard speaking out against apartheid, for gay rights, women's equality, fair votes so that everyone's voice was heard, and devolution so we didn't all have to dance to London's tune. My head was turned by the Liberals and their partners in the SDP. I was an awkward kid. I wasn't cool. I was affected by the desire to be liked but at the same time determined not to be conventional about anything. I resented any attempt to lump me into a tribe – I loved music, but wouldn't conform to one identity, not a goth, not quite an indie kid, not a punk . . . and definitely not mainstream.

It's almost as though I sought unpopularity, or maybe I was seeking attention. If fitting in makes you anonymous, perhaps standing out is what counts, even if you stand out for being a bit of a berk . . . Anyway, awkward kids don't line up behind the establishment. I'd concluded that the Tories were wicked, but that Labour were just the other half of the establishment. Stodgy and tribal. The Liberals appeared reasonable, human, radical and with no vested interests. If I was going to follow anyone, it would be them.

But then my exams got in the way. Once they were completed, I spent much of the summer of 1986 in the company of my friends – and with two of them, Robert Nickson and David Smith, I formed a band. Politics would have to wait . . .

It was a good summer. England had a decent World Cup – knocked out in the quarter finals by Maradona's handball. This was great really, because it meant that we could pretend that it was injustice that robbed us of the World Cup, rather than England just not being quite good enough. O levels and CSEs were over. I had two jobs – my paper round and helping on the farm doing hay-bailing with the farmer's grandsons, my friends and neighbours Paul and Mark Simpson.

With no school work, most evenings were free, and I had just about enough money to go to the pub. What's not to like? The best part of that summer, though, was the band. I was a fairly unremarkable child, never hugely popular, pretty pathetic with girls . . . but the friends I left school with gave me a sense of belonging that I'd maybe never had before. Robert and David were my bandmates, but we had two other non-playing members, Ian Cuerden and John Duckworth. We were a well-mannered gang, we got into no bother whatsoever, but we felt somehow edgy and important. There were no sex or drugs and it was hardly rock 'n' roll – more, as our sixth-form magazine would later describe us, 'a fourth-rate New Order'.

Robert had a new bass guitar and he'd even had some lessons. Over time, he began to acquire more and more equipment: keyboards, drum machine, sequencer . . . David was a good guitarist. In the years since, he's become very good. Me, well, I had been a pretty good treble before I hit my teens! At 16 I had one of those reedy, pained and pretentious voices typical of the era – somewhere between David Sylvian and Morrissey, but, of course, much worse than either of them.

I don't think that any of us really ever imagined we'd make the big time, but we loved every minute of it. Being in a band was just an opportunity to live out a friendship, to be big kids while pretending to be cool. It was an excuse to go to the local pub in eye-liner, and writing lyrics for actual songs seemed less pathetic and Adrian Mole-ish than writing naff teenage poetry.

The band had a variety of names: 'Portfolio', 'Fred the Girl' (after a weird dream that one of us had about a ginger-haired female fighter pilot in the First World War) and 'Paris' and 'The Voyeurs'. We liked 'The Voyeurs' because we thought it sounded futuristic. My mum then explained to us what the word meant, and so we dropped it.

We spent more time out and about dressed like idiots (in bandannas, hats, sunglasses, make-up and flouncy shirts) doing photo shoots rather than actual band practice. Someone once said that 'politics is showbiz for ugly people' so maybe that explains why I went from that pretentious egocentric lifestyle, to the one I currently have.

Once the photos were back from the developer, Robert's mum Ivy would choose the best photos and send them along with demo tapes and a nice covering letter to record companies. It never really occurred to us at the time, but Ivy was effectively our manager and developed some really good relationships with people in the record industry as a result. Years later, when I was trying to book a band for the graduation ball as the president of Newcastle University Union, it was Ivy Nickson that I turned to for contacts. As a result, I nearly booked Duran Duran but ended up with two-fifths of the Bay City Rollers. But that's another story.

Pretty much all the replies Ivy received were rejections. Then after two and a half years, in February 1989 I was at the Lib Dem students' conference at Brunel University when a phone call came through to me via the porters' lodge. It was Robert. He'd had to ring my hall of residence in Newcastle, find someone who knew where I was, find a number for Brunel, find which block we were in and ask a porter to track me down. I thought, 'This must be serious!' It was. Island Records wanted us to come and do a recording session at their studios in London. But the date they wanted us clashed with my exams and I bottled it, so we didn't go to London. Robert and David have always been relaxed about this and very understanding. They've never blamed me for screwing up our best shot – at least never to my face. We're still friends anyway! But I look back and think, 'What if we had taken that chance, where might it have got us?' Probably nowhere, but it's intriguing to ponder that my life might have been very very different.

But back in 1986, as the summer drew to an end, absolutely no one was interested in signing us. We didn't care much as we were having too much fun anyway. My CSE and O-level results had turned out well, and so in September, I went to the huge further education college down the road in Leyland to begin my A levels. Runshaw College was (and is) a massive place. It serves two boroughs in central Lancashire, where almost all the secondary schools are without sixth forms. Almost everyone went to Runshaw. David and I went to do A levels, Ian a BTEC in business studies, and Robert and John vocational courses. Runshaw had a students' union which was heavily politicized. There was an excitement, almost a sense of danger at the weekly union meetings. On 16 September 1986 I went to the college 'societies fair' not having the first idea what to expect. I remember two conversations that I had there. The first was with Derek Draper on the Labour Club stall. Derek had just finished at Runshaw and was heading off to study at Manchester University. He went on to be a leading New Labour spin doctor, and became no stranger to controversy. On arrival at Runshaw I already knew that I wasn't a Conservative. I was pretty sure that Labour wasn't for me either. They were too conventional, too establishment, too conservative.

My chat with Derek Draper confirmed that view. I wasn't Labour, so why would I join them? I guess the only reason to join Labour would be if my main objective was to become an MP and have a political career. I'd already grandly formed the view that any old mediocrity could join Labour or the Tories and have a political career – so there was nothing special about those options. To be yourself, a free-thinker, an individualist, a liberal . . . Now that sounded like the kind of quirky thing that would be worth doing and worth being. I liked David Steel (the Liberal Leader), but I *loved* David Penhaligon (the MP for Truro in Cornwall). I loved his humour, his anti-tribal radicalism, his human way of speaking. I didn't think about it much, but if in my subconscious there was an idea of what a liberal was, what a liberal politician might look like and what kind of liberal politician I might aspire to be, then David Penhaligon was that idea.

Conservatives in Cornwall to this day both admire and resent Penhaligon. They resent him because he set the bar of what was deemed an acceptable work rate and local focus for an MP far too high for comfort. To me, the Penhaligon way is how you should serve as a parliamentarian. In 1986, he was subconsciously and vaguely my model. Today, in my life as an MP, Penhaligon *is* my model, consciously and precisely. He spoke for his community ahead of his party, he seemed to find his job a joy not a chore, and he looked relaxed being himself rather than trotting out a line.

Please don't think I made a calculated choice that day in the drama studio where the fair was being held. Essentially, all I did was say goodbye to Derek, wander next door to the Liberal Society stand and hand over £1.50 to Tim Pickstone to join a party that 'felt right' to me. I wasn't a socialist, I wasn't a Tory, I was a liberal. I hadn't read and imbibed every tenet of John Stuart Mill's writing, or understood the nuanced differences between Hobhouse's liberalism and social democracy. This wasn't a scientific conclusion. In the years since, I have been tempted to make my joining of the Liberal Party seem the consequence of a more detailed analysis of political ideology. Let's be honest, it wasn't. It was a thing that I did at 16. At 16, I joined a party. At 16, I also formed great friendships. You can dismiss those developments as invalid because of my age. But in the following thirty-odd years those friendships have lasted, as has my political choice.

You might vote for a party on the rational analysis of its policy programme. But you commit to a party because of something far deeper. I joined the Liberals because they felt right, but I stayed in the Liberals because I fell in love with the party, its people and its culture.

I may not have joined the Liberal Party as a result of a careful analysis of party doctrines, but you can be sure that once I had joined, and once I felt comfortable, I made it my business to understand liberalism, what it meant in theory, what it meant in practice and what it meant to me.

The liberalism of John Stuart Mill, penned mostly in the 1850s and 60s, seemed to make sense of how a fair society ought to operate. The language was a bit dated, but the concepts struck me as fresh, lively and relevant. To Mill, freedom is the key. The freedom to make our own choices so long as they don't damage the freedoms of others. It was a social liberalism that contrasted with what I considered to be the shallow classical liberalism of Mrs Thatcher, or the libertarianism of many of the young Conservatives I came across at sixth form and university. Their concept of freedom was about absence of economic restraint or the absence of formal curbs on liberty. But that struck me and still strikes me as an incomplete liberalism that undermines true freedom. Adam Smith spoke of an 'invisible hand in the market place' that ensures that a right balance is struck and that right outcomes are achieved in a free market, laissez-faire economy. But even the most cursory of glances at real life should tell you that this isn't how things really work.

There is an invisible force in the market place, but it is more like gravity: more and more goes to those who already have the most. Those with the least lose what freedom or power they had in the circumstances of a small, weak, laissez-faire state. The family I grew up in and the community to which I belonged had many freedoms in theory and under law – the rights to own a home, to work, to send children to university or to own part of a formerly nationalized company in Margaret Thatcher's emerging share-owning democracy – but those rights meant nothing without the financial wherewithal to make them a reality. An absence of restraint does not constitute freedom if you can't in practice make the choices that, in theory, we are free to make. Economic freedom must then mean that we have the ability to exercise choices, which is why a strong welfare state, the ability to have a safe and decent home, and the realizable opportunity to educate your children, are central to true liberty. But freedom must also mean that you are free to think and free to be whom you choose to be. If you aren't free to think, or do, or be, why is that? Sometimes it can be the law that restricts your freedom. Male homosexual practice had been legal for around twenty years at the time I joined the Liberals, but the age of consent for gay men was still five years above the age of consent for straight people. That constituted a continued restriction to liberty, but a far greater restraint was society's failure to treat gay people as equal. This inequality was enshrined in law but the greater constraint came from the unlegislated attitudes of society. The same was true for people of faith, something that I only came to realize much later. The law may say that we are free to love whom we love, or to worship our God and to live in accordance with the teachings of scripture, but if we are sneered at and treated as a social pariah for doing or even thinking those things, then we are not free. And those who do the sneering are not liberals. John Stuart Mill understood this perfectly. In 1859 he wrote:

> In this age, the mere example of non-conformity, the mere refusal to bend the knee to custom, is itself a service. Precisely because the tyranny of opinion is such as to make eccentricity a reproach, it is desirable, in order to break through that tyranny, that people should be eccentric. Eccentricity has always abounded when and where strength of character has abounded; and the amount of eccentricity in a society has generally been proportional to the amount of genius, mental vigour, and moral courage which it contained. That so few now dare to be eccentric, marks the chief danger of the time.
>
> (*On Liberty*, Longmans, Green, Reader, and Dyer, 1878, p. 39)

Societies that close off debate are not liberal societies. When you close down someone because of their faith, their lifestyle, sexuality – or for their opinions on any of the above – you have stopped being a liberal.

In 1988 I started at Newcastle University and soon got into Student Union politics there. The first big debate of the academic year was the proposal to ban a first-year student from entering the Union building on account of his membership of the British National Party. As I learned about this character, I began to see that this was no naïve knucklehead, but an incredibly bright believer in racial ideology who led and directed the activities of dozens of far-right activists. He was dangerous, no doubt. But he was to be banned from the Union, not for his actions but for his thoughts, and for possessing a BNP membership card. Liberals are against that sort of thing. If you only defend the rights of people you like or agree with, you cannot claim to be a liberal. When an Islamic militant tells me, a Christian, that I am an infidel worthy of judgement and death – I should defend his right to do so. The offence we cause, or are caused, does not equate to physical injury. If you challenge my world view or my sense of identity, then that is your right and it is my duty as a liberal to accept that offence. It is your duty too. If we treat offence as though it was injury, then we stifle freedom.

My political hero understood that, and she taught me well. Neva Orrell was the first Liberal elected to the council in Leyland in Lancashire for 50 years. When she won in 1960 by 13 votes, the Conservatives were so staggered that they didn't ask for a recount. Neva represented wards on the local district and county councils over a period of 42 years. Having won her seat in 1960 and 1963, Neva lost it in 1966, got it back in 1967, lost it in 1970, got it back in 1973, lost it in 1977, won it back in 1981 and then remained a district councillor until the age of 89 in 2002 when she passed away in her sleep following a planning meeting. She didn't like planning, so she'd have cheerfully gone before if she'd had the choice . . .

Neva was a never-say-die Liberal community activist. But there was much more to her than pounding the pavements fixing municipal problems. Neva joined the Liberals in 1949. She was pregnant at the time with her second child. By her own account Neva was a woman riddled with the anxieties of that age – she had just lived through a war which had left a profound mark upon her. She had seen the newsreels of the Nazi death camps, while closer to home she had comforted distraught bereaved relatives and lost loved ones herself. Neva was in no doubt as to who was to blame: the wickedness of extreme nationalism, fractured relationships and suspicion between countries, the aggression of armies bent on subjugating others, and the cruelty and narrow-mindedness of a political creed. Later she would read George Orwell's *1984* and understand a little more of the horrors of a society where your very thoughts are policed.

In 1949, Neva's next-door neighbour was the local doctor. He was a Liberal. One night he was off to a local party meeting to discuss European co-operation. Neva learned of this while she chatted with the doctor in his garden. She went inside, spoke to her husband Ken and explained that she was going out for a couple of hours, announcing that she was taking a sixpence out of the housekeeping because she would be joining the Liberals. Neva explains it thus: she had lived through a war caused by nationalism, racism, fascism and aggression. She chose to join a movement that she felt was the antithesis of all of this: internationalist, egalitarian, liberal and peaceful. She wanted a party that stood for the kind of values that would make a repeat of the horrors of the years 1939 to 1945 least possible. She joined the Liberals. Neva then spent the remaining 53 years of her life campaigning for cleaner streets, mended potholes and better council houses. Was this a let down from her high-minded resolve to join the Liberal Party in 1949? Absolutely not. What is a liberal? It is someone who believes in the rights and freedoms of the individual. Anyone can say they believe that, but Neva proved that she believed in the rights and freedoms of the individual by getting her hands dirty and serving the individuals she saw every day with her own eyes. She did this for half a century.

Neva's story is one of service, of authentic radicalism, of real liberalism. She became a great friend. After leaving university in 1992 I returned to Lancashire and succeeded her as County Councillor for Leyland while Neva stayed on the district council. We were a formidable double act. A six-foot lanky, ginger kid and a sub-five-foot tangerine-rinsed old lady.

The sin that tempts politicians the most isn't one of the salacious ones that the tabloids tell you about. It is pride. Vanity. Ego and self-importance. Neva didn't have a shred of any of that. She didn't see people as vote-units, or as members of some kind of class-bloc. Her ideology meant that every human mattered and that is why she served them. She set my standards way too high. I confess that I find it hard to respect other politicians in the light of my experience of Councillor Mrs Neva Orrell MBE. The shallowness, transparency and venal qualities of the rest of us seem all the more glaring when held next to her example.

There is no one quite as keen as the new convert, so, back at sixth-form college, within weeks of having joined the Liberals I was off to the Union of Liberal Students conference at Cardiff University, and then to the National Union of Students conference in Blackpool. I discovered that the Liberal students were nerdy, pleasant and thoughtful. I returned from Cardiff glad that I'd been but not overwhelmed. The NUS conference in Blackpool was something else. It was about fifty times bigger than the Union of Liberal Students event. It was full of edgy, extreme and intolerant people the likes of whom I'd never seen before. But I confess that I was intoxicated by all this. There were about ten different Trotskyist groups there, all screaming betrayal at one another. Not to mention the anarchists, the Stalinists and the far-right Federation of Conservative Students seeking to enrage everyone else by wearing 'Hang Mandela' T-shirts and the like. The relatively sensible NUS president Vicky Phillips sought to keep order among the raucous madness on the conference floor. No one at that conference seemed to speak. They only ranted. As I looked around the conference floor, I caught the eye of a few others like me, not necessarily Liberals, but folks who by their expressions were clearly not zealots and were instead either appalled by this whole nonsense – or, as in my case, strangely amused and excited by it all.

So, for the following six years, I fell into the glorious diversion that is student politics. I don't regret it at all, and I made good friends during the ten NUS conferences I went to. Most of those who were involved in student politics, I discovered, didn't engage in real politics. They weren't knocking on doors in council elections or anything of the sort. But for me, that was proper politics. Student politics was fun. It helped me to develop communication, leadership and campaigning skills, but it didn't carry the authenticity of what we Liberals call 'community politics'.

Community politics is the essence of practical liberalism. It is about immersing yourself in a community and serving it by empowering it. By communicating to, and with, a community you can equip those who live in a community to hold their council and their MP to account, help them to make a difference to their area whether it be cleaner streets, safer roads, more play facilities, better housing or improved health services. Liberals should never consider one group of people to be their 'tribe' to the exclusion of others. We should always see above people's class or other identities and seek to serve them. Liberals want to empower the individual, and that's an active enterprise. We don't sit around waiting for Parliament to legislate to give people more power. Instead, because knowledge is power, we inform people of what the council is or isn't doing (by regular newsletters and door step surveys – this is pre-Internet) and give them the ability to then work together to get the council to do something else or to do it differently.

Through my student years I spoke to hundreds of socialists. I respected and liked most of them. They'd sit in the Union bar or the cafeteria talking about a political theory that would give us a better world. Meanwhile, I was spending my time on the streets actually doing something that might make at least my bit of the world a little better. Liberal community politics was (and is) unglamorous, but it is authentic. Other parties have tried to copy it, but it can only truly be practised by a party that is essentially liberal and believes that individuals and communities have intrinsic dignity which requires them to be served and empowered – not herded as tribal identity groups.

All this made me a very weird mixture. I'd go drinking with my friends who thought politics was dull and stupid, then go and organize a Liberal jumble sale with some pensioners. I'd do band practice with Robert and David, and then be engaged in some bitter partisan row at the Students' Union general meeting. I'd be studying hard for my A levels, and then doing some hay-bailing on the farm to pay for another under-age drinking spree or for a recording session.

Our first recording session took place as a result of a crime. An act of breaking and entering. We didn't realize this until some time later.

Robert had found us a recording studio, owned by a guy who would also act as our engineer. You have no idea how exciting it felt as Robert picked up David and me at 9 p.m. and took us for an overnight recording session at Silent Sky Studios in Preston. The studio was in the basement below a café. The engineer – another David – met us outside and immediately apologized that he'd 'forgotten his keys'. He forced the lock on the front door and we went downstairs to the studio. In the main part of the studio there were stacked chairs from the café upstairs and huge bags of potatoes, onions and other veg. 'I let them keep them down here, it's good for the acoustics,' he said. We accepted this, why wouldn't we? We recorded five songs, with me singing from within a large cupboard under the stairs. It turned out that Dave had been hired as an engineer to work on the new Katrina and the Waves album and had therefore relinquished the lease of the studio some weeks earlier to the café upstairs. The reason we had to do our recording between 9 p.m. and 3 a.m., and the reason that Dave didn't have keys, was because he had no right to be there. He hadn't been able to retrieve his recording equipment because of an ongoing dispute over unpaid rent. Anyhow, he got 70 quid out of us that night and we felt like we were The Clash.

A few weeks earlier I had been ditched by my first proper girlfriend, Sam (the lads called her Sausage Woman because she worked in the local chippy). I was beyond morose. I made Morrissey look joyful by comparison. I lost about a stone due to self-pity. I was pathetic. To this day I don't think I have ever felt so utterly hopeless and miserable as I did in the months following my being dumped. Anyhow, turning up to sixth form the morning after with bleary red eyes and a cassette tape featuring our night's work gave me a deep sense of meaning, triumph and satisfaction at what was a bleak time. Sam came up and asked me, 'Were there groupies there?' I replied that there were, that I was so overwhelmed by the waves of lasses that we'd not been able to complete the album and would have to go back again.

There weren't any lasses. There was just Rob, Smithy, me and a bloke called Dave who'd broken into a studio that he no longer owned . . .

Being miserable after a relationship breakdown can have differing effects on people. For me, it helped me to throw myself into my A-level revision. If I failed and had to re-sit, I'd be in the same classes as Sam and I couldn't cope with that thought. It also made me value my friends. We continued to write together, drink together and play Subbuteo together.

There was a lad at sixth form called Jack. He was 'the college Christian'. Jack was also the treasurer of the Students' Union. I recall that for a long time he had misunderstood the meaning of the word 'approximately' and believed that it meant 'precisely'. He would give the weekly report at the Students' Union meeting saying, 'The Union has in its current account, two hundred and thirty-six pounds and twenty-seven pence, approximately.'

My favourite memory of Jack was sitting in the coat racks outside the Union office as – the first time for both of us – we read *Viz*. *Viz* can only be described as an 'adult comic'. It is satirical, scatological, foul-mouthed, puerile . . . and the funniest thing I had ever seen in my life. *Viz* was – and is – a product of Newcastle culture, and I confess that it featured highly among my motivations when it came to applying to the university there.

Jack was a Christian. A 'born-again Christian'. People liked Jack, but they mocked him. He was pictured on the front cover of the college magazine, sipping a beer at some college night out, and the caption underneath it read 'It's a sin!' I admired Jack, and I really liked him too, but I thought his faith was weird, restrictive and unattractive.

What I never expected was that a few months later, I would become a Christian myself.

5

Being picked

In the spring of 1988, as I moped over Sausage Woman and got stuck into my revision, Mum came home one evening with some unexpected news. She and a number of colleagues from Preston Polytechnic (now the University of Central Lancashire) were to be seconded to run, and teach at, the new English College in Singapore. The prospect of going to Singapore was thrilling. It was another thing that helped me knuckle down and revise.

Three weeks after I'd finished my A levels, we flew out. I'd only been abroad once in my life before that, and that had been a week-long package holiday to a Spanish island when I was 12. This was beyond anything I had ever experienced before. Singapore was hotter than anywhere I'd ever been, and it felt exotic and different in every way. My sister Jo, Mum and I were settled along with a friend and fellow lecturer, Ian, in a detached house in the south of the island, an area called Bukit Timah. Mum and Ian had been an item in the past, but not at this point, so they of course refused to share a room. This caused a slight problem. This was a house with only three formal bedrooms. There was no question that either Jo or I would tolerate sharing, which meant that the storage room was quickly reconfigured as my bedroom. All the junk was taken out and stored in the outhouse, but the bookshelves and their contents remained.

I accepted the junk room rather than fighting to force Jo to take it, partly because I'm not that mean and partly because I was going to be the first of us to leave Singapore five weeks later. I had to go back to the UK for my A-level results. For Mum and Jo, the future was a little less certain. Mum's commitment was indefinite at first and Jo was very open to continuing her education in Singapore.

In Singapore, I wrote letters most days to either my friends, my grandparents, my dad, Sam, Sam's friend Fiona (because I knew it would get back to Sam and that it would wind her up) and I also wrote loads of songs that I still have somewhere. I'd go into the city, I'd go drinking with Ian, or take my sister swimming, but there was still a lot of time to fill and no work or studies to fill it with, so I'd listen to music and read. It rains a lot in Singapore, or more accurately when I was there it rained once or maybe twice a week. But when it rained, it rained a lot. I'd never seen rain like it. Dirty marble-sized drops that hit the ground and seemed to explode. If you were outside when it rained you didn't just get wet, you got hurt. It was another reason to spend time inside and read, read and read.

I ran out of books pretty quickly. I hadn't brought much material with me, so I turned to the books on the shelves in my junk room. The house belonged to the College and the previous tenants had been lecturers. They were a Christian couple and the books on the shelves were theirs.

The first book I began to read had a huge impact on me. I hated it. I was offended by it and didn't finish it. It was called *I Once Loved a Girl* – a great title for a song by the way, and I ripped it off accordingly. The book itself was the account of a pastor in Africa teaching the teenage boys in his care about sexual ethics – no sex before or outside marriage. 'Get knotted!' I thought. How dare this bloke seek to constrain the natural desires of these young men? I was outraged . . .

Outraged, but intrigued. Christianity seemed to be something more than cultural. It seemed to make a claim on how people lived their lives. I felt hostile to the writer of *I Once Loved a Girl*. But there were plenty of other books on those shelves, so even when the weather became scorching and sunny again, I took some of those books and sat outside.

At the time, the writing that really captivated me focused on the colossal number of Old Testament prophecies relating to the coming of the Messiah, all of which are fulfilled in the person of Jesus Christ. Until this point, I'd shrugged off Christianity as not relevant, a bit boring and unlikely to be true. Jesus was an interesting and good bloke, a wise teacher but no more. Now, I saw that there was something more to this Jesus. I also began to see the Bible with new eyes. I had previously seen it as an old book full of interesting teaching, wisdom and some fairly brutal matter that we shouldn't take too seriously. To believe that the Bible is true was, in my opinion, laughable. Only extremely credulous and weak-minded people would believe that.

But it also occurred to me that if there is a God, then which is easier to believe? Is it more likely that there is an almighty God who can create the universe and be trusted to communicate his will to us through his word . . . or that there is a half-time, low-wattage Happy Shopper God who might be able to create the universe but somehow can't manage to leave us a reliable word so that we might know him?

Looking back, what gripped me most about those books was their insistence that Christianity is a dynamic faith: that God's purposes weren't finished, that the universe is on a trajectory, and that each of us human beings is involved. I was also gripped by a growing awareness that Christianity was personal. Jesus had died for me. He was not just seeking followers but people with whom he would have an eternal relationship, fulfilling our very deepest, all-pervading need.

Of course, I could have avoided the obvious, but it became clear that God's appeal was directed straight at me. As I considered the stated purposes of the eyewitnesses who wrote their accounts of Jesus, I had to ask myself 'What are they saying to me?' Some words towards the end of the Gospel of John made it clear: 'these are written that you may believe that Jesus is the Messiah, the Son of God, and that by believing you may have life in his name' (John 20.30).

There is no faffing about here. These are not vague bits of philosophy. This is a clear and forthright appeal to believe that Jesus really is who he says he is, that he really did die and rise again and that we should put our trust in him. If it's true, everything changes. Much that you thought was wrong is right, and much that you thought was right is wrong. Stop everything now. Nothing else matters.

I had always assumed that the Gospel stories about Jesus in particular and the Bible in general were, at least partially, mythological. It's now clear to me that the only thing that the Gospels cannot be is myth. They're a hoax, or a big mistake, or they're true.

I began also to see that Jesus' claim to be the Son of God was unique and exclusive. It was explicit and not vague. That's why many of the religious authorities at the time considered him to be a dangerous blasphemer, worthy of death. It is also why so many who heard him concluded that he was who said he was and put their trust in him.

Some of the above occurred to me in the months and years that followed. Please don't think that I left Singapore with all this fully worked out, but it provides the gist of what I confronted in Singapore in July and August 1988. Some time in the early hours of 2 August 1988, I committed my life to Jesus Christ, repented and believed . . . and amazingly did not become perfect. To paraphrase someone wiser: 30 years on and I'm still not perfect, I'm not even good . . . but I'm better than I used to be.

My family thought I'd gone a bit mad, of course. I prepared to leave Singapore in mid-August having made this tumultuous decision. During the summer, I'd enjoyed the feeling of being terribly grown-up, of going out with Ian or my mum, drinking in the exciting bars of the city and smoking my mum's rather elegant More Menthol cigarettes. They were long, brown and seemed terribly sophisticated. As I boarded the plane to Heathrow at Singapore's Changi Airport, I decided to book a seat in the smoking section of the plane (yes, those things existed back then). It was a 16-hour flight. I sat in the window seat next to a couple of Glaswegians who chain-smoked Benson and Hedges all the way to London.

I felt almost overcome by the smoke in that section of the plane. I am sure that the purest air I breathed during that long flight was when I smoked my three More Menthols . . .

I got off the plane feeling woozy, not just from the long flight but from having passively inhaled half a tobacco plantation from the serious smokers around me. My grandparents came to meet me at Heathrow and we caught the train north.

My A-level results were still two days away, so I immediately reconnected with my friends. Ian, Robert, John and David were somewhat bewildered by my conversion, but it nevertheless provided a new and interesting conversation topic to add to our usual repertoire.

Results day came, and I was utterly relieved and ecstatic that my A-level grades were good – I'd more than met the entry requirements for Newcastle University's politics department. One of my tutors tried to persuade me to take a year out and apply for Oxford for the following year, but I hadn't applied for Oxford or Cambridge in the first place because of a rather juvenile antipathy to those places. I didn't want to be one of those stuck-up people surrounded by privilege and entitlement. I wanted to go to a real university with real people. My sincere apologies to the many perfectly decent people who have been to either of those good institutions. I'm just telling you how my mind worked back then. Anyhow, I was itching to get away and start afresh in Newcastle. The thought of waiting another year was completely unappealing.

The night of 30 September, we had a get-together at my grandparents' house (Mum and Jo were still in Singapore and our family home was temporarily rented out). Around came Ian, Robert, John, Tim Pickstone . . . and Sam. David had planned to come round but he rang to say that his 16-year-old sister Susan had gone into labour. Later that night she gave birth to Lianne.

The next morning, I set off for Newcastle. In the two months since I had become a Christian I hadn't spoken to a single fellow believer. Then, on my first night in Newcastle, there was a knock on my door from my neighbour in our hall of residence. Pete Carrington was a second-year medic, and he wanted to invite me to a Christian Union event later in the week (he had no idea I was a Christian). He also invited me and a new friend out for a pint that night.

We went to a local pub and Pete ordered 'a pint of Scotch'. Blimey, I thought, this bloke is an extremely serious drinker. I then became aware of the existence of 'Scotch Bitter', a sickly and unpleasant beverage favoured by Geordies. I have rarely drunk it since . . .

I bedecked my room with posters that I'd bought at Affleck's Palace in Manchester a few weeks earlier. I had posters of Prefab Sprout, The Smiths . . . and one of Jo Grimond, the iconic former Liberal Leader. The Grimond poster was visible to anyone looking into my room from outside.

A few days later I went down to breakfast, wearing – of course – my Lib Dem badge. I was about to sit down at a table full of people I didn't know, when a rather diminutive young woman looked at me and my badge with eyes wide open and with excitement in her voice. She exclaimed: 'You're the one who lives on the other side of the Quad with the Grimond poster!'

'How do you know?' I asked.

'Well,' she replied, 'there can't be three of us!'

This was Lucy McKeever. Years later she would be my best man when I married Rosie. A committed Liberal, a pop music anorak (the youngest of six children, she had the most exotic music collection fuelled in part by her three punk- and new-wave-obsessed brothers) and a football fanatic (Birmingham City). As C. S. Lewis said in *The Four Loves*: 'Friendship is born at the moment when one says to another "What! You too? I thought that no one but myself . . ."'

So it was – and still is – with Lucy.

Alongside Lucy and about a dozen others, I got hugely involved in the Liberal Democrats at university, spending at least as much time in Student Union politics as I did on my degree. I was also going to the Christian Union a couple of times a week. Incidentally, I didn't go to church at all during my first year as a Christian because I got the fellowship I needed in the CU. That wasn't necessarily a bad thing at the time. Realizing that I needed to belong to a decent church didn't come until quite a bit later.

Everyone at the CU knew that I was heavily into politics. One Saturday afternoon about 20 of us were at the house of a Christian lecturer. Another CU member, Adrian, was chatting to me and said out of the blue, 'As a Christian, are you sure you should be involved in politics? It's a mucky business . . .'

The words we say to one another can be really powerful. Adrian's were to me though I'm certain he didn't realize it, which has been a lesson to me that I shouldn't say things lightly. In the months that followed, as I threw myself energetically into local elections, parliamentary by-elections, Student Union elections and the round of meetings and conferences that are the lot of the party activist, I would mull Adrian's question over in my head. Should a Christian be involved in this 'mucky business'?

I came back home for the local elections in 1989 to help Neva. The year 1989 would turn out to be the low point for the Liberal Democrats. Even the cataclysm that befell the Lib Dems in 2015 after the coalition wasn't quite as bad as 1989. In the June European elections, we lost all but two deposits in the whole country (which means that we registered less than 5 per cent almost everywhere) and came fourth behind the Greens. The local elections in May were almost as bad, and Charles Kennedy referred to the whole business as 'a damage limitation exercise'.

One of the places where we limited the damage was Leyland. Despite the disasters for the Liberal Democrats across the country, Neva managed to hold her seat with a hugely increased majority, taking 59 per cent of the vote. As I listened to voter after voter telling me that they were enthusiastically voting for Neva because she helped them in one way or another, it occurred to me that politics was not an especially 'mucky business'; instead, it was a unique way of serving people. Of course, it attracted its fair share of venality, dishonesty, vanity and selfishness but there were a thousand other professions or vocations just as susceptible to those things. If Christians were to steer clear of politics, then they might as well also steer clear of bus-driving, journalism, mining, the law, teaching, retail or professional sport.

But if being a Christian and being involved in politics is acceptable, what about being a Christian and being a Liberal?

To many, liberalism and Christianity seem strange bedfellows. I've never understood why this should be so. After all, those who founded the Liberal Party in the UK were mostly Christians. Indeed, they were mostly evangelical Christians – non-conformists who fought against the power of the established church, which deprived those who were not Anglicans of many fundamental rights and dictated the terms of whom you could marry, where you could study and where you could live.

William Ewart Gladstone, the Liberal Party's greatest and most successful leader, was a committed Christian. Indeed, following the Liberal Party's near annihilation after 1945, the party's disappearance was only prevented because of its staying power in those parts of the UK with concentrations of 'low church' affiliation in mid-Wales, the south-west of England and the Highlands and Borders of Scotland.

To be a liberal is to believe in the equality and fundamental dignity of every human being. It is to believe that neither state, church nor any other institution should be able to dictate how we live, work or worship. Liberals believed that in the 1860s and they believe it today, or at least they should do.

The view that liberalism and Christianity are incompatible arises from two developments. One is the rise in religious illiteracy, and the other is the increasingly dangerous tendency of liberals across the Western world to be tolerant of everything apart from those things they disagree with. I've described this latter development as 'liberalism eating itself'.

Being a liberal means fighting for the rights of all – including those whose world view you do not share. That's what the great nineteenth-century liberals did. Fighting for the rights of people who are like you, or whose world view you share or agree with, does not make you a liberal. Any Conservative or indeed any fascist would take that position. That's why, as a Christian, I not only feel that liberal values best reflect my desire for equality, dignity, compassion and service, but I also feel that liberalism best preserves the rights of those whose world view is off-centre or 'eccentric' as John Stuart Mill would describe it. Christians who fear that their rights are under threat should therefore instinctively be inclined towards the liberal cause. And those who belong to other minorities should seek to defend the rights of religious minorities, especially when those minorities believe things that jar with their world view.

If liberals fight for the rights of minorities then would it be true to say that Christians are a minority? If so, are they an oppressed minority?

I could make an in-depth analysis here of the places where Christians are under threat – North Korea, Syria, China and Iran. The reality is that in each of those places, Christianity is spreading like wildfire. Christianity tends to grow when it is most under pressure. I suspect that in societies where life is easy – economically or politically – we are more likely to be suckered in to worship the gods of prosperity and self-realization. In North Korea, what do the Christians there do? Do they plot or even pray for the downfall of Kim Jong-un? No, they pray for Kim Jong-un, that his heart may be softened and his eyes opened to the gospel. If that is the reaction of the persecuted church in North Korea, what on earth are Christians in the West thinking about when they complain about being dissed on Twitter? Jesus taught that when someone strikes us, we shouldn't hit them back, or whine about them hitting us, but turn the other cheek towards them so that they could hit us again. Christians are called to do all they can to help right the wrongs of this world but are given no encouragement to seek to preserve their own rights.

This doesn't let liberals off the hook. To sneer at or seek to marginalize those who hold a world view that you disapprove of, means you cannot be a true liberal.

The fact that Western liberalism has become so polluted with authoritarianism and self-righteous judgementalism does not make me despair of liberalism – it makes me all the more desperate to see real liberalism fight back. It does, however, make me sad for those whose liberalism has 'eaten itself', sad that they claim a creed that they do not live by in practice.

In short, I tend to think that Christians should behave like Christians, accepting offence with grace. And I think that liberals should behave like liberals, actively respecting and defending the rights of those whose world view they do not share.

These things matter, but I still find myself much more disturbed by other issues. There are over 2,000 children living in poverty in my constituency alone. There are 3,000 families on the waiting list for a home in our area. Further away from home, hundreds of thousands of families are rotting in refugee camps while the West looks the other way.

Given that no one is truly free if they haven't got the means to make basic choices, this is a far greater affront to me than the fact that some people on social media are nasty about Christians.

The Liberal Democrats doubled in size while I was Leader, principally because of the stand we took on the UK's departure from the EU. Many of those who share my sadness at this development do so from a sense of lost identity. I respect that and, to a degree, share the sentiment. However, my main motivation in speaking out as I have is that I fear the UK's exit will make our country poorer. Those who lose the most when a country becomes poorer are those who were already poor to start with.

It isn't the loss of the EU flag that troubles me so much as the probability that families who are only just keeping their heads above water, barely being able to afford to pay the rent or the weekly shopping bill, will end up sinking. This is where social liberals differ from classical liberals – we care about actual freedom rather than notional freedom. In the midst of the aggressive flag-waving on either side, it is the reality of lives lived at the margins that should motivate us.

It is those realities that brought me into politics and into the Liberal Party as a teenager. Those realities are my main motivation today. Winning elections is not, to me, an opportunity for my team to beat the other team and impose our identity on society. Winning elections is the way we gain the ability to liberate people from poverty and the oppression that always comes with it. That is what drives me in every election. The 2017 campaign was no different.

6

War and fees

Without any doubt, the biggest problem facing the Liberal Democrats in the 2017 general election was the result of the 2015 general election. Being reduced from 56 MPs to a rump of just 8 in 2015 meant that, no matter how strong our electoral message may have been in 2017, we simply didn't have the credibility to be the major players we had previously been.

The 2015 general election result saw David Cameron's Conservative Party returned with only a small majority. This result ended the Conservative–Lib Dem coalition government of the previous five years. David Cameron's success was built almost entirely on a cleverly executed plan to wipe out Liberal Democrat MPs by taking advantage of two developments.

First, many voters feared a fabled ragtag coalition including the Labour Party and the newly resurgent Scottish National Party. By implication, the Liberal Democrats were to be part of this imaginary coalition.

Second, support for the Liberal Democrats had evaporated following five years of it being in an actual coalition with the Conservatives. Most Liberal Democrat MPs had relied on the votes of people who would otherwise have voted Labour but who chose to use their votes tactically to support the Liberal Democrats in order to keep out the Conservatives. After five years of sharing power with the Conservatives, many of these left-leaning voters felt no inclination to lend their support to the Liberal Democrats on this occasion.

The party's identity had been submerged into the co-alition and, by the end of our five years in government, we simply had no message to draw people to us. We were easy pickings. For the Conservatives and Labour to take seats off the Liberal Democrats in 2015 was like taking sweets from a baby. They very nearly took the whole lot. I'd argue that the party's rout in 2015 was largely undeserved, utterly predictable and probably preventable.

The 2010 election had resulted in a Parliament where no party had a majority, the first time this had happened since 1974. In the days that followed the result, I had reluctantly supported the Liberal Democrats entering a coalition with the Conservatives because, like most of my colleagues, I couldn't see a plausible alternative. The only other option seemed to be that we should step back and allow the Conservatives to govern alone as a minority adminis-tration. This was an unattractive choice because it would probably have led to a second election in the autumn of that year which the Conservatives would most likely have won.

Labour had too few MPs to allow a Lib Dem–Labour coalition to be formed. That didn't stop me, Ed Davey, Chris Huhne and others urging our then party Leader Nick Clegg to open negotiations with Labour to see what might be possible.

This rather optimistic endeavour ended pretty swiftly because Labour's hastily assembled negotiating team informed their Liberal Democrat counterparts that they were not interested in even exploring the multi-party arithmetic that might have seen a non-Conservative coalition gaining a majority.

One Lib Dem negotiator told me that Labour had essentially said, 'We'll talk to you, but we aren't touching the nationalists with a barge-pole.' The only route to a non-Conservative majority involved Scottish and Welsh nationalists getting on board. Once Labour had ruled this out, there was no longer a way forward.

In the heady days of the coalition negotiations a lot of factors were at work. Liberal Democrat MPs who had never dreamed of holding ministerial office could now see this prospect lighting up in front of them. Some were mesmerized by it and saw it as the holy grail of a political career. Most of us understood that for the Liberal Democrats, joining the Government was a huge step and one that we ought not to pass up lightly. If you insist on standing for election, then getting into government is an occupational hazard. Indeed, to stand for election and to not want to take power is dishonourable. It can be very easy to take opposing positions that make you feel self-righteous, but surely, doing good is better than feeling good. Going into the Government was, then, the honourable thing for the Liberal Democrats to do. I am proud of us for doing so. Having joined the Liberals as a 16-year-old, I had slowly – subconsciously – developed the assumption that we would remain outsiders and in opposition for ever. There was something utterly exhilarating, then, about the prospect of joining the Government.

On Monday 10 May, around 30 Lib Dem MPs crowded into the downstairs of a Thai restaurant in Pimlico to consider our options. Many of those MPs had been elected for the first time just four days earlier, so their heads were spinning more than most. None of the party's negotiating team (Danny Alexander, David Laws, Andrew Stunell and Chris Huhne) were at that dinner. We would meet them later that night when they returned from their discussions with their counterparts.

Most of us in that downstairs room had our say that night, with the general feeling being that the prospect of joining the Government was too big an opportunity to dismiss. People with very marginal seats seemed to have lost their usual fear of electoral consequences. The 30 of us left the restaurant feeling bullish and excited as we headed for Westminster Hall to meet up with the rest of our colleagues.

The meetings of the Liberal Democrat MPs that took place in the days following the 2010 election lasted long into the night. The meeting in Westminster Hall on 10 May was no exception. The mood was hubristic. Having kept my thoughts to myself at the Thai restaurant, I felt that it was important that someone should sound a note of severe caution. I stood to speak and asked my colleagues to weigh seriously the likely reality that our choice to go into a coalition with our age-old adversaries, the Conservatives, would toxify our party's brand for at least a generation. I reminded the room that over the previous 30 years, many voters had refused to consider supporting the Liberals or their successors, the Liberal Democrats, because for 18 months in the late 1970s the party had propped up Labour Prime Minister Jim Callaghan's administration in what was dubbed 'the Lib–Lab pact'. If the Lib–Lab pact that took place when I was eight years old was still costing us votes, what would a full-blown coalition with the Conservatives do to our support in the future? We would surely be dismissed as 'the Tories' little helpers' and our chance of winning seats against Labour, or retaining Labour tactical votes in our contests with the Conservatives, would be much diminished.

Two days later, filled with foreboding, I voted for the party to join the coalition for the want of a less dreadful alternative. My colleagues John Leech and Charles Kennedy were the only Lib Dem MPs to vote against the deal with the Conservatives.

Despite this, I still think that the Liberal Democrats did the right thing for the country in joining the coalition. We provided stable government, introduced many progressive policies and held back the worst excesses of the Conservatives. We did the right thing for the country, but perhaps the wrong thing for the Liberal Democrats. The question is: might protecting the future of the Liberal Democrats have also been in the national interest?

My fears for our future as a result of joining the coalition didn't appear to be shared by too many of my parliamentary colleagues. Understandably, these were intoxicating days as the party looked to form part of a government for the first time since the all-party administration during the Second World War.

Eighteen Liberal Democrats took ministerial office, including five members of the Cabinet. The party took secretary-of-state positions in Energy and Climate Change (Chris Huhne), Business (Vince Cable) and the Scottish Office (Danny Alexander). In addition, David Laws became Chief Secretary to the Treasury – a cabinet post, but as number two to Tory Chancellor George Osborne. Nick Clegg became Deputy Prime Minister with a roving brief across government and special responsibility for constitutional affairs.

I was clearly nowhere near to being in the mix for a cabinet post but, as a member of the Liberal Democrat Shadow Cabinet (I held the Environment, Food and Rural Affairs brief), it seemed quite possible that I might be given a junior ministerial role. It wasn't to be. Alistair Carmichael, the new Chief Whip, rang me on the Saturday after the coalition was formed to let me know that I hadn't made the cut this time. It's instructive to analyse one's immediate feelings when given news like this. Looking back, I confess that I felt slighted at being overlooked . . . but also somewhat more relieved.

As the months went on, I became all the more grateful to the leadership for deciding that my face didn't fit.

Those who took ministerial office often found themselves cut off from their constituency parties as they spent more and more time in their departments or on official business around the country. They were also obliged to toe the government line at all times even when it meant being on the wrong side of public opinion.

As a third party, the Liberal Democrats had become

experts in insurgency, challenging the established order and being a thorn in the side of many a previous government.

Our popularity in the first decade of the twenty-first century had been based on our principled opposition to the Iraq War in 2003 and on a number of key domestic policy areas. Most notably, the party's opposition to the Labour government's introduction of tuition fees had placed the Liberal Democrats, effectively, to the left of Tony Blair's Labour Party and proved immensely popular with students, their parents and the public-sector middle classes more generally.

For the first time in decades, the Liberal Democrats had developed a 'constituency' that was represented by more than just traditional liberals from 'the Celtic fringe'.

But as we began our time in government, it seemed to me that the party was embarking on a strategic programme of alienating almost every group of people who had voted for us over the previous ten or 20 years.

The first act that alienated many of our supporters was simply to go into government at all. Being in power appeared to convince the public that the party was no longer the 'none of the above' option for voters. We had become 'one of the above', part of the establishment, insiders rather than outsiders. That was a very large section of our USP taken out in one go.

Even so, in the first few months of the coalition our poll ratings were still fairly healthy, sitting in the high teens. As we went into the autumn of 2010, it seemed that most if not all of our voters were prepared to keep the faith and stick with us.

One issue above all was to horrify those who had backed us in the election and would see the party lose half of its 2010 voters before the year was out – the trebling of university tuition fees.

It is often said that the Liberal Democrats did better in the coalition negotiations than our Conservative partners. One reading suggests that almost three-quarters of our manifesto became coalition government policy – not bad for a party with less than a quarter of the vote. Also, key manifesto policies were adopted by the Government, including the raising of the income tax threshold which would see a million or more low-paid workers exempted from paying tax on their income.

The truth is that many in the party leadership had been reluctant to keep the policy to scrap university tuition fees in the manifesto, so when it came to the coalition negotiations, fees were not treated as a priority. Nevertheless, the policy was still a major reason why so many people had chosen to support us. Whether we liked it or not, so much of the Liberal Democrat brand was centred on this one policy. It was totemic and pointed to a wider commitment to education and the public sector. Added to this, almost all the party's MPs had publicly signed the pledge to scrap tuition fees during the 2010 campaign and gleefully posed in photo-ops holding placards containing the pledge. You don't need to be an expert in British Government and Politics or in Political Behaviour to work out that breaking that pledge might not be the brightest thing to do . . .

The coalition inherited, from the previous Labour government, the work of the Browne Commission into the funding of higher education. It concluded in September 2010 that tuition fees would have to rise significantly. Anticipating this, the coalition agreement contained a clause that tied the new government to introducing the findings of this commission, while giving Liberal Democrat MPs the right to abstain in the event that an increase in fees was proposed.

Few identified this fly in the ointment at the time, but, looking back, one has to wonder what the negotiating team were thinking of to allow it into the agreement, knowing as they must have done what a huge impact it would have on the party's standing. The leadership didn't like the policy on fees, and the negotiating team clearly didn't fight for it when the coalition agreement was being drawn up. I assume that they thought that the Conservatives would get the blame for this.

The matter would blow up in October 2010. Before that, at the end of May, Vince Cable stepped down as Liberal Democrat Deputy Leader.

There was a sense that the party's Deputy Leader – elected only by MPs and thus only truly the Deputy Leader of the parliamentary party – should not be a minister. Vince was now Secretary of State for Business. A number of colleagues suggested that I should run to be Deputy Leader, something that genuinely hadn't occurred to me. It became clear, however, that the leadership's preferred candidate was Simon Hughes. Simon is one of my greatest friends in politics, a mentor to me and, on the two occasions that he had run to be party Leader in 1999 and 2006, I had been actively involved in his campaigns. Running against Simon went against the grain, but I decided to run anyway. If nothing else, it would show that I was not planning to sit on the backbenches, politely waiting my turn.

One alarming feature of the early weeks of the coalition was the apparent sense that we were to be presented as a single entity rather than as two very distinct parties. Prime Minister David Cameron and Deputy Prime Minister Nick Clegg had launched the new government in the Rose Garden at Number 10 Downing Street in what became a defining event for the coalition. This seemed to be a partnership that looked a bit too close and friendly for many of us. I watched the televising of the Rose Garden launch in the office I shared in Parliament with Greg Mulholland, the MP for Leeds North West. I was quite shaken by the spectacle and turned to Greg and said, 'It's like seeing your wife run off with another bloke.' Greg agreed. Our boy looked like he'd sided with the enemy. Nick Clegg spent five years fighting in the trenches, winning policy battles and delivering liberal ideals while blocking Conservative excesses. He deserves enormous credit for his time in government. I count him as a friend and I am proud of him. But the imagery around the coalition launch left an unpleasant taste in the mouth and it helped to bracket the Liberal Democrats as 'Tory poodles'.

Running to be Deputy Leader came largely from my desire to put this right – to make sure that the coalition was not to become an assimilation. As a centre-left Liberal, I didn't want the coalition shifting the centre of gravity of my party to the centre-right. After a short campaign, I was defeated by Simon fairly comfortably by 36 votes to 18. Given that it became clear afterwards that all the party's ministers had been strongly encouraged to vote for Simon, that wasn't such a bad result – if you were to remove the 'payroll vote', it would have been a dead heat.

Following the campaign for deputy leadership, I declined the offer to chair the party's Campaigns and Communications Committee. Norman Lamb, Nick Clegg's Parliamentary Private Secretary, rang me to make the offer. The gracious and servant-hearted thing to do would have been to accept, and looking back, I know that I should have done that. However, in the days following the result, I felt pretty aggrieved that the upper echelons had so energetically blocked my attempt to be elected to a post that I actually wanted. I didn't have a problem with losing, especially not to Simon. I was, however, pretty cross at having been organized against by those at the top.

Before the summer recess began, there was a drinks reception at Number 10 for Liberal Democrat MPs hosted by David Cameron. As we filed in through the famous black door, we were asked to hand over our mobile phones. I was taken aback but – thinking quickly – I submitted my Blackberry, while keeping hold of my personal phone. I did this partly because I can be an awkward person and partly because the 2010 World Cup had begun. John Leech and I sneaked behind a book case to check the scores from time to time.

While I was at the reception, the party's President, Baroness Ros Scott, took me aside and told me that she was not planning to seek re-election to the post in the autumn.

She further suggested that I should think seriously about standing for the position myself.

I went on to give the matter consideration but, once the summer recess had begun, I immersed myself in constituency events. Every summer I do my surgery tour when I take my A-board pavement sign to every town and village in Westmorland and Lonsdale to listen and speak to local people. I made sure that the 2010 summer tour was more extensive than ever. I had two weeks in France with Rosie and the children, but apart from that, every spare minute was spent out and about in my local communities. Of course, I should have spent some of that time preparing a presidential campaign.

When Parliament returned in the first week of September, Ros confirmed that she would not be contesting the presidency. I quickly decided that I would run for President and began putting together a campaign team, but it was not until the party's conference in Liverpool in the third week of September that things really got under way.

On the first night of the conference I was in the bar chatting with friends when Jonny Oates rushed in looking very flustered. Jonny was Nick Clegg's Chief of Staff, an immensely capable operator, a decent man and an experienced Lib Dem campaigner. The first night's party rally was about to start, and its star turn, Charles Kennedy, had failed to show. Jonny asked me to stand in with 20 minutes' notice.

I thought about it for about five seconds and said yes. Jonny and I ran to a room behind the auditorium and with the help of Phil Reilly – at that time, one of our press team – I put together the bullet points of a rabble-rousing speech.

The speech wasn't properly written down and I can't recall much of what I actually said, but the audience reacted extremely positively. It was clear that I'd had to wing this one, and so the members at the rally gave me credit for that and for the back-of-a-fag-packet one-liners which, randomly stuck together, constituted my speech.

On reflection, taking this chance and pulling it off was what helped me to win the party presidency. That, and my decision to find a campaign manager who knew what they were doing. I have many failings, but over the years I think my greatest skill has been to identify and appoint brilliant people.

As we were packing up to leave at the end of conference following Nick Clegg's closing speech, I noticed Chris White sitting in the lounge next to the bar working on his laptop. Chris has been a successful councillor in St Albans for many years, a great strategist and – significantly – he had been Ros Scott's campaign manager when she had won the presidency two years previously. I knew at once, 'Chris is my man'. I ran into the bar, sat down at Chris's table and popped the question – 'Will you do the same job for me that you did for Ros?' He said yes. After I'd left, Chris turned to our mutual friend Susan Gaszczack, who was with him, and said, 'Did that really just happen?'

The next few weeks involved rushing around the country speaking to local and regional party meetings as the campaign for the presidency got under way. My opponent was Susan Kramer who, by her endorsements, seemed to be the choice of the party's establishment. Susan was an excellent candidate as a former MP, a baroness and – as it would turn out – a future minister.

The role of Party President is, effectively, to be the internal head of the party, while the Leader is the external head. However, our Leader was now part of government and busy running the country rather than promoting the party. Within the Leader's close team, it had clearly been decided that there would be no breaking ranks with our Conservative coalition colleagues, and that we would be presented as a single entity. I remember a conversation with one of the Liberal Democrat whips, which helped me understand the thinking of Nick's inner circle. They wanted to prove that coalition government worked so that voters would feel more inclined to back the Liberal Democrats in future. They were also terrified of rocking the boat and causing an early election.

I understand this line of thinking, but I think in both cases the logic was flawed. You don't vote for a coalition. You vote for parties. Those who supported the Government would vote for the larger party in government, the Conservatives. Those who were against the Government would vote for opposition parties, not the junior partner in government. Our failure to present ourselves as a distinct entity from the very beginning of the coalition meant that our brand was eclipsed and replaced by whatever our opponents or the media decided to hang around our necks. That our motivation for submerging our identity into a unified coalition brand came from a fear of causing another election, is even more difficult to swallow. No one feared an early election more than David Cameron and George Osborne. They had sold themselves as the Tories' answer to Blair and Brown, as the modern voter-friendly antithesis of all that had gone wrong for the Conservatives since 1992. Cameron and Osborne's entire platform was based on the premise that they could win and would deliver a Conservative majority. Despite Labour getting the worst result of any incumbent party since the Second World War, the Conservatives had failed. Conservative MPs and the party at large were furious with their leadership. While there were a mere 18 Lib Dems taking ministerial posts, there were at least 118 Tory MPs seething, convinced that they would have been ministers had Cameron not snatched defeat from the jaws of victory and been forced to do a deal with the Yellow Peril.

If the coalition had not been formed or if it had crashed in its early months, then David Cameron and George Osborne would surely have been removed by the Tories as a result. The Tory high-command knew that. It is why Cameron made his 'big, open and comprehensive offer' to the Liberal Democrats. We had a much stronger hand than my colleagues believed. We acted like the Tories held the aces when, in reality, we did.

In terms of our image to the outside world, the Liberal Democrats ran the risk of morphing from insurgent, centre-left outsiders, the party of the young and the public-sector middle classes as well as those who considered themselves 'anti-establishment', into supine insiders delivering nothing of note to those groups who had supported us the most.

I ran for Party President because I thought someone needed to deliver the pure and unadulterated Liberal Democrat message. I felt increasingly angry that our distinctive voice had been drowned out and lost amidst the noise of the coalition. We no longer seemed to have an independent identity in the eyes of the public. This was not intentional, but it was clearly happening and I could see that the consequences for the Liberal Democrats could be catastrophic. Like so many others, I feared that we were sleepwalking into oblivion. I wasn't sure I could stop it but I wanted to take hold of an office that would allow me to do my best to save the party, even if it was only to 'rage against the dying of the light'.

It would be right, then, to say that anger drove me to stand for the party presidency. Or rather an indignation that, for all our achievements in government, our very survival was at risk by our being so focused on the business of government, so much so that we overlooked the growingly obvious electoral peril that we then found ourselves in.

Sober judgement and the advice of wise friends led me to the same conclusion, which was that if I was President, I could use the role to help protect the party's distinctiveness and independence. This mattered and was worth doing for two reasons.

First, the electorate could hardly be expected to vote Liberal Democrat if they didn't know what we stood for and believed in, if they only ever saw us as part of the coalition government. Maybe I could – as one who was outside the bounds of collective responsibility and ministerial office – project our pure and independent message?

Second, our members needed to believe in us and be inspired. We lost a third of our membership in coalition and about half of our elected councillors. We weren't just losing votes, we were losing infrastructure. I wanted to be the one to inspire our members, activists and councillors to keep going, to maintain their passion and to be proud of what we were doing in government.

Looking back, I think I can claim success in the second of those two objectives. We later reversed the decline in membership and, among our activists, we retained astonishing unity and positivity against all the odds. But any hope I really had of achieving the first was torpedoed in the early days of the presidential contest.

On Saturday, 9 October 2010, I was visiting the Scottish Liberal Democrat conference in Dunfermline. Susan Kramer and I were at a hustings there and I spent the day with colleagues, taking part in the debates and talking to delegates. Towards the end of the day, we got word that Vince Cable, the Business Secretary with responsibility for higher education, had put forward a new plan for student financial support. In essence, this meant that universities would be permitted to increase the upper limit for tuition fees from £3,000 to £9,000 per year.

The business of the conference was over by the time that this news filtered out on the Saturday evening, but delegates were beside themselves as word spread. All of us knew the electoral toxicity of such a decision if it turned out to be true.

Thanks to the Liberal Democrats' time in the Scottish coalition government between 1999 and 2007, tuition fees were abolished north of the border. Even though the trebling of fees would not touch Scotland, no one I spoke to was naïve enough to think that this move wouldn't poison the party's brand in every part of the UK.

The irony of all this was that it was our party's ability to force Labour to accept our policy of scrapping fees in Scotland in 1999, that protected us against the less popular decisions we had to take during that coalition. The scrapping of fees in Scotland was evidence that we'd maintained our integrity and made a difference. Trebling them in England would be seen as evidence of duplicity and weakness.

I also spent the following Monday in Scotland at a presidential hustings with Susan in Glasgow, followed by a gathering of my supporters in Edinburgh. Members in both places were incredibly nervous about the rumoured proposals over fees. Sufficient uncertainty at that point meant that people were more anxious than angry. The anger would come later. After the Edinburgh event, I went to the station and caught the sleeper train down to London.

I use the sleeper train three or four times a year. It always feels the most exciting and romantic way to travel – but if I had to do it more regularly, I'm sure it would kill me. I'm always knackered afterwards because 'sleeper' trains are a misnomer in that you rarely get that much sleep.

Bleary-eyed, I made my way to Westminster on Tuesday 12 October. As I arrived, the news had been confirmed that the Government was to put the proposal to treble fees to Parliament. That morning, Ming Campbell and I had a chat in the tea room. He was very clear that he could neither vote for such a proposal, nor would he abstain.

I served as Ming's Parliamentary Private Secretary during his time as Leader. He is not a troublemaker, he is by instinct a loyalist and knows the compromises one has

In Dad's back garden with Dad and my sister Jo, 1981

On holiday with Mum, 1982

The band with many names, 1987. Robert Nickson (keyboards, left), David Smith (guitars, right) and some prat in the middle wearing his mother's hat

Right: Campaigning in the snow for myself and fellow Liberal Democrat Jo Hart outside the Newcastle University Union Society building, early 1989. The elections were for the Newcastle delegation to the 1989 NUS conference

Below: My first Liberal Party membership card, September 1986

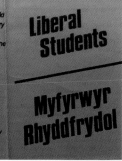

Speaking at a Lib Dem party conference, 1995

Leading the Lib Dems on the pro-EU march in London, 2016
© Paul Smyth/Alamy Stock Photo

The Lib Dem battle bus: my home for much of the 2017 general election campaign
© Bettina Strenske/Alamy Stock Photo

Rosie and I prepare to go to Buckingham Palace to meet HM The Queen and the King
and Queen of Spain, July 2017. It was my last formal engagement as Leader

A sombre moment as I pass on the treasured Leader's mug to Vince Cable, July 2017

Sitting in the famous leather chair for *Celebrity Mastermind*, December 2017

Feeling pleased with myself after finishing the 2018 Langdale ten-kilometre trail run, aka the 'Christmas Pudding Race'

to make when Leader. He had the highest regard for Nick Clegg. Seeing Ming so instantly resolute in his decision to rebel on this matter made it clear to me how big a disaster the trebling of fees would be.

Ming's view was that while the party might not have been entirely wise to have made the pledge to scrap tuition fees, nevertheless that pledge had been made. Breaking it would be a disaster. That had been my gut-feeling since the news had leaked out over the weekend but hearing it from the incredibly wise Ming Campbell confirmed to me that my gut-feeling was right. The scrapping of fees was in our manifesto, and it was one of the few Lib Dem policies that was both well known and popular. To cap it all, all but one of the Liberal Democrat MPs had signed the NUS pledge to scrap tuition fees and many were pictured holding a sign bearing the pledge.

Surely, I thought, if enough of us made it clear that we would vote against the Government on this, something would give?

The problem was this: the coalition agreement, which almost all of us had signed up to, included provision for Liberal Democrat MPs to abstain on any proposal that might see an increase in tuition fees. In the end, 21 Liberal Democrat MPs voted against the fee rise. Had the number been much greater, the Government's majority might have been at risk. Alistair Carmichael, the party's chief whip, and Nick Clegg both warned me that if we insisted on voting against the Government then the Liberal Democrat members could not be afforded the luxury of abstaining. They would have to vote with the Conservatives for the fee increase.

War and fees

Alistair asked me, 'Do you want the Government to lose the vote? This could bring down the Government!' As I sat in his office squirming like a scolded schoolboy, it occurred to me that, actually, I did want the Government to lose this vote. The Government's proposal looked set to destroy my party's brand for years to come. I reckoned that the fallout from a successful backbench rebellion would be a walk in the park compared to that. If, in the unlikely event that the Government had fallen as a result of such a rebellion, we would still have found ourselves in a far healthier position than we eventually did in 2015.

After a close-fought and very good-tempered contest with Susan Kramer, I was elected President of the party in November 2010 and took office on 1 January 2011. From the point that I became 'President-elect', I seemed to become the go-to person for those in the media who wanted a Lib Dem voice that would be critical of the Government. However, I didn't want to be that kind of voice. I reasoned that I could be a critical friend of the coalition. I was seeking, as I told members during the presidential election campaign, to be 'supportive of the coalition but besotted by the Liberal Democrats'.

In December 2010, undercover journalists working for the *Daily Telegraph* infiltrated the constituency surgeries of a number of Liberal Democrat MPs who held office in the coalition Government. Their mission was to trap my colleagues into saying negative things about their Tory partners, to record those comments and to then make a splash about splits in the Government. It was hardly a challenging mission.

If you ask a Lib Dem MP for their opinion of Conservatives, I would hope that they would give a view that was polite and gracious but honest and therefore critical. That is exactly what colleagues such as Vince Cable, Ed Davey and Sarah Teather did when they were recorded secretly in their constituency surgeries. When tempted to say critical things about Conservatives, they obliged. Of course they did. I would have done!

To think this was ever considered a story at all says much about the utter banality that pollutes our political discourse. Journalists are at least as responsible for this as politicians.

Nevertheless, the 'sting' did indeed become a story.

The morning the story broke, I went to the BBC studio in Kendal to do a morning round with Radio 4's *Today* programme, the Radio 5 Live *Breakfast* show and others. My job was to deal with the negative flak that had been generated, which was being spun as the opening of deep fault-lines within the Government. I dismissed the whole business, ridiculing the news item as 'the shocking news that Liberal Democrats disagree with Conservatives . . .'

It was one of those rare media rounds that I emerged from feeling that I'd comprehensively done a good job. As I took off my headphones and headed out of the studio, I was sure that I'd put the ball in the back of the net.

My next job that morning was to drive to Sedbergh, about ten miles east of Kendal in the spectacular Dales. One of our councillors, David Evans, came with me. I had no working hands-free mobile phone kit at the time, so when the phone rang as I was arriving in Sedbergh, David answered the phone for me. He turned pale and, turning to me, said, 'It's the Prime Minister's office!'

'I doubt it,' I smiled, 'It'll be the Deputy Prime Minister's office – someone in Nick's team.'

Dave earnestly called back, asking, 'Do you mean the *Deputy* Prime Minister?'

I could hear the stern voice on the end say very clearly and sharply, 'No! The Prime Minister. *Is* Mr Farron available to take his call?'

I stopped the car and took the call. I was of course somewhat taken aback that I was then put through to David Cameron, but more affected and amused by David Evans's reaction to all this. He had volunteered to join me on an outdoor surgery at Sedbergh market, not to be triaging calls from the PM!

I was genuinely impressed that Cameron had called. It was a nice touch. I was President of the Liberal Democrats but unlike my opposite number Grant Shapps, the Chairman of the Conservative Party, I wasn't a member of the Government. As a result, I didn't come into contact with the Prime Minister on a one-to-one basis all that often. That's what made his call all the more a surprise. He simply wanted to congratulate me on handling the story well.

This was after all an early version of the 'Lib Dem and Tory coalition partners at each other's throats' story that journalists would seek to resurrect from time to time throughout the 2010 to 2015 government. That morning I had dealt with what could have been a damaging story with a robust shrug. Why *would* you be surprised by the 'news' of differences of opinion between two parties that believe different things and therefore don't agree with each other on most issues? The parties had agreed to work together in the national interest as a result of an electoral accident, but they hadn't changed their views or ideology. Lib Dems and Tories were co-operating and behaving like grown-ups. We weren't merging. The rest of Europe manages to understand this, so what's our problem?

In the following four years I used my role as President to be the voice that went out to the media to explain what the Government was doing from a Liberal Democrat point of view.

For instance, the Liberal Democrats had increased the threshold at which low-paid people began paying income tax, and we raised the threshold by more and at a quicker rate than we had originally stated in the coalition agreement. This move took millions out of poverty and gave a boost to all low- and middle-income earners.

The Conservative Chancellor George Osborne, however, extracted a price for this over-delivery. He insisted that the Conservatives had to have a win too. He therefore proposed to reduce the top rate of income tax for high earners from 50p in the pound to 45p. The coalition presented these two policies drily, giving no narrative of the fact that they constituted a quid pro quo of one progressive Lib Dem policy matched by one regressive Conservative policy. As expected, we ('we' the coalition *and* 'we' the Liberal Democrats) drew heavy criticism for the reduction of the top rate of tax.

My task was to explain simply that this was a deal, a transaction between the Lib Dems and the Tories. The Liberal Democrats had successfully delivered a tax cut for up to 20 million low- and middle-income workers, but the price we had to pay to achieve this was to permit George Osborne to cut the taxes of a few thousand wealthy people, most of whom I suggested were known to him personally and on his Christmas card list. This example of quid pro quo showed you everything you needed to know about what – and who – were the priorities of both the Liberal Democrats and the Conservatives.

During the coalition years, it became my mission to do more like this – to distil the Liberal Democrat achievements in coalition and promote them, and to defend Nick Clegg and the rest of our ministers with language more colourful and less compromising than ministers themselves felt able to do.

It also meant being the voice that spoke for the Liberal Democrats on electoral matters. The first opportunity to do this came a fortnight into my time as President, just as the Oldham East and Saddleworth by-election reached its final fortnight. The by-election took place in unusual circum-stances, after an electoral court had disqualified the Labour MP Phil Woolas who had been elected with a tiny majority of 103 votes over the Liberal Democrats. Elwyn Watkins, the Liberal Democrat candidate from 2010, was selected to stand again in the by-election.

The campaign took place over December and January amidst ice, snow and bitter temperatures. The HQ we had established in Shaw was a freezing-cold stone building without any serious heating. Part of the building had served as an abattoir. I imagine that most of the animals would have died of cold before they reached their slaugh-terers (handily pre-frozen for retail purposes).

The by-election had become the major focus for party members right across the country. The press team and the HQ campaigns department had been shipped up to Oldham East en masse. My abiding memory is of the press team wearing thick dressing gowns over their day clothes in an attempt to stay warm.

Fighting a by-election over the Christmas and New Year holiday was tough, but the party pulled together and put on a good campaign. We had spent six months being vilified and now appreciated the chance to go on the offensive, defend our record and fight back.

In the end, Labour held the seat with an increased majority of around 3,600. This was hardly surprising, given that the tuition fees disaster had happened at the beginning of the campaign. However, the Liberal Democrat vote share stayed pretty static at over 30 per cent, and in view of the bruising nature of the previous six months, I made the case that we should actually be reasonably happy with the result. As I spoke, one after another, to the media outlets at the count on the night of 13 January, I stood my ground and suggested that the Liberal Democrats could count this as a 'score draw', a result that wasn't a win for us but from which we could take some encouragement.

There are few more tedious clichés in politics than the poor MP for the losing party who has to put a positive spin on a terrible result. On this occasion, though, I think I was justified in making the point that a decent second constituted an acceptable outcome.

It was a reasonable result, but it may have done us more harm than good. It lulled us into a false sense of security.

The Conservatives pulled their punches in that campaign and, in those early days of the coalition, it felt as though they really wanted us to do well for the sake of our new government. I had a meeting with Michael Gove, then Education Secretary, the Monday before polling day on a constituency matter. As we finished the meeting, he asked me in some detail and with apparent concern about how things were going in Oldham and wished us good fortune in the by-election. Call me naïve, but I sensed that he was sincere.

The next by-election came in Barnsley two months later and it brought us down to earth with a bump. Dominic Carman was a first-class candidate, but he was not honoured with a first-class result. It was sixth, to be precise. Having come second in the previous election, we slipped back four places, taking 4.2 per cent of the vote. This was the election that saw the UK Independence Party or UKIP begin to make a significant showing at parliamentary elections, rising to second place behind Labour. From this point on, the Liberal Democrats would most regularly be in fourth place in the opinion polls, behind UKIP. As Party President I was again sent to do the job of talking to the media as the face of Liberal Democracy in adversity as I defended our performance. I was interviewed by BBC Radio 5 Live (famed for its sports coverage) and said, 'Well, I'm a Blackburn Rovers fan. We *dream* of coming sixth!' I got away with this on 5 Live, but the presenter on Radio 4's *Today* programme didn't see the joke.

It was to get much worse for the party. Two months later in the Scottish Parliamentary, Welsh Assembly and local government elections, the Liberal Democrats were battered. In Wales, we managed to stand our ground and hold 5 of our 6 seats but in Scotland we were crushed, losing 12 of our 17 seats. I didn't try to put a brave face on it as I was interviewed in the early hours of the Friday after polling day. Dozens of my mates had lost their seats and they deserved better than someone trying to spin away their defeats as 'mid-term blues' or regrettable collateral damage. I was gutted and I didn't shy away from wearing my heart on my sleeve as I spoke to the various journalists.

At this point, in 2011, there was a sense that we were being punished by those who felt that we had let them down by going into coalition with the Conservatives, or for going into government at all and especially for breaking our word on tuition fees. The referendum on Alternative Vote was held on the same day as these elections. The Government held the referendum as a result of the coalition agreement. Liberal Democrats had always favoured a change in our electoral system to one that was proportional and fair. In the negotiations with the Conservatives in May 2010, the compromise was that the electorate would be asked to support the introduction of the Alternative Vote as the new electoral system for Westminster elections. AV is not proportional, and while it is fairer than our current first-past-the-post system, it isn't a huge improvement. Indeed, Nick Clegg himself had described AV as a 'miserable little compromise'. I wasn't in the coalition negotiations, but it always seemed to me that this was our party at its most naïve. In the coalition negotiations we had the chance to push for the Liberal Democrat holy grail of electoral reform and came away like Jack in *Jack and the Beanstalk*, with a handful of beans in exchange for our prize animal. We should only have accepted AV if it was granted without a referendum. Proportional Representation might require a referendum, but the minor tweak that was AV should never have needed to clear that hurdle. The AV campaign was also the Conservatives' first demonstration of seriously bad faith during the coalition. Their agreement to acquiesce over the AV referendum was broken about six weeks before polling day as they began to fund and fight the 'No to AV' campaign. Conservatives had woken up to the possibility that AV might lose them seats, and so they decided to kill it using a well-resourced campaign and the weight of their friends who own so much of the print media.

Their principal weapon was Liberal Democrat Leader and Deputy Prime Minister Nick Clegg, who was deployed as the bogey man. The AV campaign was presented as Nick's campaign and so the voters had an opportunity to punish Nick – a bizarre but sadly effective tactic. Chris Huhne, the Liberal Democrat Secretary of State for Energy and Climate Change, threatened legal action against the Conservatives in an angry cabinet meeting in April over alleged untruths in their messages. The honeymoon period of the coalition was most certainly over. In the end, the uninspiring 'Yes to AV' campaign and the negative but effective 'No to AV' campaign conspired to produce an outcome where 77 per cent of voters rejected this change in the electoral system.

The voters were angry with the Liberal Democrats and wanted to punish us. But it was to get much, much worse.

Later in Parliament it felt that we weren't getting punished so much as simply being ignored as an irrelevance. The 4.2 per cent vote in Barnsley in the March 2011 by-election compares favourably with the 0.9 per cent we took in the by-election in Rochester and Strood in November 2014.

When Chris Huhne was forced to resign his Eastleigh seat in February 2013, we faced another by-election. Chris had been charged with perverting the course of justice over a historic speeding case from 2003. He was eventually sentenced to eight months in prison after his ex-wife Vicky Pryce gave evidence against him and heart-breaking angry text exchanges with his children were submitted to the court. For Chris and his family, this was a terrible tragedy. I prayed for them all, and I wrote to Chris in prison.

For the Liberal Democrats, though, it led to our electoral high point of the coalition years. We actually managed to win something. I spent a vast amount of time at the by-election supporting Mike Thornton, our candidate, visiting on no fewer than six occasions during the three-week campaign. In the end, Mike was elected by a majority of 1,700 with the Conservatives slipping to third behind UKIP.

Eastleigh was a seat where we were relevant. We had a track record locally where we ran the council and held the parliamentary seat, and voters could choose to vote to endorse that record. We were also – so it seemed – the only plausible challenger to the Conservatives. If voters didn't like the Conservatives, they could vote for us to stop them. The problem was that around the country, in seats where we weren't already first or a good second, there was simply no reason to vote for us.

The 0.9 per cent vote in Rochester was the sign of a party evaporating.

If my main role as President was to motivate and to inspire members and activists, then you could say that my job just got more and more challenging as the results got worse and worse.

I think it is fair to say that I didn't make myself entirely popular with some of my parliamentary colleagues during this time and was viewed with suspicion by the leadership.

On rare but well-documented occasions I did not vote with the Government. The issue over tuition fees was not the only time I rebelled. I rebelled on the Health and Social Care Act and on the Bedroom Tax, among others. Those were votes that weren't popular with some of my parliamentary colleagues, but they were popular with the party around the country. Standing up to the Conservatives and staying true to Liberal Democrat principles gave rank-and-file Lib Dem members heart and encouragement. Many told me that they only remained in the party because I (and others) had stood up for some of those key issues where members felt we should not have compromised.

I enjoyed making rabble-rousing speeches. I enjoyed speaking from the heart and I often looked like I was enjoying being a rebel a bit too much. It probably looked like I was parading my conscience, being able to speak without the nuance that collective responsibility brings with it. The party needed this, but some of my colleagues didn't like it.

Some around the leadership thought that I was planning to challenge Nick for the leadership. They were quite wrong, but it didn't stop them briefing against me. Since I stepped down as Leader, a number of journalists have opened up to me over the staggering extent to which my colleagues in the House of Commons and the House of Lords, and some of the Special Advisors, were briefing against me to the media. A great deal of the content of these 'off-the-record briefings' related to my faith. I was a weird Christian, not a proper liberal.

'What is there about the treacherous, sanctimonious, God-bothering little shit, not to like?' suggested one anonymous colleague to a newspaper journalist. I thought this was extremely funny at the time, and in my constituency office we seriously considered making T-shirts bearing the slogan.

But it gave me a window into what people were saying about me, and what they thought about me. It gave a clue as to what tactics might be used against me in any future contest.

There were some in the party who distrusted me for my religious beliefs. But mostly I think the motive for seeking to undermine me through these anonymous briefings was that I was seen as either too left wing or not possessing sufficient gravitas. An additional factor, though, was that some were angry with me for standing firm on the Chris Rennard Affair.

The party's former Chief Executive and Campaigns Director, Lord Chris Rennard, had been accused by a number of women in the party of being guilty of sexual harassment. I had taken this matter seriously and treated the women's complaints seriously. Chris Rennard had been a great servant to the party and, among the House of Lords' group especially, has many close friends. I greatly respect Chris's achievements. However, the accusations against him could not be dismissed. As a party we needed to be clear and decisive in tackling harassment and the alleged abuse of power-relationships. Taking the stand that I did made me plenty of enemies within the Lords' group, and fuelled much of the briefing which continued against me throughout my time as Leader.

All of this raises the question, how should a Christian respond to this kind of thing? The 'treacherous, sanctimonious, God-bothering little shit' label deserves deconstructing a bit. My 'treachery' was to vote against increased tuition fees and the Bedroom Tax – in line with what our party members believed. I'd argue that those votes came from an attitude of loyalty. Loyalty to our party and to the thousands of members who had elected me as President. So I reject that charge.

On tuition fees, I think my faith did make a difference to the stance that I took. In reality, the reformed system of fees that was proposed made some sense. The system was arguably fairer than the system it replaced, in that it reduced repayments for lower earners and increased them for higher earners. Why not vote for it then? Well, because I had made a promise, a pledge, not to increase fees. If you make a promise, you should keep it. 'Nothing so disillusions the voter than backing the winning candidate,' wrote Mark Twain. Quite, because we always tend to be disappointed. People assume that politicians are dishonest, so surely our job is to confound that assumption rather than confirm it? Essentially, I rebelled on fees because you should keep your word.

The 'sanctimonious God-botherer' part is interesting. To be sanctimonious is to be self-righteous and to demonstrate moral superiority over others. Opposing tuition fees probably looked like a sanctimonious act to some. But self-righteousness is the opposite of what it means to be a real Christian. You only become a Christian if you realize that you are a sinner in need of redemption. And if you become a Christian you are ordered to look down on no one and to forgive everyone who crosses you, including people who brief anonymously against you. Whoever you are, I forgive you!

If you reference your faith at all as a UK politician, you will get labelled. If you let it influence your actions and your approach to politics, then you will be scrutinized all the more. I am often asked how Christianity affects my politics. It is usually asked from a standpoint that assumes that it's not liberal to 'impose' your faith on others. I would agree that it's not liberal to force people to adhere to a faith that they don't believe in or to treat society as if it believes things that it doesn't. But what people mean by 'don't impose your faith' is that I should not allow my judgements or world view to be in any way affected by something that is central to who I am. To any atheists, agnostics, or secular humanists reading this, I ask you to consider how valid it would be if you were asked to leave your world view and your values at the door before entering any discussion?

Must we begin every debate with an empty head? I am simply saying that we ought to be careful not to slip into lazy thinking when it comes to separating your deepest beliefs from your public life.

In reality, though, maybe the most important impact of my faith on my public life is that I understand that all things are temporary. Significantly, that they are temporary in the context of there being such a thing as eternity. My time in Parliament is temporary, the rise of populism is temporary, referendum results are temporary, Jeremy Corbyn's ascendancy in the Labour Party is temporary, the Conservatives winning at elections is temporary. Every empire, regime, era, system, epoch, movement . . . every defeat and every victory are all temporary. The Bible is really clear that, in the end, every knee will bow and every tongue will confess that Jesus Christ is Lord (see Philippians 2.10–11). That includes the knees and tongues of Trump, Juncker, the Clintons, May, Corbyn, Hitler, Stalin, Farage and Farron, no matter what we currently say we believe.

If we know that our time on earth isn't for ever, and that there is an eternity that we fit into, then it will follow that any and every defeat, disappointment, setback – yes, even every tragedy – can be seen from a different, much larger perspective.

This means that everything that happens in this life matters, but it also means that you can hold those things lightly. Triumphs and disasters alike are not permanent. You can therefore rise above them both. I promise you that this is a lot easier said than done. I do not live in the state of serenity that this might imply – but faith in Christ does provide a way to keep the successes and the setbacks in proportion.

Another question I faced as a Christian politician was that given that Christians are meant to be humble, self-sacrificing and putting others before themselves, what room is there for ambition? The answer, I believe, is that it depends on the motives behind your ambition. I have to confess that my motives were mixed, and probably best summed up as being a fusion of duty and vanity.

During my time as President, it became clear that I was in a strong position to be the next Leader of the party. I was the bookies' favourite from 2011 onwards. The chance to lead the party that I love was a hugely attractive proposition. As I saw my party slump in the polls and in almost every election during that Parliament, I saw the need for someone who could rebuild and inspire our party after what seemed an inevitable electoral disaster in 2015. Maybe I wouldn't have been a great Deputy Prime Minister, but I felt that my skill set very much suited the job of a campaign leader who would have to fight back from the depths and achieve the survival and renewal of the Liberal Party cause. My ambition to be Leader grew during that time.

I always felt, though, that my faith would bring me down. During this time, I mentioned this to a couple of friends, one Christian and one non-Christian. They both thought I was being slightly vainglorious. I meant what I said, though, because to hold to biblical teaching as a British politician in this era is considered at best to be 'odd' – even if you are, like me, a liberal who accepts everyone, judges no one and believes that you have no right to impose your morality on others.

Once upon a time, the hot-button issue where Christian teaching would jar with the culture was slavery. Another time it would be materialism, legalism or attitudes towards militarism. Today it is in the area of sexuality and sexual identity. In a hundred years' time, it will be something else.

In 2013, the hot button got pressed by the coalition. The Liberal Democrats ensured that the Government presented the bill for equal marriage to enable same-sex couples to tie the knot.

From the moment that this entered Parliament, I received a massive amount of correspondence from people opposed to this legislation. Many of those people were Christians. I was challenged at church – gently, lovingly and politely, but regularly.

The view that those opponents of equal marriage presented was simply that to ensure equality for LGBT people did not necessarily mean that the law needed to redefine marriage, given that marriage has a specific meaning. It's a respectable viewpoint and one that should not be elbowed out of the public square. Nevertheless, I took the view that, whatever I believed, I did not have the right to expect people who were not Christians to live as though they were.

Marriage in the sight of God cannot be amended by Parliament. But civil marriage in a secular society can be something different, whether one likes that or not.

In the vote for the second reading of the bill for equal marriage, I voted in favour. In the weeks that followed, however, I felt increasingly uneasy. As the report stage of the bill came to the Commons, there were some areas that I felt particularly concerned about from a liberal perspective. First, I supported an amendment that would have allowed registrars to quietly pass on their duties for a same-sex marriage to a colleague if their conscience did not permit them to perform such a ceremony. The precedent for this is the conscience clause that allows health professionals to decline to be involved in an abortion and to pass the responsibility to colleagues. The amendment was defeated.

Second, I know many transgender people who were distressed that the retention of the spousal veto meant that the existing husband or wife of a trans person had the right to prevent the straightforward dissolution of their marriage (should that be what one or both wish), giving the non-trans member of the relationship greater power than the trans member. It struck me that if we were going to legislate to allow equal marriage, then it should be equal for all, not just for some. The Government would not, however, remove the veto in this bill.

My uneasiness at these liberal blind-spots within the bill meant I felt that I just couldn't vote for it at third and final reading.

I must be honest, though, as underlying all of this was my inner turmoil about what the Bible says of marriage. I knew that the bill, for all its faults, was in many ways a liberal move, one that enabled equality. I also knew that it would pass with a large majority and that it didn't need my vote to put it on the statute books. Could I close my eyes and walk through the 'aye' lobby despite my liberal and spiritual misgivings? I experienced real anguish as I weighed this up – I had well-meaning Liberal Democrat colleagues giving me interesting stabs at theology to 'help me out' . . . and others being somewhat less charitable.

I was quite conscious also that if I was to equivocate on this totemic bill, no matter what my reasoning might be, it would in all likelihood kill off my leadership ambitions.

On the night of the third reading, I voted for some of the amendments and then as the division bell rang for the third reading on the final bill, I breathed deeply, collected my bags and walked steadily out of the Commons and got on the Tube to head for Euston. When the bell rings in Parliament, MPs have eight minutes to get to the Chamber and file into either the 'aye' lobby or the 'no' lobby. As I stood on the Tube, I checked my watch. When the eight minutes were up, I knew then that my abstention would be noted, and that there was no way to undo what I had done (or, indeed, hadn't done).

I always knew that I wouldn't vote against someone's right to get married to the person they loved, but for all the reasons above, in the end I just couldn't vote for it either.

That night and in the days that followed my social media feeds were full of bile – bile from people who preach tolerance.

Indeed, I also got a lot of stick from Christians, Muslims and others who felt I was wrong not to have voted against. Interestingly enough, most of those who thought I should have voted 'no' were more liberal, tolerant and understanding than those who thought I should have voted 'yes'.

I remember an article by a leading Liberal Democrat blogger and activist, Mark Pack, a few weeks earlier. Mark had written that he was suspicious of me because he felt that I had never made a difficult speech or done a difficult thing in a parliamentary vote – he feared I was a people-pleaser. In his article he wished for me to make a speech or do something that he would disagree with. On the train home I re-read Mark's article. 'Happy now, Mark?' I thought to myself.

In many ways, I regret not voting 'yes' at the third reading – only because it gave people the wrong idea of me and gave my opponents, in the party and outside it, the chance to categorize and demonize me as some kind of homophobe. But the attacks received by some of my colleagues who had voted against equal marriage at the third reading were far worse. Those colleagues aren't homophobes either. Disagreement is not the same as hatred or fear. The misuse of this term is bogus and counterproductive. To bandy it around whenever someone presents a world view on sexuality that differs from yours is to sleepwalk into the adoption of a sinister 'newspeak' vocabulary. It is also to substitute mindless insults for understanding and debate. Liberals beware! So, I utterly reject that I am a homophobe, but I am more offended by the lazy and illiberal thinking that is behind such a charge than I care about any personal insult implied. My agonizing over the bill came mostly from my desire not to sacrifice the need for good liberal scrutiny and healthy scepticism about legislation by joining in a wave of unquestioning approval. I'd humbly argue that my motives in not voting for the third reading were at least as liberal as those who voted in favour. Nevertheless, this predictably provided an excuse to some to claim that I was unreliable on LGBT rights and on equality – a thoroughly inaccurate claim, but a claim that stuck.

Maybe that was the moment I ought to have chosen the easier path and left ambitions of leading the party to others.

7

Langley Park . . .

In the first week of July 2013, about ten of us gathered at Wainwright House, a hotel in Kendal owned by a friend. We'd been out for a meal the night before and we sat outside in the spacious garden with flip charts, marker pens and post-it notes for an event that had been in the diary for a few weeks, enigmatically entitled 'Langley Park'.

From Langley Park to Memphis is Prefab Sprout's third album (some would say fourth because *Protest Songs* was recorded before *From Langley Park to Memphis* but was released afterwards. You're glad you know this, aren't you?). Prefab Sprout are my favourite band. To call them an 80s indie act doesn't do them justice, but the NME once described them as 'the Smiths for people with A levels'. Lyrically and musically sublime, they had the cleverest lyrics ('words are trains for moving past what really has no name') and transcendent melodies. I fell in love with them the first time I heard the track 'Appetite' on the radio in 1985. My mum bought me their second album *Steve McQueen* for Christmas in 1985 and I've never looked back. That original vinyl copy of *Steve McQueen* remains my most treasured material possession.

So when I was asked by Kiran Horwich, my researcher at the time, what she should put in the diary to describe this 'thing', I thought it a wonderful opportunity for self-indulgence and began the process of thinking my way through the entire Prefab Sprout canon, settling on 'Langley Park' mostly because it sounded more innocuous than 'Swoon', 'Steve McQueen', 'Andromeda Heights', 'Protest Songs', 'Let's Change the World with Music', 'Jordan: The Comeback' or 'The Gunman and Other Stories' (*Crimson Red* hadn't come out at that stage)!

So what was 'the thing' that necessitated an enigmatic code name in the diary? It was, of course, my embryonic campaign to be the next party Leader.

That first al fresco gathering of the Langley Park group in the Kendal sunshine was chaired by Ben Rich. Ben is one of my oldest friends in politics. I first met him when I ran successfully for the National Union of Students' National Executive Council. I was the first Lib Dem ever elected to that role, and Ben, as my campaign manager, was a major part of that achievement. Ben's a fixer, a networker, a strategist – and most importantly he's a loyal friend. We'd remained so over the years and met again for a coffee in the café overlooking Waterloo Station concourse in May 2013. I'd come to the conclusion that when the leadership became vacant, I wanted to be in a position to be a serious runner even if – in the end – I decided not to enter the contest. So, in the coffee shop at Waterloo we decided that it was better to plan for something that might not happen than to not plan for something that might. Langley Park was born.

There were ten of us gathered together that weekend in Kendal. I felt incredibly awkward planning a campaign that was so centred on the individual (that individual being me). I've stood in many elections, but there is quite a difference between being a candidate for the council or for Parliament where you are carrying a message and a set of policies on behalf of the whole party, and being the candidate for internal office where your message is focused on your own personal characteristics and values.

When Nick Clegg ran for Leader in 2007, I supported his campaign. His launch speech was at the National Liberal Club in Whitehall Place. As I sat in the audience listening, I was irritated by the number of times he self-deprecated, talked himself down and even apologized for being there. 'I am here because I think you're great,' I told him later. 'Don't go telling me that you're not!'

As I sat in on that first Langley Park meeting, I understood how Nick must have felt – all those people turning up for you, pinning their hopes on you. You'd have to have serious ego problems not to find that a bit difficult to handle.

Probably the one person with us that day who felt even more awkward than me was my friend Paul Baxendale. Everyone else in the Langley Park group was a seasoned political campaigner of one kind or another.

Paul, however, is the pastor of our church in Kendal. I wanted him there so that he could give me feedback afterwards and to contribute during the day as a different voice from the others.

The following day, Paul said he was impressed by how committed everyone at the Langley Park day had been, and how determined they were by a desire to do good. It had struck him, however, that everyone else was looking for hope in someone or something else other than Jesus. Of course they were. All of us are. In politics, it is so easy for us to seek our ultimate meaning in the form of an ideology, a manifesto, a party or a person. Paul pointed out to me that our ultimate meaning, and humanity's ultimate hope, is in something way above party politics.

It was a reminder that religion and politics speak different languages and have different priorities, and that means that we need to work harder than we do to understand one another. Mind you, too often believers and sceptics alike don't seem all that interested in understanding the other side. For Christians, this is a shameful state of affairs, because you cannot love your neighbour if you don't take the time to consider how they think and treat them with respect. For me, I should have begun to understand that this 'speaking different languages' could become the means by which I got into trouble later in my career. I was surrounded by the most amazingly talented and decent people during my time as President and Leader, but most of them were not practising Christians. They were helping me to formulate my words and yet they spoke a different language. I am bilingual to a degree – as a liberal, knee-deep in liberal sensitivities and the language of liberation and identity, and as a Christian who sees his ultimate meaning in life in following Christ. I'm at the narrowest intersection of the Venn diagram. It's a privileged place to be, and yet during my time as President and Leader I didn't use that privilege to reach across the divide – I kept my Christian life in one box and my political life in another. I couldn't bring myself to translate what I believed to the non-Christians who supported me so strongly and who were keen to help me communicate. I should have had more faith in them. I should have taken the risk of explaining my faith in Christ and been prepared to accept that the consequence of this might have been that they dropped me and looked for someone else.

I am still living in that intersection of the Venn diagram. I am grateful to have a second chance now to use my experience and my voice to speak from that almost unique location. I don't intend to waste that opportunity.

The Langley Park weekend was over. We'd identified my strengths and weaknesses (incidentally, my faith was considered to be both) and developed a campaign slogan: 'a fresh start' which – sadly and accurately – implied that we would have had a hammering in the general election that preceded a leadership contest. The slogan also carried with it a sense of putting the years of the coalition, and in particular tuition fees, behind us. Not because the coalition had been a bad thing but because one of my key objectives as Leader would be to re-establish our own distinctive identity.

Not once did I consider even the possibility of challenging Nick Clegg for the leadership. I am a Nick Clegg fan, aware he spent five years taking incredible stick for stepping up to do what was right for the country. I was comfortable with Nick staying on as Leader for as long as he wished. I had decided that I wanted to be Leader but I wasn't really in any rush.

The assumption we made was that the party would suffer at the 2015 general election and that Nick would take that opportunity to step down. I was to be a candidate in the subsequent leadership contest.

The other assumption was that I was to be the candidate of the 'left' and that there would be a 'continuity' candidate – someone who was less critical of some of the policies of the coalition, and who was on the centre-right of the party. It looked likely that the continuity candidate could be Ed Davey, Danny Alexander or Norman Lamb. Norman was becoming increasingly high profile and looked to be the potential rival candidate who was most prepared. Norman also struck me as being the candidate who would have the best chance of beating me in a contest. His strengths lay in his being an extremely personable colleague, a first-class campaigning constituency MP and an effective health minister who had done more than anyone else to put mental health issues on the map.

The fixed-term Parliament and the stability of the coalition meant that we could be 95 per cent sure that there would be no general election until May 2015 and therefore no leadership contest before then either.

There was always a five per cent chance of a leadership contest happening sooner. That chance nearly came to pass in May 2014.

The local and European elections took place on Thursday 22 May. A joint campaign with a single polling day meant that this would be the biggest electoral contest before the general election.

Nick had asked me to chair the 2014 election campaign – a poisoned chalice if ever there was one! I accepted and we decided that our job was to pour resources behind council seats that demonstrated a serious inclination to win in order to minimize local election losses. On Europe, we made the bold decision to do something quite unusual – we decided that our European election campaign message would, for once, actually be about Europe. We styled ourselves as the party of 'In', the party that was in favour of our being in the EU and working with our partners to create prosperity and maintain peace. Our slogans during the campaign were variations on a theme, such as 'In Europe, in work'.

The fact that it seemed such a risk for the party to adopt an unashamedly pro-European slogan for a European parliamentary election campaign gives you an insight as to how, two years later, the UK voted to leave the EU in the referendum. It was considered a given that the UK was a member of the EU and always would be. Of course, there were plenty of politicians who played the populist card and opposed the UK remaining in the EU but surely, they'd never get their way? Most of the electorate seemed to acquiesce over Europe rather than being overtly hostile towards the institutions, but very few people seriously warmed to the EU either.

Those parties and politicians that were pro-Europe were therefore too nervous to come out and make the case for staying in the EU, for fear of losing votes.

Our national opinion poll ratings had steadily slipped. We had secured 23 per cent of the vote at the 2010 election, and in the months after the coalition was formed this dropped to 15 per cent. After the tuition fees debacle, the poll ratings for the Liberal Democrats fell further to around 10 per cent. By New Year 2014 we had fallen further, to around 5 to 6 per cent. It felt like the hatred, which the party had incurred over tuition fees and the decision simply to go into coalition with the Conservatives at all, had faded away but that our relevance had slipped away too. People had stopped despising us and in doing so had also stopped caring about us. It's a reminder that no situation is so bad that it can't get worse.

With this in mind, Nick and I agreed that selling ourselves as the pro-European party gave us the chance to register on people's radar, make some kind of impact and get a hearing. After all, it's better to be 'Marmite' and upset some people while inspiring a few, than to be blancmange and neither offend nor impress anyone.

Simply saying that we were pro-European wouldn't make much difference though – we'd need to do something reasonably newsworthy. We decided to challenge 'the anti-Clegg' Nigel Farage, leader of the right-wing, anti-European UK Independence Party. Farage was very happy to accept the challenge. Two debates took place a week apart. We prepared Nick well in the days beforehand. I had the joyous honour of playing the part of Nigel Farage in the warm-up mock debates that we held at the Ministry of Sound nightclub near the Elephant and Castle in London. Three of Nick's press team were loaned to me so that I could prepare for 'being Nigel'.

During the debates, I would throw all sorts of figures at Nick – for example, the number of people suffering while languishing on waiting lists for NHS surgery, council houses, preferred local schools . . . all because of the number of immigrants coming in and swamping the country. After one of the mock debates Nick was concerned, asking me, 'How did you get those figures?' I replied, 'I just made them up, boss, that's what Farage will do!'

The thing about being a populist is that you can say anything you like because the market you are playing to is one that responds to emotion and not logic. If you are angry at the system, you won't be overly concerned about the integrity of the politicians you vote for, as a way to smash that system. If you want to break a window then you won't care much about the moral character of the rock that you pick up and throw at it. If it's big and heavy enough to break the window, you'll celebrate when the glass shatters, no matter what.

When the Nick versus Nigel debates took place, Nick's logic was no match for Nigel's emotion. Nick was deemed to have lost both debates. However, he performed well and won the endorsement of between 25 and 40 per cent of those who watched or listened to the exchanges. When you are polling at 5 per cent, you should take that as a win.

In the European elections of 2014, the Liberal Democrats managed to poll 7 per cent. Given the evaporation of our brand and of our electoral credibility, we could easily have suffered the same fate that we did later that year when we took just 0.9 per cent in the Rochester by-election. The strategy of choosing to be the party of 'In' gave at least some people a reason to vote for us and avoided total oblivion. It must therefore be seen as a moderate vindication. Nevertheless, of the 12 European parliamentary seats that we defended, we lost all but one.

The local and European elections took place on 22 May with the local election results declared overnight. Those results saw us hold barely half of the council seats we were defending. The European election results were to be counted across all 28 states on the Sunday evening, so we had the long wait over the weekend to discover our fate. The indications were that those results would be as bad as they indeed turned out to be.

As these were the last elections before the general election of 2015, speculation began to focus on how many Westminster parliamentary seats the Liberal Democrats could reasonably expect to hold in that election. For four years, we had seen vast losses in councils, the Scottish Parliament and the Welsh Assembly. Our numbers in Parliament (56 MPs – a strong third party force) remained untouched only because we had faced no contest since the coalition was formed. A hammering in the European elections would mean that we were on a 12-month countdown to annihilation at Westminster too.

On Saturday 24 May, as speculation grew about the European election results to be announced the following evening, Rosie and I headed down to Wolverhampton. We were attending the wedding of my press officer Paul Butters to his fiancée Gemma. Paul, as I've described earlier, is a legend in his own lifetime. He has an extraordinary talent for the ability to do deals, place good stories and snuff out bad ones. I imagine that a lot of press officers like to think of themselves as a reincarnation of Tony Blair's apparently omnipotent press secretary Alastair Campbell – but Paul comes the closest I have ever seen to pulling this off.

Respected and feared in equal measure, he remains a real friend . . . and believe me, you wouldn't want him as your enemy.

The ceremony took place soon after midday, and we then made our way to a lovely hotel in the Shropshire countryside for the reception. The speeches were good. Paul put away his acerbic persona and gushed with touching sincerity about the lovely Gemma. All thoughts of impending election results were banished as the evening do kicked off. Or so Gemma thought . . . At around 10 p.m. while Paul and I were dad-dancing to The Clash, I felt my phone vibrate in my pocket and out of habit I reached for it to see who it was. It was Nick Clegg. I showed the caller-display to Paul, who stopped bopping and said, 'Outside.'

We sneaked out of the hotel and sat at a picnic table as I called Nick back with Paul listening in. Nick appeared in good humour as he answered. I told him where I was, and he asked me to pass on his good wishes to Paul and Gemma. Paul nodded. After a few more pleasantries, Nick said that he knew the results were going to be very bad on Sunday night, worse even than the local elections had been the previous day. 'If you think I should step aside now, please tell me,' he added. I wasn't expecting that. Maybe Paul was but it hadn't occurred to me that Nick's state of mind had reached that point. He went on to say that he feared that the electoral disaster owed much to people not trusting him as Leader and therefore discarding our message.

Reception wasn't great at the hotel and in the middle of this conversation the call failed. Paul cursed and we rushed around to the front of the hotel where we found a better mobile signal. I was about to call back but Nick rang first. In the minute or so that we had been off the phone, Paul and I considered my response so, when my conversation with Nick resumed, I let him finish what he had to say and then I responded.

I told him that the personal grief that he and his family had had to endure over the previous four years was something that no one should have to experience. That I was proud of him now as I was when he trounced David Cameron and Gordon Brown in the 2010 leaders' debates. If he wanted to step down, then he must feel no guilt in doing so. But I explained that I didn't think that he needed to do so. If Nick were to step down following these results, what would happen next? I speculated that if there were to be a leadership contest, we would then throw ourselves into a two- or three-month internal campaign which would divert the attention and energies of every member from the more important job of committing to the fight of our lives in the constituencies we were defending. The only alternative to a contest was a coronation, where the party would unite around a single candidate.

I explained my view to Nick that the only person who could plausibly be the 'coronation' candidate would be Vince Cable. I am an admirer of Vince, and he stood out as the one Liberal Democrat in government who most jarred with the Conservatives. He could present a more distinct image for the party and maybe – just maybe – he could do something to improve our fortunes.

The problem with Vince was twofold. The first was that while Vince was seen by the media as a more left-of-centre and anti-Conservative figure, he was nevertheless the minister who had shepherded through the tuition fees policy. Up until this point, the anger at the fees debacle was directed at Nick in a very personal way. However, I suggested that it would take the media five minutes to change tack and very plausibly pin the blame on Vince. His honeymoon wouldn't even last as long as Paul and Gemma's.

The second problem with Vince is that, while I could see some merit in a desperate throw of the dice to try to revive our standing for the last year of the Parliament, there were many other colleagues who would not accept that. Paul understood from his contacts that Danny Alexander, and possibly Norman Lamb and Ed Davey too, would see a vacancy as their chance to run for the leadership. The 'Orange Book' wing of the party didn't think much of the more social democratic and Keynesian Vince Cable.

For readers who are not immersed in the internal landscape of the Liberal Democrats, the *Orange Book* was a collection of essays, edited by then MP and future minister David Laws and investor and philanthropist Paul Marshall, and written by Liberal Democrat politicians including Nick Clegg and Vince Cable, in 2004. The book has been seen since as an attempt to move the Liberal Democrats towards a more centre-right, pro-market position. While not an entirely fair characterization of what was an important and interesting contribution to thinking in the party, it nevertheless stuck and the term 'Orange Book' has been since used to describe the party's centre-right. Although Vince was one of the authors, he has largely been considered to be 'to the left' of the majority of the *Orange Book* contributors.

As I stood outside the hotel, with the music from the disco providing the backing track to our conversation, my advice to Nick was, 'Don't resign unless you really feel that you need to for the sake of your family.' If Nick had resigned, I suspect that there would have been a lengthy and divisive contest that would do us far more damage.

Nick seemed grateful for my frankness and loyalty. I'm never sure whether he trusted me or not. I have always hugely admired him for his decency even more than for his political skills (which are considerable). My guess is that Nick's view of me must have been coloured by the suspicion in which I was held by many of his advisors.

As we ended the call, I wondered what he made of my motives in giving him the advice that I did. Did he think I was playing some kind of game, or that I was calculating in my own interest? In reality, I simply told him what I genuinely thought.

Of course, Paul's immediate response once the call was over was, 'If he goes, will you run?'

I don't know how seriously Nick intended his offer to step down. I suspect he simply wanted to test the water and see what colleagues thought, but that his inclination and desire was to continue in the job. In the end he did just that, but the story didn't quite end there.

The following morning, Paul had arranged for a fleet of satellite trucks from the various Sunday political programmes to come to the hotel to allow me to speak on behalf of the party as we speculated exactly how much of a hammering we were in for that night. Gemma looked down upon us from the balcony of their room as her husband moved among the journalists spinning and schmoozing like the absolute pro he is. I wonder what she thought of all this . . .

That night I attended the count for the North West European parliamentary constituency at Manchester's Town Hall. My job was, once again, to be the face of the party in adversity. To be that bloke on the telly who pretends that a complete and utter disaster is actually not all that bad . . . When you lose all but one of your Members of the European Parliament, that's a pretty tough gig.

I got back home to Milnthorpe in the early hours of Monday morning and packed a suitcase. After many weeks of campaigning, we were going on a short family holiday to the Highlands. After a short night's sleep, I got up and five of us – plus Jasper the spaniel – piled into the car and headed up to Fort William, then turned left on the road to the Isles. We had booked a chalet by a loch near Arisaig and had a blissful four days without any phone signal or Wi-Fi. I went running, we climbed a couple of hills, had a day trip to the Isle of Rùm, played cricket on the beach and ate lots. It was a fabulous break.

Meanwhile, back in the bubble, it was all kicking off. As I continued my holiday incommunicado, cut off from the world, a furore had blown up concerning the leadership of the party.

Lord Matthew Oakeshott, a long-time critic of Nick Clegg and friend of Vince Cable, had leaked some polling that he had paid for which showed – if you asked the right questions – that Vince would be a more electorally successful Liberal Democrat Leader than Nick.

The media loved this, of course, and I suspect Matthew rather enjoyed it too. Vince and Nick didn't. I was relatively high up on the call list for mischief-making journalists. (Actually, to be fair, on this occasion the mischief was all 'made' by folks within the party. The media simply reported on it.) Likewise, as President, I ought to have been the one on the airwaves giving the party's response to this and pouring oil on troubled water.

I was genuinely uncontactable. Paul Butters was on honeymoon and my constituency agent Paul Trollope – the one person who could have furnished the Press Office with Rosie's number (because she did have phone reception) – decided that I deserved a break and that I should be left alone.

By the time I returned from the Highlands, Matthew Oakeshott had been sacked from the Liberal Democrat group in the Lords, Vince had been forced to distance himself from his friend, and Nick's position – if it had ever been in doubt – was now secure given that this rather half-baked coup had flopped with traditional Liberal Democrat amateurishness.

The one potential 'coronation' candidate was, for the time being, bounced into pledging loyalty to Nick and stating that he was not seeking to be Leader.

With the benefit of hindsight, was Nick right to continue for that final year? Or would a change at the top have helped us avert the disaster we incurred in May 2015? You could argue that with a new Leader at the helm, the 2015 result could hardly have been much worse. Relegation-threatened football teams often remove a talented but beleaguered manager with a dozen games left of the season in the hope that a new boss will provide fresh impetus to turn things around. Indeed, this often works. The problem was that the Liberal Democrats did not have a large field of potential leaders with the right experience to choose from. The coalition-enthusiasts or 'Orange Bookers' all shared two traits. One was that they were just as tainted by the tuition fees issue as Nick was. The other trait they all shared was that none of them were as talented as Nick Clegg. Not many of us saw much point in replacing Nick with a less capable replica. In which case that left only two likely potential replacements: Vince Cable and me.

While Vince might have had a chance of being offered the leadership uncontested, there was absolutely no way that the party hierarchy would have tolerated me as Leader and Deputy Prime Minister without a fight. Liberal Democrat ministers, whips, major donors and the like would consider me much too big a risk to be handed the job on a plate. I don't blame them for thinking this.

As I have said earlier, I would not have considered challenging Nick for the top job, but would I have put my name forward in the summer of 2014 if Nick had decided to step down? I'm not sure I would have. At that time, I didn't think that I possessed the skills or the experience necessary to be Deputy Prime Minister. I believe that I did have the skills to be a campaigning leader who could rebuild the party after an electoral defeat. That meant that 2014 was not the right time for me. Who knows whether I might have been persuaded into running if a vacancy had arisen at that time, but I'm pretty sure I would not have been. Instead, I would have remained neutral and above the fray as the party's President, while casting my secret ballot for Vince.

Nothing that happened in the months that followed suggested that the party was likely to stage a late recovery as the general election date got closer.

We were diverted from the existential threat to the party in September 2014 by an existential threat to our country. Namely the referendum on independence in Scotland. I know and am genuinely fond of a number of Scottish and Welsh nationalists in Parliament, but I have always found nationalism to be an utterly illiberal and destructive creed. Someone once said that 'patriots love their country; nationalists hate their neighbour'. This is a harsh, but generally accurate barb in my experience.

To me, as a Northerner who considers himself at least as much British as English, Scotland, and Wales and Northern Ireland, are an integral part of my identity and of the country to which I belong. I took part in the referendum as a foot-soldier more than as a politician. I joined the fight for UK unity because I cared deeply about the result. I knew, however, that English voices in that referendum campaign might have played into the nationalists' hands, and so I restricted myself to leafleting and canvassing in the Scottish borders. There were to be no big media appearances or speeches this time.

As a white person, I have never experienced racism in my life. But during that referendum, I was regularly told to 'F*** off back to England!' by 'Yes' voters. Having been in coalition government with the Conservatives for four years,

I was used to hostility on the doorsteps but never the kind of venom that this toxic identity politics brought with it.

One evening I spent a long session knocking on doors in Hawick in the Borders. After my night on the doorsteps with half a dozen Scottish colleagues, we went to the pub to swap notes on our experiences. The Scots around the table had encountered around 40 per cent in favour of independence, 10 per cent against independence and 50 per cent who wouldn't say. I, on the other hand, had 40 per cent for independence, 50 per cent against independence and 10 per cent who wouldn't say. We concluded that 'No' voters were too nervous to tell a fellow Scot how they were voting for fear of exposure and social disgrace . . . but that they were more relaxed about telling a 'neutral' Englishman with a northern accent. Maybe.

The other observation I made following that evening session was that 'Yes' posters outnumbered 'No' posters by five to one, even though, in the end, Hawick voted more than two to one against independence.

It felt as though the 'tyranny of opinion' here was that one could not truly be Scottish unless one was pro-Independence.

A friend of mine in her eighties who lives in the Hebrides confided in me with sadness, 'The worst thing is that they've stolen our flag.' She felt that all things Scottish now belonged to the nationalists and that those who opposed independence were somehow unpatriotic. To this day I remain bewildered that so many otherwise liberal and social democratic people can fall for such divisive and intolerant hogwash.

As the referendum campaign got into its last two weeks, I was not the only opponent of independence who was getting increasingly alarmed at the prospect of the vote going the wrong way. Polls began to show 'Yes' in the lead. It struck me that the voices of the 'No' campaign were lacklustre and that the strongest pro-Union voices were not being heard.

At that time, the two most popular pro-UK voices in Scotland were former Liberal Democrat Leader Charles Kennedy and former Labour Prime Minister Gordon Brown. Neither was being deployed very much. I felt that they needed to be drafted in immediately to give those who were unsure how to vote some emotional and logical reasons to vote to remain in the UK and to undo the momentum that the 'Yes' campaign was enjoying.

As a friend and colleague, I was able to reach out to Charles, but his health problems prevented him doing more than he already was. I had no real route to contact Gordon Brown, but I did know Peter Hain, the former Labour cabinet minister, and I asked him whether pressure could be put on Gordon to get more involved. Peter said that he would do so and that there were many others in the Labour Party who were also encouraging Gordon to be more prominent in the final few days of the campaign. A week before polling day, I bumped into Gordon himself during a vote in the Commons and flattered him (sincerely) by saying that he was the most popular politician on the pro-UK side and that we could really do to hear more from him in the crucial final few days.

When at last Gordon Brown did enter the ring, it's fair to say that he delivered a knockout blow. As I watched

Gordon Brown's speech on the eve of the referendum on 17 September, I was brought to tears by the utter passion and intelligence of his words, and by his delivery. It was one of the greatest pieces of oratory I have ever seen and probably the most effective. It's quite possible that Gordon's 13-minute speech was the event that won the referendum for 'No' the following day. I was out on the streets of Galashiels on polling day, and the Brown speech was mentioned by countless voters from both sides, but mostly those voting 'No'. What was great about Brown's speech was that it ticked every box. It dealt with the logical reasons to vote 'No', the reasons to vote 'No' if you were still uncertain given that this vote was 'for all time', but it was the emotional appeal that was the greatest aspect of the speech. In the sing-song tones of the preacher, he brought us to imagine the Scottish, English, Welsh and Northern Irish soldiers who lie side by side in cemeteries in Europe, who fought for our freedom together. He said that we had done more than win those wars together; we had built the peace together: the NHS, the welfare state. He talked about the Scottish values of sharing versus the un-Scottish values of breaking apart.

For those of you who do not know Gordon Brown, let's just say that this was not his usual style. Brown's speeches had been known for their emotionally detached, detail-heavy qualities, laden with gravitas, and certainly empty of the pulpit passion Gordon showed on that day. It is a reminder that when you strip politicians of ambition and invite them to pick a side based on principle rather than on political calculation, the resulting authenticity can be mind-blowing.

In the early hours of 19 September 2014, 'No' defeated 'Yes' in the referendum by 55 per cent to 45 per cent. A clear win for a continuing United Kingdom – but the SNP developed their grievance politics intelligently in the weeks following. The Nationalists received a large and sustained bounce in the opinion polls as those who had voted 'Yes' fed off the SNP's argument that the Government had not kept the promises it had made to Scottish voters in the referendum. As the May 2015 general election came closer into view, the SNP's polling strength seemed, if anything, to be growing.

Suddenly, Labour MPs in safe seats in Scotland began to understand that they were in danger of losing to the SNP. The same applied to the Liberal Democrats. Had it not been for the SNP surge, then the Liberal Democrats would have held 5 or 6 of the 11 seats we had won in 2010 rather than hanging on to just the one (Orkney and Shetland). Incidentally, Labour went down from 41 Scottish MPs to just one, with the Conservatives keeping the solitary seat they had previously held.

Not only did this revolutionary change in the dynamic in Scotland damage the Liberal Democrats in Scotland, it also proved instrumental to the Conservatives' winning message throughout England and Wales and led to our obliteration in Parliament. The spectre of a much larger SNP parliamentary party meant that Labour couldn't really hope to gain an overall majority of their own, which provided the Conservatives with the opportunity to say to the electorate that the choice was between stability and certainty with the Conservatives and the instability of a chaotic coalition of Labour, SNP and the Liberal Democrats.

Even before the Conservatives happened upon that message, I noticed that the mood of Liberal Democrat MPs became increasingly sombre once the dust had settled on the Scottish referendum.

Having remained positive throughout the coalition, a large number of my colleagues began to resign themselves to losing their seats. The triumph of hope over evidence that led so many in the party to rush to vote for going into coalition in May 2010 was evaporating. It is a real testament to our mutual loyalty and togetherness as a team that no one defected or resigned, no one in the parliamentary party spoke out against the leadership, even if some of us had misgivings over the choices that the party had made in power.

Our message for the campaign had been chosen some months earlier: 'Stronger Economy, Fairer Society'. On one level, I liked this slogan – it summed up the party's approach to competent governance combined with compassionate social policies. It summed up nicely what we were about and implied that the other parties were in favour of either a stronger economy or a fairer society, but not both. However, it was also a weak slogan. There was nothing emotional about it. 'Stronger Economy, Fairer Society' would have been an excellent title for a manifesto, but as a strapline, it moved nobody.

The message was weak, but the strategy was pragmatic and sound. The strategy was to do what I had been urging us to do from day one: the 'multiple by-elections strategy'. In other words, given the trashing of our national brand, the one thing we could realistically do was to pour our limited resources into the seats that we held and treat them all like parliamentary by-election campaigns, as full-on targeted local campaigns that focused not on our national message or brand but on our *local* message and brand. In most constituencies, we had a popular MP who was standing for re-election, and we hoped that we could focus enough on that positive in order to deliver victory.

The problem with this approach was that our Conservative, Labour and nationalist opponents were also treating Liberal Democrat constituencies like by-elections, considering our seats as relatively easy pickings. The other problem was that the party's general election campaign group, nicknamed the 'Wheelhouse', seemed to be somewhat deaf to the realities on the ground. As the campaign began in March 2015, the party was still aiming to win up to 40 seats.

All the evidence indicated that we had no chance of holding so many seats. With limited resources, I felt that we could now only realistically hope to hold up to 20 seats. Nevertheless, the Wheelhouse Group, chaired by former Leader Paddy Ashdown, continued to fight on a much broader front than what – to me – seemed sensible. My term as Party President ended at the turn of New Year 2015 as I made way for my successor, Baroness Sal Brinton. I thus ceased to be a member of the Wheelhouse and no longer attended the meetings thereafter.

During my time attending Wheelhouse meetings, I witnessed the group agonizing over whether they could 'de-target' held constituencies.

On one occasion they brought themselves to drop three seats – all of which were completely beyond our ability to hold. That we even needed to debate this struck me as a sign of a body that lacked the instincts needed to actually affect the outcome of the election. In the end, once it was agreed to drop these constituencies, I was the one given the job to go and break the bad news to the three sitting MPs involved. It was an unpleasant task, but I accepted the responsibility.

After I stepped down as Party President, Nick offered me the role of Foreign Affairs Spokesperson for the Liberal Democrats. We didn't have a minister in the Foreign Office, which meant that a non-minister needed to take on the portfolio for the party. I enjoyed the role, but I spent most of the remaining weeks of the Parliament working hard in my own constituency and helping out in other seats as the election got closer.

In the run-up to the election, I belonged to the party's manifesto working group, chaired by the immensely brainy and capable David Laws. David, by this time, was back in government as a minister of state in the Department for Education. He chaired the working group well and was inclusive of opinions across the party. David was deemed to be on the party's right, with me on its left, but I had little sense of any attempt to drag the party away from its traditional liberal and social democratic foundations. The problem for me was that the Liberal Democrats always come up with an impressively costed, detailed, comprehensive and responsible manifesto. At every election we have the best manifesto – and at every election we lose. Manifestos can be a dreadful banana skin as Michael Foot found in 1983 and Theresa May found in 2017. They can lose you an election, but they never win it for you. The excellence of our manifesto just showed up all the more starkly the complete absence of any message or unique selling proposition.

8

. . . to Memphis

Just before Christmas 2014, Paul Baxendale and I went for a walk with Jasper the spaniel in the woods at Sandside near my home in Milnthorpe. We talked about the months ahead. In just over four months' time it was likely that the Liberal Democrats would be out of government and looking for a new leader. I was the favourite, but was I really going to put my name forward?

I was so used to enthusiastic voices telling me that I must stand for Leader when the moment came, that Paul's words came as a refreshing contrast. Paul was sceptical – could I retain integrity and grow as a Christian while leading a political party? Most importantly, could I serve as a good dad and husband? Paul talked about bishops he had known who rose to that position while being faithful believers of God's word but who had become worn down and ineffective by the pressure of the daily requirement to compromise in their elevated role. Would I face the same pressure?

Nevertheless, I continued to plan for Langley Park to become a reality. Every Tuesday morning at 8 a.m. at a small Langley Park planning meeting, I was building up towards a campaign that might begin the day after the election or maybe not at all.

It was very clear that Norman Lamb was preparing to run for the leadership too and was spending at least as much time on the rubber chicken circuit as me (rubber chicken for Norman and rubber tofu for me).

The realities of what was to come became all the clearer as the Liberal Democrat 'shadow cabinet' met on 4 March to look at polling that showed us losing seats we had hoped to be among our most safe. Eastleigh, Hazel Grove, and Ross, Skye and Lochaber all looked to be irretrievably behind for us. The Liberal Democrats were to go down from 56 seats to just 8 in the 2015 election – my prediction never quite went down that low but by polling day my estimate was that we would return with 14. The problem was that the Wheelhouse was still throwing resources at seats that were now well beyond hope. Hilary Stephenson, the party's unsung hero of elections over the past twenty years and the Director of Campaigns, urged realism but she wasn't able to persuade others to narrow our targeting strategy in order to give us a chance of hanging on to more than a handful of MPs.

The Liberal Democrats' spring conference took place in Liverpool on the weekend of 15 March. Lib Dems take their conferences seriously, probably too seriously. I mean, who thinks it's a good idea to spend a weekend away from home drinking and talking about things that will never win us any votes when you are six weeks from a crucial polling day?

I gave an interview to *The Observer* on the eve of conference which ended up overshadowing quite a lot of it. This was no one's fault but my own. When asked how I would rate the party's performance in government, I told the reporter, 'I would give us 8 out of 10 for policy and 2 out of 10 for politics.' Looking back, this line was so neat, so accurate, so memorable . . . and such a stupid thing to say. Of course, no one reported the '8 out of 10' bit.

Paddy Ashdown hit back in the media saying that I had poor judgement. Vince Cable said something similar. I had to take that on the chin. I could hardly complain about the stick that I got from within the parliamentary party as a result.

I am very sorry that I gave that interview and said those words at that time. However, I think that those words usefully summed up our five years in power. We had done a lot of good: the pupil premium, the raised income-tax threshold, the Green Investment Bank to name but three successes, not to mention the fact that we had brought good and stable government and prevented the Conservatives delivering the worst of the cuts to the most vulnerable of people.

At the same time, we didn't get credit for any of it. In the end, those who had voted for us in 2010 either weren't aware of what we had achieved in government or else they weren't interested. They had written us off as 'Tory poodles' because of the political errors we made in the first six to 12 months of the coalition, especially regarding tuition fees and the Health and Social Care Act.

As Parliament dissolved and I went back to my constit-uency I felt increasingly cut off from my colleagues as they focused hard on trying to hold on to their seats. I visited other constituencies such as Sutton and Cheam, Cheadle,

Bermondsey, Southport, and Berwickshire, Roxburgh and Selkirk. When I compared these visits to the feeling on the doorsteps in Westmorland and Lonsdale, most of them felt colder, more in the balance, and I sensed fewer people were giving me straight answers.

In the midst of all this, I got a text one Saturday night in the middle of April from Robert Nickson, my old friend and bandmate. As if it was 1988 and the most natural thing in the world, Robert told me he'd written some music and wondered if I'd like to put some words to it. I spent a joyous evening penning lyrics and chatting to Robert online. For a couple of hours, I was a teenage wannabe popstar . . . rather than a middle-aged wannabe leader . . .

A week before polling day, I went to help Greg Mulholland in Leeds North West, and afterwards joined the 'spin team' as party leaders David Cameron, Ed Miliband and Nick Clegg took part in the televised leaders' debates. Actually, they weren't debates at all. Each leader was subjected to a series of questions from a live audience but none of them actually got to debate the other. Nick did really well. In fact, I'd say that he comfortably was the best of the three, but by then our poll ratings seemed to be anchored in single figures. At this late stage it felt as though our brand – in so far as it still existed at all – was so toxified by the coalition that this counted for very little.

As I left the studios and walked to the car, I got a call from Martin Horwood, our sitting MP for Cheltenham and – in all likelihood – my campaign Chair for the leadership campaign. The data he was now seeing showed that he would lose his seat by quite a margin. Apparently, Ryan

Coetzee, the party's Director of Strategy, had told him, 'Don't worry Martin, you'll be fine. If we're losing you then we really are stuffed.' Indeed.

I was astonished. Cheltenham was one of our best seats and Martin one of our best campaigning MPs. If Martin was in trouble, everyone was in trouble. In fact, if Martin was in trouble, most of the rest were already toast.

Having since experienced the joys of the Leader's tour from the inside, I have much more sympathy now for those who told us we were getting a last-minute Leader's visit in 2015.

Nick was a fantastic Leader, but on the eve of poll you don't need a Leader's visit if you are defending a parliamentary seat. All it does is underline that you might be in danger. A Leader's visit to a non-held seat does the opposite, as it suggests that you might be in with a chance. However, in both cases, a Leader's visit creates a lot of work when maybe that effort would be better employed leafleting and canvassing.

Nevertheless, with two days to go, we were told that Westmorland and Lonsdale would be the midway stop on the Leader's John o' Groats to Land's End bus tour on the last day of the campaign. We met Nick's team at 5 a.m. and went to visit a bakery at Plumgarths, just north of Kendal. We got great coverage and we also had the benefit of three of Nick's advance team staying behind with us after the battle bus headed south, so we took them to a very wet Sedbergh to deliver leaflets for the next few hours.

As we prepared for polling day itself, three very important people turned up to help. Ben Rich, Jo Owen and my dad.

Ben was my campaign manager for any leadership contest that might occur. Jo is a friend and top-class leadership coach, wonderful at providing clarity and engendering calm in a stressful environment. My dad is the best person in the world for keeping me grounded. If I'm being an idiot, my dad will tell me that I'm being an idiot . . . while slipping in that he's proud of me . . . but that I'm still an idiot.

I don't remember much about polling day – it was the normal blur of running around the streets reminding people to vote. Most of them didn't need reminding. One thing that does stick in my memory is that the party's chief executive Tim Gordon rang me mid-afternoon to say that his figures showed that Westmorland and Lonsdale's figures looked very healthy and so please could my telephone volunteers switch their work to help Mark Hunter instead? Mark was our defending MP in Cheadle near Stockport. I trusted Tim's judgement, and I knew from my own figures – and my gut feeling – that whatever was happening to my colleagues across the country, Westmorland seemed to be in a political microclimate of its own on this occasion. I felt that I could take the risk of allowing our local volunteers to lend a hand to our colleagues down the road.

We worked hard, talking to voters in Kendal right up until the polls closed. I then drove to collect Ben from his hotel. I can't have had the radio on in my car, because I was unaware of the exit poll. Ben was breathless and wide-eyed as he got into the car and said, 'Have you seen the exit poll?' He then proceeded to tell me that the estimate was that the Liberal Democrats would end up with 10 MPs, down from 56. Paddy Ashdown was in the BBC studio as the poll was announced. He mocked it, saying that he would eat his hat if the poll was accurate. Paddy was right. This dismal exit poll was not accurate. The reality turned out to be even worse.

Ben and I drove to my home and joined Rosie as we watched the results come in. Much of my time was spent thinking about what I would say to the media amassed at Kendal Leisure Centre where my count was taking place. Ben, Jo, Paul Butters and I had thought through the potential scenarios – none of which were quite as bad as the party ending up with just eight MPs. Whatever the outcome nationally, it seemed that my result in Westmorland would be comfortable. The five years of coalition would mean that the majority of 12,264 I had achieved in 2010 (up from the wafer-thin 267 by which I had gained the seat from the Conservatives in 2005) would be reduced. In the end, I won by 8,951. I was the only Liberal Democrat in the country to get above 50 per cent of the vote in what turned out to be a nationwide massacre.

Knowing that you are going to be OK, while simultaneously knowing that your friends and colleagues were going through nerve-shredding recounts and much worse, engendered a sense of guilt. It also felt slightly unreal.

There was a full national media presence at the count in Kendal. It was understood that the party would have a very bad night, that I would be one of the survivors and that the party might officially or unofficially be looking for a new leader by the end of the night . . . and that I might ultimately be a candidate for any vacancy that would arise. I was potentially the subject for one of the stories that the media might develop over the course of the night. The journalists were keen to speak to me and my team was keen that I spoke to them – so long as I said the right thing . . .

In my interviews I defended the Liberal Democrats' achievements in coalition, spoke of my personal sadness for colleagues who had lost, and of my strong admiration for Nick and all he had put himself through in the previous five years. When asked whether Nick should or would resign, I said that he shouldn't, but that whether he did or not was up to him. I added that he had earned the right to continue and I would support him if he were to carry on in the role.

All of which had the advantage of actually being true.

I wasn't desperate to be Leader, but I had now resolved that I would be a candidate should the opportunity present itself.

As we kept an eye on the Westmorland ballot papers stacking up, we were given news of defeat after defeat. Some were expected, but many were not. To lose Twickenham, Kingston, Yeovil, North Cornwall, North Devon, Thornbury and Yate, Cheltenham and Cheadle left us reeling. I think I was mentally prepared for us to go down to fewer than 20 seats, but not fewer than ten!

As the scale of the disaster mounted, I received three calls in relatively quick succession. I went outside to take them.

The first call was from Willie Rennie, Leader of the Liberal Democrats in Scotland, and the second was from Kirsty Williams, Leader of the Liberal Democrats in Wales. Both urged me to be ready to stand for the leadership and offered their strong support. They were both devastated by the results but were impressively determined that we should fight back. I was grateful to them and promised that I would keep in touch over the coming hours.

The third call impressed me yet more. It was Jo Swinson. She had just lost her East Dunbartonshire seat. She also knew that her husband, Duncan Hames, was about to lose his Chippenham constituency. Despite these huge personal blows, which she'd only had a few minutes to digest, she rang me and told me to run for Leader.

My response to all three was that I was grateful, that I was seriously considering running but that I would not do or say anything unless, or until, Nick Clegg clarified his intentions. At that time (I took the calls around 2 a.m.), Nick had said nothing on the matter. This was understandable given that his Sheffield Hallam result had still not been declared.

Nick stepped down some hours later. I don't remember exactly when. I just remember that the sun had come up again, that I was standing outside my home with Jasper, sipping a cup of tea and keeping an eye on the updates on my phone when the news came through. I was incredibly moved by Nick's words. It was the most emotionally charged, dignified, classy and effective resignation speech I'd ever heard.

His delivery made a good speech great. At the end of his resignation statement, Nick's closing words were the most moving of all:

> Fear and grievance have won, liberalism has lost. But it is more precious than ever, and we must keep fighting for it. That is both

the great challenge and the great cause that my successor will have to face. I will always give my unstinting support for all those who continue to keep the flame of British liberalism alive.

On the morning of the most crushing blow to the Liberal Democrats since our Party was founded, it is easy to imagine that there is no road back, but there is – because there is no path to a fairer, greener, freer Britain without British liberalism showing the way. This is a very dark hour for our Party but we cannot and will not allow decent liberal values to be extinguished overnight.

Our Party will come back, our Party will win again. It will take patience, resilience and grit. That is what has built our Party before and will rebuild it again. Thank you.

That speech had two tangible results. First, it triggered a leadership contest within the Liberal Democrats. Second, it sparked a huge rise in the party's membership. We saw a net increase of 18,000 new members as a result, taking us above 60,000 members for the first time since the coalition was formed.

There is something terribly British about falling in love with the noble loser. Liberal Democrats are certainly used to losing but we hadn't experienced all that much love in recent years. Amidst all the horrors of the election result, that boost to our membership, that never-say-die spirit and enthusiasm of those who had joined us, provided an immense tonic for a devastated party.

Eight of us had survived: Alistair Carmichael (Orkney and Shetland), John Pugh (Southport), Mark Williams (Ceredigion), Tom Brake (Carshalton and Wallington), Norman Lamb (North Norfolk), Nick Clegg (Sheffield Hallam), Greg Mulholland (Leeds North West) and me.

I took the weekend to decide for certain whether or not I would run. On the Saturday I spoke to Norman, to catch up with him and to ask him – directly – if he was likely to be a candidate. He said that he wasn't sure, and that he would let me know. I was clear to him that I very probably would run. It was a friendly chat, but I sensed that Norman had already made up his mind to put his hat in the ring.

Norman Lamb had been my mentor when I first became an MP. Having won his North Norfolk seat four years earlier with a similarly small majority, it was Norman who showed me the ropes and helped me see how I could best use my time in Parliament to serve my communities back home. Norman imparted much of this wisdom over a dinner in May 2005. I scribbled down notes during that dinner and went back to my office later on to type them up. I still have them by my desk, entitled 'Norman's Top Tips'.

So, having stood against one of my mentors, Simon Hughes, for Deputy Leader five years earlier, I now faced the prospect of standing against another for Leader. I don't know if this felt awkward for Norman, but it did for me.

That weekend after polling day, as we prepared to put the Langley Park battle plan into practice, I knew that there was trouble ahead. Running for Leader would expose me to scrutiny, my family to pressure and my local party to a need to make sacrifices. Did I have it in me to do this? My life would be so much easier if I just stepped back. After all, Norman would be a fine leader. I didn't have to do it.

On the Sunday afternoon after polling day I had a moment of doubt – or was it a moment of clarity? I am a Christian who seeks to trust God and the Bible, in an age when these things are sneered at. I reasoned that there was no way that the media and my opponents were going to ignore this. Of course they would see this as a golden seam to be mined and mined. I faced the hard truth: if I was to stand, my faith would be used against me and my life would be harder because of that.

I prayed about this, but not really for very long. Was I prepared to do the opposite of what I wanted to do if I felt God was telling me to do so? I was unlikely to get a clear steer from God if I wasn't prepared to let go of my prejudices, of my preconceived preferences and genuinely asked for guidance.

In reality, I don't think I gave enough time to counting the personal cost of running for Leader. It was too easy to dismiss these doubts as 'vertigo', the perfectly normal misgivings that anyone in my position would go through on the verge of something so potentially huge and exciting.

Let's not overlook what it was that I was on the cusp of achieving, and how much it meant to me personally. I had been immersed in the local and national life of my party for three decades. I was fully part of that family, I had imbibed the culture of the movement and I was utterly proud of and committed to the party that I had served since my teens as a foot-soldier, as a candidate, a councillor, an MP and as the Party's President. The opportunity to follow Gladstone, Lloyd George, Grimond, Steel, Kennedy and Ashdown would be a huge prize and it now felt as if it was within reach.

To add to this, Rosie urged me to stand. Her motives were the same as when she encouraged me to stand for Party President. 'You have to stand to save the party,' she said – again!

Doubts put aside, I came to see that this was what I needed to do. My mission was to stop the party dying, to revive, inspire and rebuild.

The party was no longer one of government, it was barely even a party at all. As I returned to Parliament the week after the election, I saw many of my former colleagues clearing their offices and realized that the huge influx of new SNP MPs meant that they had now officially become the third party instead of us. The Nationalists had acquired the Liberal Democrat Leader's office on the committee room corridor and our former whips' office next to the Members' Lobby.

No longer did the Liberal Democrat Parliamentary Party meet in the large Committee Room 11 in the Commons. Instead we gathered around a single table in a meeting room on the corridor where the eight of us had our offices.

It became clear that the new Leader would matter less in Parliament than any of his or her predecessors, but that the Leader would matter more out in the country and among the membership than all those who had gone before. The new Leader would have to bind up and inspire a broken party. That would be my role if I was successful.

By the middle of the week after polling day, both Norman and I had declared as candidates.

I made my announcement in Otley market square with Greg Mulholland and an excellent crowd from his local party and further afield. The message was that this party of Gladstone and Grimond was not going to die on our watch. Liberalism mattered now more than ever but we had no automatic right to survive, so we had to energetically, joyfully but deliberately fight for our right to exist and then to do more than just survive – we needed to thrive and, some day, to govern again.

Among the parliamentary party, Greg Mulholland, John Pugh and Mark Williams came out in support of me. Tom Brake supported Norman, which left Nick Clegg as former (and acting) Leader and Alistair Carmichael as Chief Whip who remained publicly neutral.

There were of course many more former MPs and serving members of the House of Lords whom Norman and I sought to persuade to be declared supporters. Having endorsements from well-known senior members isn't the most important thing in a Liberal Democrat leadership contest, but it certainly helps build momentum in a campaign.

Many who wanted the party to stay true to the Liberal Democrat messages and policies of the coalition years rallied around Norman. Those who wanted to see us move on from that and return to a more centre-left place on the spectrum tended to support me.

There was another dynamic in all this too. Norman had been a minister, I hadn't. Indeed, Norman had been a very successful minister, especially effective in the area of mental health. My experience as Party President was perhaps more relevant to the job of Leader at that stage, but Norman's experience in government was probably more impressive to some.

Both of us were grassroots campaigners, capable of winning a constituency against the tide, but my case in this contest was that I had the ability to be an insurgent leader, able to motivate a growing membership and put in place the central and local infrastructure that we would need to start winning again.

As the great and the good lined up to support one or other of the candidates, I got a call from Alan Beith. Alan had stood down from Parliament after 42 years as MP for Berwick-upon-Tweed, having served as the party's Deputy Leader. He had been appointed to the Lords in the days following the election.

Alan told me that he would be supporting me. His words were:

> You are the right man for this job. If we'd held 30 seats and were looking at being in coalition again, I might have supported Norman. But we've got eight seats and you're the one to bring us back from the brink.

I suspect his analysis was right. A different result might have required a different Leader.

The dividing lines were getting clearer: experience and continuity versus insurgency and a fresh start.

The campaign for the leadership started that first week after polling day and concluded with the declaration of the result on 16 July. Norman and I toured the country and got bored of hearing ourselves giving the same speeches over and over again.

As the campaign got under way, we were dealt the cruellest blow. Early on 2 June, it was announced that Charles Kennedy had died at the age of 55. Charles had led the Liberal Democrats from 1999 to 2006. He was the party Leader when I was first elected as an MP in 2005 and, more significantly, he led us through the turbulent period of the Iraq War. Charles's integrity and his clear opposition to the Blair Government over Iraq contrasted with the Conservatives' failure to provide any opposition to or critique of this unlawful military adventure. The bold stance that Charles adopted took us to – at that point – the highest membership our party had ever had and led to our most successful period electorally. Winning 62 MPs in 2005, Charles was the party's most successful Leader in modern times and deservedly so. He was often described as being unusually human for a politician. He was warm and funny, had not an ounce of pomposity about him, and had the most engaging style of oratory. Charles's speeches were funny, passionate and conversational. Elected at the age of 23 for the beautiful constituency of Ross, Cromarty and Skye, young Charles had gained a seat from a Conservative minister despite the Liberal candidate only coming in fourth in the previous election. Charles, who stood as the Social Democratic Party candidate (with support from the Liberals under the terms of the new Alliance), remains the only SDP MP ever to gain his seat at a general election. Every other SDP MP had either defected from another party, or else had been elected in a by-election.

Charles's alcohol dependency took a huge toll on his health and of course it led to his being forced to relinquish the leadership in January 2006.

As the Scottish National Party swept to victory in all but three of Scotland's constituencies in May 2015, Charles was one of the dozens of MPs who lost their seats.

Charles's death seemed so unfair. His ten-year-old son Donald looked down from the gallery in the Commons as he sat with his mum Sarah and heard the tributes to his father the day after Charles had died. Many of us from different parties shared our memories of Charles, but as I rose to speak and saw Donald watching us, my heart broke. I felt real anger that a son should be robbed of his father at such an age.

The leadership campaign continued, but it all felt very much put into perspective by the loss of Charles. I headed down to Cornwall, to Newquay, Truro and Falmouth before joining Norman in Plymouth for a hustings.

Campaigning against a friend is always really awkward, but the two of us got on fine on a personal level, and the Plymouth debate was good-natured. There were times during the contest, however, when our supporters engaged in aggressive behaviour. From my side, some members who couldn't forgive the tuition fees incident would be very personal about Norman who, as a minister at the time, had voted for the rise in fees. There were many in the party who wouldn't forgive the party – and Nick especially – for the coalition in general and for the fees issue in particular. For those people, Norman was the proxy figure on whom their wrath was poured. I neither consented nor acquiesced to this, but I am extremely sorry that it happened.

Similarly, from some who supported Norman, there was a clear attempt to make my faith an issue. Indeed, Norman's campaign slogan was 'Real liberal' which I am certain was a conscious choice to imply that the other candidate (me) was a fake liberal, or at least a bit more half-hearted about his liberalism.

In mid-June, just as leadership ballot papers were being posted out to the members, two of Norman's supporters were caught out doing 'push polling' to communicate negative messages about me. The questions deployed by the phone bank were of the 'Did you know?' variety, intended to plant doubts in voters' minds about my views on abortion and LGBT rights.

Norman's campaign was formally rebuked by the party for this, although I am sure that Norman knew nothing of it himself.

In one sense, this form of aggressive campaigning was fair enough. I mean, if you are trying to beat the other candidate, it's reasonable to go for his weak spots and expose his failings to the electorate. The problem with that approach is that if – to use a football analogy – you play the man and not the ball, in an internal contest you run the risk of creating a toxic atmosphere in the aftermath. Worse still, though, is the fact that if you rake up controversial things about your opponent in an internal election, it means that you have effectively done the dirty work for the other parties and the media. In other words, if you throw dirt at your opponent in a leadership election, you will have very generously provided other parties with plenty of juicy material to use against the new Leader.

Of course, if you wanted to paint me as intolerant or illiberal, you could distort the facts easily enough to make your case. I had abstained on the third reading of the equal marriage bill for all the reasons I stated earlier. My record on the other hot-button issue of abortion was somewhat 'mixed' too – at least from the viewpoint of those who think that liberalism means that only one understanding of the meaning of freedom is tolerable.*

The fact that I'd gently questioned the unquestioning 'pro-choice' approach to this issue was used as a point to prove my lack of liberalism. And, of course, if you believe what the Bible teaches on sex, you can't be a liberal either.

In so far as the media took much interest in the leadership campaign at all, these matters were increasingly brought up – especially after the 'push polling' incident.

The thing is: my record on LGBT rights was and is strong. I'd been on 'Scrap Clause 28' marches in 1988, voted for equal marriage on second reading in 2013 and been a loyal member of the most pro-gay-rights party in the UK for 30 years, so it would take a spectacular level of spin to pin 'homophobe' on me.

It would be wrong to say that issues to do with my faith dogged me during the leadership campaign. They came up relatively rarely – although they were raised with a little more intensity towards the end of the contest.

My tactic was to keep smiling, defend my record and move on to talk about the issues that ought to be central to the leadership. Namely, how do we rebuild a party that has almost been wiped out?

Only once did I seriously take up the challenge of contradicting the charge that being an evangelical Christian rendered me an incomplete liberal. At the hustings in Bristol – a huge event held in the Gloucestershire County

---

* See Chapter 3 for details of my interview for *The War Cry*.

Cricket Club's main conference room – a member asked, fairly aggressively, whether God was more important to me than the party or my liberalism.

It was a hot day and maybe I should have just smiled, dodged the question and given an inane answer. Instead, I challenged the questioner. Did he have the first idea about who had founded our party in the first place, or why they had done so? Did he realize that we were established by those desperate for religious tolerance and that, if being a liberal means anything today, then it means that we must not be cowed by law or by social pressure into dropping our religious – or irreligious – convictions? My answer went down well, probably because I was robust and didn't equivocate. Maybe I should have learned from that and done it more often.

I was interviewed by Andrew Neil on 7 June, and he chose to base his questioning around my faith. As I responded (ironically, I was interviewed down the lane from the park just behind my church – I had nipped out from our Sunday service), I looked slippery because I didn't want to be sidetracked into constantly talking about this issue, and I didn't want to hand the media or my opponents a 'juicy' phrase.

I think I was wise to conclude that if I took on any of these journalists and gave a robust defence of why a liberal can indeed choose to live in accordance with values that are not permissive in nature, then I'd just generate sensational and negative headlines.

That is why Andrew Neil asked those questions, and indeed why all the others asked them too. It was not because they wanted to understand, but because they wanted to expose. I itched to take them on, expose the shallowness of this line of questioning and tackle their two-dimensional conception of liberalism, but I also knew – or at least I felt – that I would be jumping into their trap if I did so.

And so, too often, my approach to such questioning was to duck and weave, rather than punch back. My job was to win the leadership and save the party, not to fight over what genuine liberalism looked like. I accepted that, but it was hard for me to just shrug and tolerate what struck me as a growing blind spot afflicting the Liberal family – that you cannot have an active faith and be a liberal, or you cannot choose to live by a non-permissive set of standards and be a liberal.

You see, I have always had a problem with those who seek to impose a world view or a current strand of thinking without daring to actually have the argument. It's what made me an awkward kid who thought it better to be laughed at or ignored, than to cop out and follow the crowd. It's an awkwardness I carry into my adulthood and political life.

I hated the brainless deification of Tony Blair's New Labour in the run-up to the 1997 election. I continue to be appalled at the unquestioning adoration of free markets since the days of Margaret Thatcher, and I am deeply concerned about the sinister groupthink theory of today on matters to do with faith, sex and identity.

People who are liberals and who should know better seem too often to be like the fawning courtiers celebrating the King's splendid new clothes. The sexual revolution increasingly reminds me of other revolutions we have known. We are now past the joyous flag-waving stage, and are well into the purges, the show trials and the thought police.

The nationwide tour during the leadership contest took me as far north as Aberdeen and as far south as Falmouth. I really enjoyed the campaign – the hustings were full of people who defied what might have been expected of party activists who had just been crushed at the ballot box. At every event, the 'Lib Dem Newbies' were asked to raise their hands to identify themselves, and rapturous applause followed. Often they made up half of the audience.

In the midst of the incredible schedule that Norman and I faced, I tried to maintain sanity by spending time with Rosie and the children. We managed three days on the island of Gigha in the Hebrides in late May, my daughter Gracie joined me for a day of campaigning in Tower Hamlets, the whole family came with me for a campaigning visit to Birmingham, and on 25 June I met my brother-in-law Ivan for a big breakfast. Ivan, my sister Jo and their three children live in New Zealand. We hardly ever see them these days, so the chance to spend time with Ivan (who was in the UK for an academic conference) was a real blessing during this busy time.

Ivan and I chatted about how the campaign was going. By this stage, it was increasingly looking like I would win the election – not by a landslide but by a clear ten per cent or so, as our polling was consistently showing that level of lead over Norman.

I mentioned to Ivan that I was seeing Decca Aitkenhead from *The Guardian* later that day for an interview. I had already been interviewed by Decca a week or so earlier and the piece had yet to appear in the paper. On hearing this, Ivan – jokingly – said, 'Perhaps she hasn't enough material to stitch you up with and wants to come back for more?'

Decca is a brilliant writer – a great journalist, but an astonishingly good writer. She captures her subjects with such warmth and depth and exposes them for better or worse. Decca was very honest with me during our second interview, saying that when she had showed *Guardian* colleagues her draft piece on me, they had told her that she needed to come back and have a second go because she hadn't dug into my faith enough.

We had a really good discussion, but the one bit that really sticks in my memory is when she asked me, 'As things stand, am I going to hell?'

I didn't lie to her, but I didn't give her a straight answer. With all respect to Decca, she wasn't asking me so that she could clear up in her mind a theological point that might lead to her deciding whether to put her faith in Christ. No, she wanted a colourful line from me to spice up the article. Fair enough, that's her job, but I didn't have to comply and so I didn't. I was seeking to be the party Leader – it wasn't for me to be making theological statements, it was to rebuild the stricken Liberal Democrats.

But what's the answer?

It's time for some more C. S. Lewis:

There are no ordinary people. You have never talked to a mere mortal. Nations, cultures, arts, civilizations – these are mortal, and their life is to ours as the life of a gnat. But it is immortals whom we joke with, work with, marry, snub and exploit.

(Quoted in Art Lindsley, *The Case for Christ: Insights from reason, imagination and faith*, Inter-Varsity Press, 2005, p. 179.)

The Bible teaches clearly that every human being exists into eternity. Hard to believe? Well, if you can believe that the universe can be created by accident, in an instant out of absolutely nothing, then I reckon you can suspend your disbelief for this too, at least for a moment.

There are two kinds of people in the end: those who reject God and those who fully humble themselves before him. The problem is that only one human being who ever lived fits the latter category.

The rest of us fall into the first category, because all of us, to a greater or lesser extent, reject God. Sin is rebelling against God. It's telling him to get stuffed and sling his hook. It's to grab all his goodies while giving him the finger.

There are individual sins, a staggeringly long list of them, but they are all the product of sin. The sin that rejects God in his own universe. That's why Christians are not better people than non-Christians: they are merely people who, by the grace of God, have understood that they need forgiveness.

There you are, you picked up a book by a British politician about his experiences in British politics and you've just had to wade through a rant about sin. That doesn't happen very often!

Imagine the headlines if I'd said any of that to Decca?

I mean, really imagine.

Exactly.

That's why I didn't give her a straight answer. I didn't lie, but I didn't jump into the big trap marked 'trap'. I tiptoed around it.

Decca asked me many other questions such as, 'Do you pray to God?', 'Do you seek his guidance?' and 'Do you believe that God has a plan for your life?' My answer to the last one was, 'Maybe God's plan for my life is that I lose a bunch of elections and learn about humility?'

Maybe so, but this didn't feel like an election that I was going to lose. As we entered July, the round of hustings and visits continued, the size of audiences increased, as did the number of people wearing 'Win with Tim' stickers (very imaginative!). We continued to sense that while the attacks on me due to my faith were having an impact, it still looked more than likely that I would win.

My last campaign visit was a question-and-answer session in a pub in Guildford. For the first time, I enjoyed a pint while speaking. I had been very self-disciplined for two months, but now I was among friends, and the end was in sight.

I headed back home, and Rosie and I celebrated our 15th wedding anniversary before I got up at the crack of dawn on 16 July to head down to London for the result. I was joined by my friend Peter Thornton, who was then the leader of the South Lakeland District Council, Paul Butters and my head of office Helen Matthews.

On the train back down to London, I felt a sense of nervous expectation. For me, this was a historic moment – the ultimate achievement. I had joined the Liberal Party at 16. I had sat and watched David Steel, Paddy Ashdown, Charles Kennedy, Ming Campbell and Nick Clegg delivering the Leader's speech, speaking for our party as its head, and I had watched with pride and admiration. And now I was potentially a few hours off following them. The butterflies in my stomach were fluttering. This was my cup final, I was a goal ahead, and the 90 minutes were almost up . . .

I was in my office in Parliament when I got the call from Tim Gordon, who was the returning officer. He told me I had won, and he gave me the figures: 56.5 per cent for me and 43.5 per cent for Norman Lamb. It was a slightly wider margin than I had expected.

I gave Tim enough time to ring Norman too and then I popped next door to Norman's office and shook his hand. His wife Mary was with him and they looked as relieved as I was that it was all over. As leadership contests go, this one had been pretty amicable.

That night in a Victorian hall in Islington, I was introduced as the new Leader and spoke to around 500 people tightly packed into a venue that had no seats. That's one way to guarantee a standing ovation of course, to ensure that no one can actually sit down. My speech was good but not so good that it should have made anyone faint – but someone standing just behind me did just that. It was a very warm evening. I checked to see that person was all right and then I continued, promising 'the most joyful comeback in the history of British politics'.

Next, I joined my campaign team in the basement of a nearby pub where we celebrated our success.

I was up at 5 a.m. to do a full round of interviews, including doing Radio 4's *Today*, with John Humphreys asking me, 'Do you pray?' I mean, Christians do . . . The round was all but done when I sat down in a studio to be interviewed at short notice by Cathy Newman of Channel 4, who asked, 'Mr Farron, do you believe that gay sex is a sin?'

The matter was raised again in the days that followed and I sought to close it down as effectively as I could: my faith is private, I am a political leader not a religious one, I don't go pontificating on theology, but I will tell you that I am utterly committed to LGBT equality and here's the proof . . .

By the time I delivered my first Leader's speech in Bournemouth at the party conference in September, my faith wasn't being raised at all. It looked like we'd put the lid on the issue by refusing to give an inch.

People in the party knew that I was a Christian, that some of my beliefs might be a bit 'old fashioned' from their perspective, but it was clear that I was an inclusive, accepting, liberal person who fights the corner of the LGBT community just as I do for every person or group that faces persecution or ill-treatment.

And so, the matter went away. Until an early general election was called . . .

9

Denial

The election campaign was about nine hours old. To be fair, they had been a really good nine hours. Indeed, for me, they were probably the best nine hours of the entire election.

Despite our habit of losing them, Lib Dems love elections. We may have been pretty stunned by the Prime Minister's announcement of an early election, but if my Twitter feed was anything to go by (and it always is) then right across the country the Lib Dems had been stunned into frantic activity.

Thanks to the very Marmite-ish position I had taken on Brexit, we had a cause and we were excited about fighting for it.

The news bulletins carried images of me standing outside in the Truro sunshine surrounded by excited activists and lots of orange placards, while Jeremy Corbyn's response was rather dead pan and from within a studio. To the neutral observer, we looked up for it and Labour didn't.

Following the announcement of the early election, HQ reported that we were already having yet another membership surge. Having visited Cornwall in the first part of the day, I was now in Bristol. Former MP and Minister Stephen Williams and I had done a rally together in support of his candidacy for Bristol mayor, which morphed into being an impromptu general election rally too. Once the meeting was over, I went out to talk to the media who were situated along the quay in Bristol.

At around 7.15 p.m. I did a live interview on *Channel 4 News* with Cathy Newman. I was Tiggerish about our prospects and the interview had started pretty well.

It didn't end well.

As we got to the end of the piece, she became distracted and almost jumpy. She was keen, it turned out, to crowbar me into a final 'off-topic' question. She returned to a theme that she'd begun with me the day after I became Leader in July 2015: 'Mr Farron, do you believe gay sex is a sin?'

Back in 2015 I had been a rabbit in the headlights when that same question was first asked. I'd offered the response, 'Well, we're all sinners . . .' which had the advantage of being honest, if a little inept. The answer wasn't good enough to appease the media then, and my similarly evasive response this time was apparently not good enough either.

Looking back, it is clear to me that my mistake, in 2015 and 2017, was treating Cathy's questions on sex differently from Decca Aitkenhead's questions on the matter of hell. While it is right to give honest answers to honest questions, it is all the same legitimate for the subject to consider the interviewer's motivation in asking the question. With respect to both of them, neither Decca nor Cathy really wanted to understand. They both wanted to expose. Fair enough. But I treated Cathy's question with far more respect than it deserved. The damage was done.

Jesus Christ is the most honest person who ever lived, and yet he dodged more questions than most politicians I've met. He didn't always give questioners the words they wanted to hear; instead he gave them the words that they needed to hear. On a number of occasions, Jesus refused to give a direct answer when he was asked vexatious questions motivated by a desire not for enlightenment but for entrapment. He often simply replied with a question of his own. In which case, one option for me might have been to challenge the interviewer, 'What do *you* think sin means?' If I am asked the question today, that it is very often how I will respond, but I am not Leader now and I can afford to take the time to draw the interviewer on to a theological journey.

Alternatively, I could have been clear that I believe in equality and have a track record that backs that up fully, and then say that people of faith should not be hounded because of their beliefs, especially if their actions demonstrate tolerance and love. The problem with this latter option is twofold – first it's playing the 'victim' card, something I never want to do. The second problem with this approach is that it assumes that our culture, my opponents and the journalists are sufficiently liberal to sympathize. My experience is somewhat mixed in that respect.

So what should I have said? I was asked this question because I am a Christian, not because of any genuine doubts about my stance on LGBT equality. As a result, I should have restated in my answer that this question was about my faith, not my politics, by saying, 'You are asking me this because I am a Christian.' I should have gently explained that I don't get to decide what sin is, but that I do get to decide how I treat people and think of people; that I am a liberal because I believe in equality and freedom, no matter your sexuality, and no matter your faith. The follow-up questions would have come of course, but I should have done 'repeat to fade' until the interview either stopped or the subject changed, while smiling with confidence and being gracious throughout.

You may not agree that this would have been the correct approach. In reality, the above is simply a better, cleaner version of what I actually did say when I was asked – at least most of the time. The real problem is that – unusually for me – I was afraid, and it showed. I was evasive and awkward. Of what was I afraid? I was afraid of the loss of approval and of being misunderstood.

On those occasions when people say nice things about me, they sometimes say that I am 'authentic'. By which I imagine that they think I'm a bit quirky, Northern, obsessed with football and pop music, and not clever enough to be slippery. However, as Decca Aitkenhead observed, as President and Leader I was open and chatty about pretty much everything, but when it came to my faith, I was nervous, and every word was carefully chosen.

My fear that people would see me as weird, intolerant and illiberal was my main problem – and it fed the interest of journalists who picked up on that awkwardness.

Looking back, it is clear that this moment in 2015 – just hours into my leadership – had provided the way in for a whole legion of journalists to make my faith the issue. I had given the thought police an 'access all areas' pass. I left the studio knowing that I'd plucked defeat from the jaws of victory. I had just risen to the greatest earthly achievement I could ever aspire to, and I was utterly miserable.

After Cathy reintroduced the issue in 2017 at the beginning of the campaign, I was asked the question over and over by journalist after journalist. My answers ranged from a strong statement of my support for LGBT equality, most recently on equal marriage, to stating that I was a political leader, rather than a religious one, and was therefore not going to be making theological pronouncements. But all my responses had one thing in common: they were coloured by the same fear.

So why didn't I just say 'No, it's not' to this odd question? Why would I choose to do myself so much damage when I could have prevented it all by simply saying 'no'? I mean, come on, what harm would it *really* do if I just said 'no'? I've been an elected politician for a quarter of a century – it wouldn't be the first time I'd given a simplistic answer to a complex question for the sake of convenience.

As Leader, I had the best press officer in the business in Paul Butters, a man who began as my junior intern in 2008 and became my senior spokesperson on my election as Leader in 2015. I'd always joked that Paul wanted me to be Leader more than I did, and that wasn't just because he'd put £50 on me to be the next Leader at 30–1 back in 2009 . . . Paul knew every journalist in the lobby, and they all loved him. He was charming, wickedly funny, helpful, Machiavellian, brutal, fiercely loyal and a man of his word. It seemed every hack owed him a favour for some reason or other. I would ask him why and he'd turn away and mumble, 'You don't want to know, boss.'

In the midst of the incessant questioning I received, one lobby journalist asked Paul, 'We know he's pro-gay rights, we know he's a good bloke, we know he's an evangelical and he takes all this sin stuff seriously . . . but it [my failure to say 'No, it's not'] is killing him . . . Why can't he just lie?'

So why couldn't I just say, 'No, it's not?'

I couldn't because sin is a word that Christians use to refer to a life lived against God's purposes – and we all do that. To a Christian, to count someone as a 'sinner' is to count them as human. I suppose it boils down to the question of what sin is. A question very few, if any, of the people who asked the question had an answer to.

So to answer that question with a 'yes' is to play into the hands of those who don't understand the question they are asking.

But to say 'no' is to insult the intelligence of those who do.

All the same I'd be lying if I said I wasn't tempted (indeed, in the end it proved too tempting) to just shrug and say 'no' anyway, even though the honest answer has to be far too complex for a soundbite.

So what was the problem? Why not just say the easy and obvious thing? Well, because I believe that God is real, that he's not a human construct, and that those who believe in him are not deluded. I believe Jesus Christ is his Son and the saviour of the human race. I believe that we need a saviour because we are sinners – every last one of us.

Sin results from human beings making themselves their own gods. Just look around at the state of the world at this moment. To put it gently, humans are not doing the best job. When we see the war, the persecution, the poverty, the dishonesty, the violence, the bitterness, the exploitation and the cruelty, we cry out for justice. Whether we have faith or not, we are desperate for justice. I am confident that justice will come and that God will deliver it universally. I also know enough about myself to be sure that I should be at the sharp end of that justice because I am a sinner. God created everything, including you and me. He created people to have a relationship with him and yet we have rejected him in his own world, including the boundaries that he lovingly set for our own good. His love is so immense that despite our rejection of the God who created us, he has bought us back at an unimaginable price. The justice we deserve is borne by God himself in the historical person of Jesus. But if we won't accept Jesus, if we are determined to face that justice ourselves, we will find ourselves separated from him for ever. That is to say, we will not just be separated from him, but also from all that is good. The word 'sin' has just three letters but it is a very big word.

It is God who decides what counts as sin, rather than you or I. To be clear, this is the essence of mainstream Christian theology. It's not just something that I made up!

My failure to have provided a clever and effective response came from my failure to share openly and confidently what I believed. I should have shared what Christianity really means with those who worked closest to me. This failure was fuelled by that same fear of what people would think of me, which left me nervous and evasive in front of the cameras.

My close team knew that I wasn't a homophobe, understood that I had – from their perspective – some slightly odd religious views that sat alongside my obvious liberalism. But as Leader, I should have been much more upfront about what Christianity means so that together we could have made better judgements in advance about the answers I could have deployed.

I'm a liberal to my fingertips. I didn't wander into the party by mistake. I joined the Liberals because they (we) 'felt right' and because they stood for the things that I agreed with and against the things that I was against.

Becoming a Christian was entirely different. You see, I didn't choose Christianity because I liked the 'manifesto'. It's not analogous to joining a party. It's not that I looked through the Bible's teaching in the 'Sermon on the Mount' and thought, 'I agree with that – how do I join?' No. I became a Christian because it struck me with an almost physical force that Christianity is true, which is a terribly absolutist and illiberal thing to say, isn't it?

I don't think so.

If something is true, it's true, and your opinion of it doesn't change its truth too much. A hedgehog may look at a steamroller heading towards it and strongly disagree with the steamroller. It may even deny the existence of the steamroller. I will defend its right to have those views. It's still going to become a hedgehog pancake.

I want to suggest that it isn't intellectually credible to reject at least the *possibility* of absolute truth. If you are convinced that it is not possible for there to be a knowable absolute truth, then paradoxically you do believe in an absolute truth (that is, there is no absolute truth). Nobody can have absolute knowledge, but that doesn't mean that we can't know *anything*. We all have partial knowledge.

With more than 500 eyewitnesses and overwhelming circumstantial evidence, the case for the resurrection ought to win over an open-minded jury. If you think that this is a bold claim, have a look at the evidence for yourself. The New Testament documents count as by far the most reliable sources of antiquity, written by eyewitnesses at an amazingly early stage, which means that there was no time for legends to build up. If you haven't already read it, I would recommend that you suspend disbelief, just for an hour, and take the time to read Val Grieve's short book *Your Verdict on the Empty Tomb* (Authentic Media, 1996).

In any other circumstances, would you dismiss something so important without at least checking the evidence for and against?

But even if I could convince you to suppose that the resurrection actually happened as a historical event, so what? Why does, or did, this affect me when under pressure from journalists to respond on tricky issues? Simply this: if the resurrection happened, it is compelling proof that there is a God and that Jesus is God. Dead people do not come back to life. Jesus claimed to be God and then did just that – he came back to life. If it is true, it changes everything. It has to.

Becoming a Christian is not just about providing intellectual assent to what the Bible tells us about Jesus.

Becoming a Christian affects you on a deeper level, it results in actions and a rethinking of the way we live – no longer seeking to live for ourselves or to please others, but to honour God by our thoughts, words and deeds.

When I say that I am a Christian, I'm not expressing my cultural identity. Neither am I showing off. It's not a way of claiming to be morally superior – in fact it's quite the opposite. For Christianity involves accepting that I cannot save myself, that I am not good enough, and that I need forgiveness. Christianity is ego-shattering and utterly humbling. It is a realization that your life is not your own.

How is this relevant to my answers to 'those' questions during the election? Well, when I am asked to say something that contradicts what I believe God has said in order to dismiss a troublesome question, I must not comply either to satisfy my friends or to confound my opponents. The question on sex was, in reality, a question about the concept of sin in general.

If – for my own convenience – I lead people to believe that there isn't sin, and that they don't need forgiveness, then they will never seek that forgiveness through Christ and so they will never be forgiven. My deep desire is that people everywhere should have that restored relationship with God. You see, then, why deploying the easy answer would be the most loveless and selfish thing I could do. That is the reason why I should not give the easy answer . . .

But a week later, I did just that.

So, is gay sex a sin or what? What's the answer? I mean, really? If you aren't a religious person, you will almost certainly think that the answer is 'no'. In fact, it won't even be 'no', because if you aren't religious, you will consider the concept of sin to be irrelevant. You can only sin if there's a god to sin against. For someone who seeks to be faithful to the teaching of the Bible, then the answer probably ought to be lengthier than a single word.

For a Christian, the answer should be that God very clearly and very lovingly places sexual expression only in the context of the married, lifelong relationship of one man and one woman. That means that the expression of sexuality in any other context is outside God's will. That includes my sleeping with women before I was married. Like I said, we are all sinners.

This doesn't mean that teaching about sex is the most important thing in the Bible. I never go on the front foot to talk about it. Rightly or wrongly, I have often avoided talking about sexual ethics because I felt that to do so simply allows people to conveniently and inaccurately dismiss the gospel as hateful and prudish.

In this matter, I feel the need to apologize to my party and my friends. I am deeply upset by the knowledge that my failure to address the issue more effectively hurt them. Moreover, the thought that people would consider me hateful, or that I judge them, troubles me greatly.

Christians sometimes make the mistake of preaching about obedience to God to those who do not believe, when instead they should be talking about God's grace – about his offer of free forgiveness of sins through his limitless love. To those who then accept that offer of grace, serving God with all our thoughts, actions and attitudes is the natural response, and *then* it's right to talk about obedience.

I know this from my own experience. In Singapore as an 18-year-old, I was appalled when I first read *I Once Loved A Girl*. It was only later, once I understood that I had been saved by grace and that God had the right to direct my life, that I humbled myself to accept his teaching and his rebuke.

In other words, if you're not a believer, it is not for me to tell you how to live, to look down on you, to think differently of you, to treat you as anything other than equal to me. It is for me to hold out the gospel to you in the hope that you will accept it.

If you do not accept it, I respect and defend your right. If you accept the gospel, it will make a very large difference to your life. It will be the most exhilarating thing you can do. It will be costly but you will be equipped to find that even the cost is a joy.

Christians believe they are called to deny themselves in a whole range of areas including their opinions of themselves and of others, their finances, their time, their priorities, and their sexual behaviour and attitudes.

I am not necessarily expecting to persuade you that Christians are right to believe this, but I do suggest that Christians have the right to hold to the belief that the God who created us knows best how human beings can flourish.

If you count yourself a liberal, then I assume that you see the need to join me on the front line to defend that right. I don't need you to agree with my religious beliefs, rather I need you to remember that your freedom is mine, and mine is yours. In fact, I don't merely expect liberals to defend the legal right to make those choices, I also expect liberals to acknowledge that these choices are reasonable and socially acceptable – even if you personally oppose them. John Stuart Mill's spectre of the 'tyranny of opinion' was constructed for just this sort of challenge. This is an opportunity then for all liberals to consider whether they really are liberals or whether they have sadly been stealthily seduced by the charms of a tyranny.

I hold firmly to what I believe the Bible teaches and equally feel that I have no right to impose what I believe on others. It is fundamentally illiberal to legislate to make people who are not Christians behave as though they were.

But in reality, this kind of consistency seems increasingly absent, which means that many of those who consider themselves liberals really aren't. To be tolerant of everything except those things that you don't consider to be liberal, is to reach a stage where your liberalism has eaten itself. In my case, the pressure came not because of anything I did, proposed, campaigned for or said but because of something it was assumed that I *thought*. Membership of the liberal movement is not compatible with membership of the thought police.

Tough talk from Tim.

But on 25 April, I didn't do tough talk, I did a cop-out.

For the time being though, I told myself that this would pass and that I needed to focus on getting our message across through the media, rallying the troops, enjoying the buzz of the campaign, and doing the job that I'd been born to do – leading the Liberal Democrats into a general election and bringing us back from the near-death experience of 2015.

After my TV interview in Bristol I finally got back to my flat in Stockwell just before midnight. As I flopped down on my settee to eat my tea, I made the mistake of looking at Twitter. It was teeming with bile following my TV interview with Cathy. Some of it from celebrities, some of it from people I respected, all of them taking the opportunity to stick the boot into me. I scrolled down to read that I was a homophobe, a nasty piece of work, a hate-fuelled prude . . . and that was just the repeatable stuff.

I confess to feeling pretty broken by this. Being slagged off by hard-right types never bothers me. Maybe it should, because some of the messages sent to me are extremely violent and threatening, but for whatever reason, it just doesn't get to me; it doesn't mess with my head.

This was different. I know I'm a liberal, I know I judge no one, I know I chose the path of most resistance and became a liberal because I am passionate about equality. So when a celebrity figure with a billion Twitter followers decides that you are 'fascistic scum' on the basis of a badly handled interview (badly handled by me, I grant you), it hurts. It also made me a little angry. I mean who tweets vacuous condemnations without taking half a second to understand the person they are attacking? Sorry, that was a naïve question. The answer is 'most of us' but that doesn't make it OK. And even then – as a friend often tells me – it's an opportunity to display grace in return.

I put down my phone, put a film on and lit a cigarette . . . and then another.

On occasions I've been a part-time, social smoker. I think I'm terribly funny when I say, 'You can't get cancer off other people's tabs' . . . but the thing is, these weren't other people's tabs, they were mine. I was becoming a bit more than part-time. (I once asked my pastor Paul whether he thought smoking was a sin. His short answer was, 'No . . . but it is incredibly stupid.')

What a first day of the campaign it had been. I had started the day looking forward to a local election visit. I'd been thrown into the first rally of a completely unexpected general election, looking every part the energetic Leader of the insurgent reborn third party in his and its element . . . then been bowled a frankly predictable googly of a question relating to my faith and seen my fairly embryonic national brand pretty badly battered as the day came to an end.

I drank a beer, I smoked a couple of tabs and watched half of *Apollo 13*, a film about three guys who were in a lot more bother than me.

I spent the first week of the election campaign batting away the questions about my Christian faith. I kept pushing the questions back, saying: 'I'm the leader of a political party, not of a religious movement, so I'm not answering questions on theology', and 'My private faith is a private matter, but I can tell you that I support LGBT equality – and here's a shedload of evidence for that . . .', and so on. All those responses were true by the way, but it wasn't making those questions go away. What a waste of valuable Liberal Democrat airtime when I should have been getting the party's message across!

I'd had another of those days, Monday, 24 April – six days into the campaign – when the matter just wouldn't go away. I was visiting an unlikely 'target' for the Liberal Democrats:

the normally safe Labour seat of Vauxhall in London. Labour's strongly pro-Brexit MP Kate Hoey had, however, provided us with an unexpected opportunity in a very anti-Brexit constituency. After my speech at the event with our candidate George Turner, the now predictable questions came, this time from Sky's Darren McCaffrey, a lovely person and one of the regulars on our bus. I dealt with the question, but with the same questions coming up every day of the campaign, it was beginning to wear me down.

That night I went into party HQ and my Chief of Staff and good friend Ben Williams came in to see me. He looked grave, in his kind and sympathetic way. He told me that my refusal to answer 'no' to the 'Is it a sin?' question was causing such trouble that senior people in the party had contacted him to say they were threatening to resign, and demanding that I answer in the way they wanted me to.

I felt under a colossal weight. At this point there were still six weeks of the campaign to go. It seemed that because of this relentless focus on the (frankly bizarre) question of whether gay sex is a sin, we were just not getting our wider message heard. Many in the party simply couldn't under-stand why I couldn't or wouldn't just say 'no'.

I concluded that I had three choices. I could give the slightly complex, but honest, answer I've given above and then tough it out. I could give the same answers and step down as Leader there and then, or I could simply say 'No, it's not' and hope that this would make the whole thing go away.

Ben told me that members had expressed frustration with me because they felt that by not saying 'No, it's not', I was just being 'self-indulgent'. I think this was the phrase that burned through my defences. I saw myself as a servant. I didn't want to be seen as self-indulgent.

As I sat in my office sifting those options at HQ, I despaired. Amidst the immense personal pressure of that evening, I concluded that if I chose to either stick to my position or to resign, the charge of self-indulgence would apply, the party would be hurt, and it would be my fault. Indeed, my guilt centred on the fear that I needed to put the party first and just say the thing that would make this constant distraction disappear.

To protect the party and give us the best chance of getting through all this, it seemed right for me to say 'no'. So I resolved to say 'no'. My gut immediately told me that this was wrong. I felt a sense of shame and bitter disappointment with myself but I buried the feeling just beneath the surface. I went to a friend's house for dinner that night, made polite conversation, tried to compartmentalize the decision I'd made and left it there – it was too painful to revisit it.

I woke the next morning, still determined to go through with it.

I chaired the shadow cabinet at 10 a.m. and explained that I was going to 'deal with the matter' that day. Most colleagues seemed pleased to hear it and eager for me to get this over with. Lord Brian Paddick, however, showed that he was one of the few people who genuinely understood my position. He came up to me after the meeting and with great sympathy said, 'Be careful – what will you do when you hear the cock crowing thrice?'

But I'd made my mind up. I had tunnel vision now so I gritted my teeth and ploughed on with my plan.

It was decided that I should do a sit-down interview with the BBC so that I could say 'I don't think gay sex is a sin' in answer to that question. Much of the media was following the Prime Minister in Cardiff that day so fixing the interview wasn't as easy as usual. Eventually Eleanor Garnier came over to Parliament to do the interview and as we began, she rightly gave me a hard time for my new answer – I mean, why hadn't I said this earlier? Wasn't this just a politically convenient answer?

The response to my 'No, it's not a sin' answer was utter relief in the party – I had grateful texts and emails from a large number of members. In Christian circles, the response was huge disappointment – although mostly it was expressed in sadness and with understanding, rather than anything hostile. My personal response was to find myself in unparalleled inner turmoil.

Following Jesus' arrest, Peter denied even knowing Jesus three times, just as Jesus predicted he would do 'before the cock crows'. When Peter realized what he had done, he broke down and wept bitterly. This is because Peter hadn't betrayed a rule, a manifesto or an ideology. He had denied his best friend. He was distraught that he had broken such a relationship. So it was with me.

To people who aren't Christian, this of course sounds bizarre, even pathetic. I do understand that. I've fallen for that depiction of Christianity myself in the past.

I became a Christian at 18, but when I was 23 I 'backslid' or, to put it more bluntly, I turned my back on Christianity.

I fell for a girl who wasn't a Christian, sex became part of the equation and I slowly and stealthily edged away from my faith. I knew I was living against God's will, and it caused me intense anguish while my church attendance fell away to nothing. I avoided Christian friends and I took weak comfort from listening to those who preached what I now regard as a woolly, permissive, unbiblical faith. For the rest of my 20s, I led a fairly hedonistic lifestyle, subconsciously reasoning that if I was going to turn my back on God on account of one sin, I might as well go the whole hog. I became a very selfish person.

At age 30 I married Rosie. While I had been raised in an unchurched household, Rosie had grown up in a Church of England family. They didn't take it that seriously, but baby baptisms, reasonably regular attendance and church weddings were pretty much expected among Rosie's clan.

So, Rosie and I began to attend our local parish church in Milnthorpe. The vicar there was John Hancock, an excellent and faithful preacher and a wonderfully kind and lovely man. His sermons challenged me a little. I reasoned, however, that now I was married, I didn't need to feel quite so bad about my previous sins, that I could just dawdle along as a nominal Christian and all would be well.

In the summer of 2002, Rosie and I took our two daughters (one 15 years and the other 11 months) on holiday to Spain. One night when everyone else was in bed, I sat outside beneath the stars with a bottle of wine and a copy of *Cosmos* by Carl Sagan.

Carl Sagan is one of my heroes. He was the passionate and humane voice of space exploration. It was his idea in 1994 to turn the deep-space Voyager probe around to point inwards in order to take photographs. The craft was hurtling out of the solar system towards interstellar space, having completed its main job of studying the outer planets. There was no scientific purpose in doing this, but it was a profound decision. As Voyager's camera pointed towards the inner solar system from which it had come, rather than the outer solar system to which it was headed, it took the famous 'family portrait'. The portrait was a series of snapshots of the inner planets, one of which was Earth. His speech, when he unveiled the photo of Earth from five billion miles away, was inspired and inspirational. Pointing to the 'pale blue dot' less than a pixel wide, he said:

> That's here. That's home. That's us. On it everyone you love, everyone you know, everyone you ever heard of, every human being who ever was, lived out their lives. The aggregate of our joy and suffering, thousands of confident religions, ideologies and religious doctrines, every hunter and forager, every hero and coward, every creator and destroyer of civilization, every king and peasant, every young couple in love, every mother and father, hopeful child, inventor and explorer, every teacher of morals, every corrupt politician, every 'superstar', every 'supreme leader', every saint and sinner in the history of our species lived there – on a mote of dust suspended in a sunbeam.
>
> (*Pale Blue Dot: A vision of the human future in space*,
> Random House, 2011)

Cosmos had been a successful television series that I'd enjoyed as a child in 1980 and carried the same wonderful blend of scientific exploration and poetic, humanistic appreciation of the universe around us as the 'blue dot' episode had done.

In the run-up to our holiday in 2002, I had come across the book that accompanied the series and decided that it would make great pool-side reading.

The book is about our understanding of space. It's an engaging, accessible and intelligent book. That night, however, I felt particularly sensitive about a theme that Carl Sagan kept returning to as I read the whole book in a single late sitting: namely, that religion in general and Christianity in particular is pernicious; that it holds back human beings and is damaging to our progress; and that our scientific advances as a species are stunted because of the church. Maybe that isn't what Carl Sagan meant to say, but my attention was acutely drawn to what felt like a repeated refrain of the wrongness of Christianity.

I put the book down and the thought very clearly appeared in my head: 'On this, I don't agree with Carl Sagan. I didn't abandon Christianity because I thought it was wrong. I abandoned Christianity because it was inconvenient.' It occurred to me ever so powerfully that I had never seriously doubted or changed my mind over any of the facts that stunned me into my conversion at age 18. No, instead I had suppressed what I knew about Jesus Christ because other things seemed more immediately attractive. Isn't that also what I did when I chose to give the easy answer in April 2017? I had chosen convenience, my own comfort and the approval of people over my relationship with the God who had made and redeemed me.

In 2002, what Carl Sagan inadvertently taught me was that my backsliding was intellectually bankrupt.

In the weeks that followed, I prayed more than once for God's forgiveness for abandoning him, and for turning my back on his truth.

I recall one night a month or so later, nervously confessing this to my great friends Phil and Jeanette Dixon, who ran the table tennis club at the Shakespeare Centre in Kendal. The local Liberal Democrat executive committee met in the same building one night and as we were both leaving our respective events, I bumped into Phil and Jeanette. I thought for a split second and then went for it, 'You're Christians, aren't you?' They nodded, so I said, 'I think I'm unbacksliding . . .' With many ups and downs, since then I have sought to live as a Christian.

In October that same year, my mum, then just 53, was diagnosed with ovarian cancer. I was immensely close to my mum. She was a mere 20 when I was born and gave up her career to care for her two young children. After my parents' divorce, both she and my dad struggled financially, no matter how hard they worked. Eventually Mum went to university – she'd missed the chance in her late teens, and no doubt my arrival didn't help. In her late 30s, she got her degree and went on to have a career as an academic. One of the proudest moments of my life was seeing my mum being awarded her PhD. Mum had worked so hard to overcome the cards that life had dealt her, and yet here she was facing a death sentence at just 53. We were all utterly devastated. For me, the thought that little Gracie would grow up never knowing her wonderful grandma was too much to bear. Having restored my faith in Christ just weeks beforehand was, I am sure, the only way I got through the 20 months that followed until she passed away on 27 July 2004. My mum put her faith in Christ before she died, something I suspect would not have happened had I not 'unbackslid' when I did.

Maybe the line of questioning on sexuality that I received as Leader of the party touched a nerve with me because it was my own sexual sin that had led me to deny Christ for so many years for the sake of my own convenience. I don't know. But I do know that as I stood in front of those cameras, I felt that saying 'No, it's not' to the question on sin was something I shouldn't have done.

It's hard to describe the emotional turmoil that I was plunged into. After I had given the 'No, it's not' interview with Eleanor, I made it clear to my team that I wasn't going to repeat the line. I was angry that I'd done it. Maybe my team thought I was angry with them. I wasn't at all. I was furious with myself – and I was utterly miserable. I felt lost.

That night, my friend Paul Levy, a church pastor in Ealing, raced across London from his home to sit and pray with me in my flat near Stockwell. We drank cheap Portuguese lager and we cried. It was liberating.

The pastor of my church in Kendal, Paul Baxendale, is also a great friend and was a wonderful support from a distance while I was on tour over the following weeks. We'd do Bible studies on the phone while I was sitting in the Pardew Boudoir™ at the back of the battle bus. It kept me focused and it kept me going. However devastated I was, I wasn't going to throw in the towel. I was determined to lead the party through the campaign, and I was determined that we were going to make gains.

But I still felt the weight of having let God down, in an almost physical way.

And then Paul Baxendale said something to me one day that just changed everything. He said, 'For the Christian, sin spoils our relationship with God, but it doesn't end it.'

When I heard that, I felt that huge weight lift. I believed that we are saved by grace and through faith in Christ, not by our own works or our own performance. I say I believed that, but I'm not sure how much I understood it. That moment, when I realized that no matter what kind of clanger I'd dropped and no matter what I'd done I was nevertheless utterly secure, was a game changer for me.

It still is. It's changed my whole outlook on everything. Intellectually, I'd accepted the concept of grace for years, but it's another matter to actually feel it. And what a feeling! What makes Christianity unique? Well, Christ obviously. But alongside Christ himself, the thing that is unique to Christianity is the concept of grace – that I am saved through nothing I have done. My salvation is God's work, not my own. That means that I can't screw it up, because it wasn't my work in the first place. When I sing 'Amazing Grace' these days, I really mean it. It *is* utterly amazing.

The intense focus on what I believed about sexual practice sometimes strikes me as comical.

I mean, to talk about it is not why I went into politics.

I am sometimes frustrated and sometimes amused at the caricature of me that has developed since the 2017 election as a result of all this. To some people I am some kind of modern-day Mary Whitehouse, tutting at the very *thought* of the Village People, pulling Kenneth Williams-style faces of horror and moral outrage, disgusted at every imagined sexual deviation and so on.

I am amused by this because it's a very silly caricature and also because part of me genuinely doesn't care very much what people think about me. We all have reputations of one kind or another – but those reputations are temporary and exist under the watchful gaze of an almighty God who sees far deeper than our skin-deep reputations. Then again, I'm pretty vain, so I do care what people think . . . a bit. And that's why it's frustrating to be misunderstood and to have your reputation dictated by others.

The barrage of questions about my faith tailed off after that first week or so. They didn't disappear entirely, but by the time I took part in the leaders' debates, the journalists seemed to have moved on.

There is a verse in the Bible that says, 'Whatever your hand finds to do, do it with all your might' (Ecclesiastes 9.10). My hand had found me the role of leading the Liberal Democrats, so my job was to stop wallowing in my misery following the events of 25 April, repent of my sin, accept my forgiveness and crack on with the job I'd been given.

I was no Gladstone, but I had Gladstone's party to lead. Indeed, I had Gladstone's party to save.

10

Redeeming liberalism

We'll get to the final few weeks of the 2017 campaign in the next chapter. Spoiler alert: I end up resigning as Leader. But just because I stood down, please don't think I have given up.

Admittedly, I have now entered the wonderfully liberating realm of the 'post-ambitious'. I no longer harbour any unfulfilled ambitions to hold high office. I do, however, possess an overwhelming ambition for my country and for the liberal movement to which I have dedicated so much of my life.

Autobiographical works are, by their nature, somewhat 'Me! Me! Me!' But this chapter is about the political creed that I signed up to when I was 16, a creed that I consider to be under very serious threat today. Liberalism is under threat from the outside – from authoritarian, populist and left-wing socialist movements. It is also under threat from the inside, from itself and from mistaken understanding of what liberalism is among people who think they are liberals. This book tells my story of a personal journey into politics, to Christian faith, to a political career, while looking at how those things can be held together.

My story is indeed personal, but it throws up two wider issues that I want to focus on in this penultimate chapter.

First, my story gives us a snapshot of the state of liberalism in the UK and in the West. My experience of being scrutinized because of my Christian faith and treated as an oddity (at best), for being, at the same time, an orthodox Christian and a liberal, may be a small example of liberalism's growing tendency not to be terribly liberal. Second, it provides a perspective on the state of the Liberal Democrats in the UK and the wider health of the progressive centre-left versus the growing populist movements on the left and right. In my time, the Lib Dems have had a record high of 63 MPs and we have been down to as low as 8. The decisions we took following the 2015 wipe-out have seen us recover and grow significantly: we are now a more credible election prospect than we have been for almost a decade – yet we are still some way from the comeback that we desire.

All this takes place against the backdrop of Brexit. I'll be honest with you, I kept putting off writing this chapter, waiting for some kind of definitive conclusion on this matter. But I have given up trying now, because Brexit will never end. It is a form of eternal punishment. All references to the matter will be out of date by the time you read this. In fact, they are probably out of date as I write because I haven't looked at the news for a whole 15 minutes now . . .

The UK faces serious challenges, including the likelihood of a smaller economy in the event of our leaving the European Union, reduced public spending capacity and therefore real hardship for those who rely on the state for healthcare, education or their retirement. These challenges should concern us all, whether or not we favour exiting the EU. But they are not completely insurmountable challenges.

The head of a large family firm in my constituency said to me, 'Brexit is a disaster. We've survived three fires, fourteen floods, countless recessions, a depression and two world wars and we'll get through this too . . . but it's still a disaster.'

Don't worry, I haven't fallen for the cheery but clueless refrain: 'We're British, so we'll grin and bear it and get through it all right!' Nevertheless, the UK will survive Brexit one way or another. There's only so much pessimism I am prepared to commit myself to.

Leaving the EU threatens to leave us poorer, less influential and probably less secure – but the UK will still exist, and we'll do OK.

I am not sure I feel quite so optimistic about liberalism.

Liberalism is in desperate need of redemption. Across the Western world today, liberalism doesn't seem terribly liberal.

What do I mean by this?

Well, if we are in favour of diversity and pluralism, then we must oppose all attempts at assimilation and forced conformity. There is nothing wrong and everything right about wanting to persuade people to agree with us and to accept our world view but, as liberals, we must not aim to build a society where assimilation and conformity are engineered via legal or social pressure. Nevertheless, this is where liberalism is seriously in danger at its own hands.

My experience of the attention I have received regarding my faith has given me an unexpected insight into this. I don't consider myself to be a victim, and I hope I haven't come across as one in this book. Being scrutinized because of my faith has, however, opened my eyes even more widely

225

to an increasing lack of liberalism and self-awareness among those who see themselves as liberals. Closing down discussion of difficult themes or airbrushing out uncomfortable views ought always to be a red rag to the liberal bull. Instead, they have too often become red meat to a liberal orthodoxy that seeks to eviscerate blasphemers.

In late 2017, a letter signed by 170 academics describing themselves as 'scholars of empire' attacked the University of Oxford for permitting a research project led by Professor Nigel Biggar entitled 'Ethics and Empire'. The crime committed by Professor Biggar and the university was to consider the 'balance sheet' of empire. In other words, Biggar would be looking at the pros and the cons – a rather challenging and counter-cultural thing to do, and no doubt uncomfortable and controversial. I admit to having raised an eyebrow when I became aware of the premise of this project. I am a liberal, so I don't think I need to expend much energy in convincing you that I think imperialism is a bad thing – but, just for the record, I do think it's a bad thing.

Nevertheless, my eyebrows rose far more in response to this large-scale attack on Biggar and his employer. Are we seriously saying that our leading thinkers are not allowed to consider the possibility that there may be some positives to empire? Jon Wilson of King's College, London, told *The Guardian* in December 2017 that 'any attempt to create a balance sheet of the good and evil of empire can't be based on rigorous scholarship'. (Note to self: I'd better not take my kids to Hadrian's Wall or Chester's Roman amphitheatre again.)

The letter was coordinated by an academic from Cambridge University, but the fact that there are signatories from across the world means that we cannot simply dismiss this assault on Professor Biggar as just being elite Oxbridge rivalry (I've worked in academia and I can confirm that it's even bitchier than politics!). What the very intelligent and purportedly progressive signatories of this letter are telling us is that we can't consider potential truth if it contradicts what we currently believe to be inviolably right.

In November 2018, we saw a concerted attempt to have Professor Roger Scruton, a traditionalist Conservative philosopher, sacked from his role as the chair of a British government housing group. Scruton is a serious academic, writer and thinker with whom I have serious disagreements, for example on his support for Viktor Orbán, the right-wing Hungarian President. Scruton has expressed extremely challenging views on sexuality, on national identity and on gender roles. He is also a leading expert on aesthetics and architecture, which is why the Government appointed him to this unpaid role. He has since been sacked from this position because some of his comments went too far, even for the Conservative Government! At the time of his appointment, though, social media was awash with calls for him to be sacked before he had even taken up the position. His 'extreme views' and comments on moral, social and religious issues were thought to make him 'unsuitable'. Opposition MPs joined in these calls. I'm no fan of Scruton but, once upon a time, the knee-jerk liberal instinct would have been to take the side of one with whom we disagree but who was subject to a coordinated hounding for having the temerity to think unfashionable stuff. What happened to that liberal instinct?

Roger Scruton doesn't have much in common with Peter Tatchell, Germaine Greer or Richard Dawkins. One badge of honour they all share though is this: they have all been 'no-platformed' on campuses in the UK or USA for holding and expressing uncomfortable views on faith, sex and gender – or else for daring to defend other people's right to hold or express such views.

In August 2018, Claire Fox pointed out in *The Economist* that the American Civil Liberties Union had amended its guiding principles for deciding which freedom of speech cases it will defend. In those guidelines, it now states, 'Speech that denigrates such [marginalized] groups can inflict serious harms . . . and is intended to, and often will, impede progress toward equality.' Of course, they are not referring to incitement to racial hatred or violence here, they are talking about anyone who challenges current thinking on gender, for example. This bastion of liberalism in the world's foremost liberal democracy now doesn't believe in defending the right to free speech of people whose views are currently felt to be uncomfortable. I thought the point of liberalism was to defend the rights of the marginalized and the unpopular. You can find authoritarian reactionaries who will happily defend the rights of people they agree with, but it takes a liberal to defend the rights of people they don't agree with. At least, that's how it's supposed to work . . .

Claire Fox is a Brexit Party member, a libertarian writer and a former leading light in the Revolutionary Communist

Party. Back in my student days, I remember Claire running for NUS President on a platform that even the Socialist Workers Party thought was 'going a bit too far'. Today, she seems to be living proof that politics is not a spectrum but a circle. It looks as though she has gone so far to the left that she has come around to the other side and reappeared as a libertarian. That's intended as an observation, by the way, not an insult. I respect communists; indeed, I respect libertarians – but I am neither! Liberals do accept some limits to freedom of speech. Hatred and incitement to violence are not tolerated in free societies. We are not intolerant of those dangers because we are afraid of opinions and words, but because we fear the consequences of those words leading to actions which would be a far greater threat to individual liberty and community safety.

Libertarians, the 'alt-right' and others have used the bogus claim of desiring freedom of speech, which makes martyrs of those whose rhetoric is contrived to lead to violence and hatred. For instance, there was the laughable attempt to make Tommy Robinson a 'free-speech hero' who was, in fact, guilty of crass contempt of court for broadcasting a video of defendants entering court for trial. There is a natural antipathy from liberals towards a libertarianism which appears to be a thin fig-leaf covering for far-right extremism.

Of course, Claire Fox – now Claire Fox MEP after her election to the European Parliament in May 2019 – might have a little of her own explaining to do. During the campaign for the 2019 European elections, Claire's party banned respected UK broadcaster Channel 4 News from their events. Their objection was that Channel 4 News had been unnecessarily critical about their donors in a previous programme. If we truly believe in freedom of speech, then we also need to be prepared to defend the freedom of those who write or broadcast critical things about us – not ban them from our rallies!

As a teenager in the 1980s, I remember the first time I watched *The Young Ones*, the alternative sitcom of four students living in anarchic squalor. It was puerile and political – and I absolutely loved it. The programme made me laugh until my ribs hurt. A regular refrain was that Rick (played by Rik Mayall) would dub anybody and everybody a 'fascist' for just about anything and everything. In response, my sister and I would scream, 'Fascist!' at each other for misdemeanours such as leaving the toilet seat up (or down), not letting the cat out or playing our music a bit too loud.

There are fascists in our midst today and we need to be vigilant about the rise of the far right. But liberals must not become twenty-first-century Ricks, pointing at every difficult or challenging point of view and screaming, 'Fascist!' It didn't do the boy who cried wolf any good, and it won't do us any good either.

The otherwise sensible Royal College of General Practitioners no-platformed the right-wing shock jock Julia Hartley-Brewer, who was originally booked to appear on a platform at their conference in spring 2019. Hartley-Brewer had expressed a positive view some years earlier about Enoch Powell's infamous 'rivers of blood' speech and, on discovering this, the RCGP withdrew her invitation.

I object to the no-platforming of Julia Hartley-Brewer because I am a liberal; of course she has a right to hold and express views that I think are plain wrong (and her views are invariably plain wrong) but my main concern is that, by seeking to silence people whose views we don't like, it simply amplifies them and makes 'liberals' look petty and stupid.

Too many liberals have grown angrily intolerant of debate and difference. My feeling is that the writers of *The Young Ones* had a healthy self-awareness. They were politically correct left-wingers themselves (nothing wrong with that, by the way), but they were aware of the slightly ridiculous and po-faced tendencies of their tribe and they poked fun at this. It would be healthier if we could have a similar level of self-awareness today.

I suspect that many on the left (a large number of whom are not liberals, of course) are only really bothered about playing to their specific audience, reached via social media. Their audience, whose approval and solidarity they crave and which lacks ability to grasp nuance and individuality, dictates how those on the left themselves react to any given situation.

John Stuart Mill is the father of modern liberalism. He spoke of many threats to liberty. Among the greatest that he identified is the tyranny of opinion – when people feel under pressure from their culture to think something other than what they *really* think. Mill's *On Liberty* was written in 1859 but it feels alarmingly relevant to this age too.

Today, we are used to being asked what our 'guilty pleasures' are, in terms of the things that we enjoy but are a bit too embarrassed to admit to. Mine is probably Duran Duran. There – I've said it: I am a post-punk indie kid, an *NME* reader, a John Peel listener . . . and yet I've seen Duran Duran live twice and I've got all their albums. Even the recent ones. I know. They're not my favourite act, but they're a great pop band and sometimes you just go with what you like rather than bothering to critique things. Enough excuses! Right, well I've just humiliated myself publicly. In return, can I ask you to do something privately that might (behave, it's not that kind of book!) make you feel uncomfortable?

Seriously though: think about yourself and your opinions. Are there things that you think, but are fearful to express? Perhaps you have opinions that you wouldn't voice out loud because you worry that they might offend others? Perhaps you don't voice some opinions, though, because you are afraid of being judged? If you have been honest with yourself, you will have come up with at least one or two views that fall into those categories. And, if we are all in that boat, what does that say about the honesty and freedom in our public debates and personal interactions?

It feels as though our society today is riddled with stark-naked emperors being lauded for their wondrous wardrobes. In the shadows, many of us have the potential to be the small boy who speaks up . . . except we don't want to offend, and we certainly don't want to be judged.

This is at the heart of what Mill was getting at. Mill says that the quality of our ideas and of our society is enhanced by free expression of competing world views. Society is stale without that. He is clear that our liberty is at risk when we all feel a pressure to start thinking the same things.

Our liberty is even more at risk when it is the express intention of powerful people to encourage this universal assimilation. For example, our cultural mediums and our education system from primary school upwards dictate that the sexual revolution of the 1950s and 1960s, and the radical individualistic world view it generated, is an indisputable good. Our culture maintains that materialism and the consumption of more and more goods and services is an indisputable good. It is a given that sincere belief in God is backward and contrary to self-fulfilment . . . and self-fulfilment is an indisputable good.

Social media now feeds this attempted assimilation. Maybe ten years ago we thought social media would lead to a greater democracy, greater individual empowerment, the flowering of thousands of unmediated, unfiltered, unspun viewpoints and opinions.

That hope sounds naïve now. I observe that social media fuels groupthink, pack mentality and depressing conformity – not to mention a disgraceful lack of civility and decency.

The tyrants of opinion have their secret police behind millions of keyboards.

Professor John Gray summed it up well in the March 2018 issue of the *Times Literary Supplement* when he wrote, 'Practices of toleration that used to be seen as essential to freedom are being deconstructed and dismissed as structures of repression and any ideas or beliefs that stand in the way of this process banned from public discourse.'

How did liberalism find itself so reduced that it has become an enemy of itself?

I am not going to do justice to something so complex but let me try to briefly make sense of it.

I think the heart of the problem is twofold: first, that liberalism's ascendancy is killing it. Second, we liberals have not been honest with ourselves about our project's failures – and so we have got ourselves into a hole and we continue to dig.

Let's deal with these one at a time. Liberalism has gained such ascendancy across the West that we often don't even call it liberalism. It is the established world view, it's the air that we breathe; we don't notice it because it is the dominant all-pervading culture of the West, both economically and socially.

Despite my best efforts, the Liberal Democrats have not yet won. But irrespective of my efforts, liberalism has won.

Be careful what you wish for.

In fourth-century Rome, Christianity won, in that it became the established world view. Up to that point there had been 300 years of persecution and exclusion for the followers of Jesus Christ.

After Christianity became adopted as the official religion of the Roman Empire, it morphed from being marginalized and persecuted to dominant and persecuting in a short time. In doing so, it lost sight of its own internal truth of reliance on Christ alone and self-sacrificing love. The state with which that church merged began to oppress different minorities, to show the same intolerance and violence towards other groups that Christians had endured for so many years.

Liberalism faces the same fate today. It feels as if we are tolerant of everything – apart from the stuff we disagree with. We are positive about diversity, so long as it's the right kind of diversity. We want to celebrate differences – but not *those* kinds of difference! We were a movement of non-conformists but it seems as though we can no longer tolerate those who refuse to conform.

The one part of the Liberal Democrat constitution that most party members can actually remember states that 'none shall be enslaved by poverty, ignorance or conformity'. Conformity, enforced by the tyranny of opinion, is the most illiberal of things. Yet it seems to be the mission of many who count themselves as liberal even though this mission ignores the lessons of history.

The second reason why liberalism has begun to eat itself is that liberalism is both an economic and social project – and the economic part of the project has failed too many people. An economic approach which involves (at best) modest state intervention, light regulation and an overemphasis on markets has not delivered prosperity or greater opportunity for the masses.

The many people who have been failed by the economic project have developed a grievance with the whole liberal project, including social liberalism. The response of liberals to this has been to double down on social liberalism, indeed becoming illiberal in the ways in which they attack those who criticize liberalism.

Western liberal democracies have seen the standards of living of their people decline relative to those in China and other non-liberal and non-democratic societies. Voters across many parties have lost confidence in the economic branch of the liberal project. Many, especially among lower income groups, now question whether liberalism works for them at all. That is certainly the case in the northern towns of England in which I grew up, where communities that have seen no discernible personal economic benefit from the liberal project voted against that project's centrepiece: membership of the EU. It is true also in the US Rust Belt where blue-collar workers, struggling to get by, have turned their back on the Democratic Party and voted for Donald Trump.

How has the globalization of our economy and the increase in individual liberty improved the life of Sandra, who earns a fraction above the minimum wage as a carer? She provides 15-minute visits to elderly people whose own children live hundreds of miles away, thanks to their acceptance of economic opportunities and freedoms. Her clients eagerly look forward to her visits, yet she has barely any time for conversation because she has to rush through her duties in order to get to her next appointment. Sandra is my age; she's spent ten of the past twelve months in rent arrears to a local housing association. She hasn't had a holiday in years. Her kids are in their late teens and early twenties and are still at home, one studying and one with a minimum-wage, part-time job. The younger child would love to be an engineer, to work in construction, but the jobs aren't there because we aren't building enough. Sandra is a lovely, kind, patient human being. She voted to leave the EU because, she says, 'Nobody listens to people like me.'

The reaction of too many liberals to this backlash against the underwhelming economic achievements of their project is to ignore the economic issues, while insisting on the irrefutable righteousness of the social aspect of the liberal creed. Those who question that creed are then denounced as 'deplorables' in the USA or 'gammon' in the UK. If you were to look closely enough at Sandra's timeline, you might find an example of something a bit off-colour that she's posted or shared (in fact, I've checked, and she has), in which case you can safely dismiss her concerns, can't you? You no longer need to answer for her economic situation if you can easily pigeon-hole her as a bigot.

I hope I am not the only one who thinks that liberalism's answer to the millions of Sandras out there is utterly unacceptable. Surely the answer to the lack of economic success of liberal governments (of the centre-left or centre-right) is to address these economic failures, rather than to judge and belittle those who question whether any part of liberalism works for them any more?

Sadly though – for the moment – it seems that many liberals are happy instead to accept that tinkering with the market is the best we can do and that attempting to galvanize national or regional identity for positive liberal aims is ugly and contemptible.

As liberalism effectively abandons serious attempts to restore its economic credibility, it focuses almost exclusively on the social aspect of liberalism and treats with hostility and disdain those who question the social liberal orthodoxy. Ignore our economic failures, we say, and look at our commitment to equality and diversity . . . although not for everyone . . .

Those of us with a religious faith are perhaps canaries in the cage, drawing fire because we are seen as blasphemers against the social liberal creed. Fodder for an undernour-ished liberalism that has begun to eat itself.

To be a Christian is to deny yourself and follow Christ, which means that Christianity rubs against every earthly culture, especially a culture like ours, in which self-actual-ization, self-determination and self-definition are the great virtues – and in which self-denial is the great sin. Christianity is therefore counter-cultural. It always has been and always will be. If you are a Christian, you should be a decent, good-mannered citizen, but you should never feel at home. You are to be a resident alien.

You don't need to be a Christian, though, to be an alien. Maybe you hold a different world view – whatever it is – or have a sense of personal identity that makes you an outsider too? In which case, you need a healthy liberalism that builds a society where people with wildly different views and values can rub along together. It may be an uncom-fortable co-existence but it can be peaceful and respectful. The problem for many liberals is that having won the freedoms they craved, they no longer have an appetite to defend the freedoms of others. Liberalism has thus become ascendant, complacent and intolerant.

Today, to many liberals, faith that is anything more than an outward expression of cultural or family heritage is derided. Those whose lives are built around a desire, for example, to follow faithfully and in full the teachings of Jesus, can expect to be mocked at best or more likely treated with contempt.

Followers of Christianity, Judaism and Islam are all viewed with suspicion – our allegiance to our country or to modern British values is deemed to be diluted, and we are seen to have divided loyalties at best. Those who have a faith blaspheme against the liberal creed by believing that we are not actually our own 'god' or even our own property, that radical individualism is not an unalloyed good, that there are transcendent values that sometimes go against the grain. We don't conform, we can't conform, and we won't conform. As such, we should be the poster boys and girls of liberalism. We're not. You see, faith is not just the canary in the cage, it is the elephant in the room. It is a massive elephant that liberals mostly try to look around and ignore, occasionally patronizing it with a nervous pat, sometimes staring contemptuously at it, wishing it wasn't so much an elephant and perhaps instead a hippo or a zebra . . . I mean why does it insist on being an elephant? How very dogmatic!

Most people on the planet have a religious faith. More than two billion call themselves Christians, and a further 1.6 billion are Muslims – those two faiths alone claim more than half of all humanity. A failure to respect or understand people with faith isn't consistent with liberalism.

I want to argue that liberals are wrong to seek to rub out faith in general, and Christianity in particular. For one thing, to do so is quite illiberal. However – even worse than that – deleting Christianity from liberal societies means deleting the very world view that created and shaped liberalism in the first place, and which sustains it today.

Liberalism's two key purposes are formed as a direct consequence of Christian heritage. First, liberalism intervenes to improve the well-being of the many because compassion and love for our neighbour is of utmost importance. Second, liberalism intervenes to protect individual freedom against the pressures to conform because Christians believe in the sacred value of every human being and know that Christianity's safety as a minority belief depends upon the protection not only of their freedoms but also of the freedoms of others.

British liberalism is founded in the battle for religious liberty. In the nineteenth century, the non-conformist evangelical Christian groups that were persecuted by a society which favoured adherence only to the established church built a liberal movement that championed much wider liberty for women, for other religious minorities, non-religious minorities, for cultural and regional minorities, and for the poor and vulnerable.

History is loud and clear: where the gospel is preached, other freedoms follow. The abolition of slavery was led by evangelical Christians, most notably Wilberforce. The drive to introduce laws to prevent industrial exploitation was led by a committed Christian, Lord Shaftesbury. The ending of the cruel practice of sati in India was the result of campaigning by Christian missionaries, especially William Carey.

This is not a coincidence. If you believe that you have been saved by grace, by a God who commands that you then show that same selfless love to others, if you believe that God created every person of equal value and dignity and in his own image, and if you believe that you are answerable to that God, then that belief will not leave you unmoved. That belief will define your values and it will define your actions. Christianity, then, is the essential underpinning of liberalism and, indeed, of democracy.

If our values are relativistic, if they are shifting, and if they depend upon the temporary norms of this age, then the freedoms you bank upon today cannot be guaranteed tomorrow. Our liberties are in the hands of unstable forces – we cannot have confidence that our rights will still be our rights from one generation to the next because we cannot call upon any authority in support of those rights.

Christianity provides the values that permit liberalism to flourish.

That does not, of course, mean that you can only be a liberal if you are a Christian. I am, however, saying that the values that underpin modern liberalism are derived from Christianity, the value of the individual, and the equality of all before God; that there are self-evident rights and wrongs, and that there should be justice to uphold individual liberties and protect the powerless from the powerful.

In discarding Christianity, we kick away the foundations of liberalism and democracy and so we cannot then be surprised when what we call liberalism stops being liberal. Relativism is not liberalism. Relativism is the gateway to tyranny.

Relativism is the belief that something can be good now but may not be good in the future; that something was acceptable then but not now. The only way to throw off relativism is to accept that values are enduring, eternal and not of our making. Yet modern counterfeit liberalism won't do that because to do so would be one small step away from accepting the possibility of there being a God.

Underpinning the growth of illiberal liberalism is the all-pervading myth of secular neutrality. For many years now our culture has considered that the absence of faith is the neutral position, and that the holding of a religious faith is eccentric. In other words, an absence of faith is the standard assumption around which we build our social structures. If you have a faith, we will consider you to be eccentric but we will tolerate you, as long as you remain on the edges.

What appears now to be happening is that while the absence of faith is still thought to be the neutral position, holding a faith is today only considered to be tolerably eccentric if it is merely cultural. But if your faith actually affects your world view in any way that puts it at odds with the mainstream, then your faith is considered to be malign and intolerable.

Many will now believe it to be unacceptable if your faith tells you that you should submit to God and, in doing so, deny yourself when it comes to your money, your time, your sexual desires, or that you should raise your children to believe that Jesus is who he says he is, or that the life of every human being matters at every stage of existence.

You may disagree with one who holds to these values but, if you are a liberal, then you will accept that, as long as these values are not imposed by force, they have equal standing. True liberalism defends the right for everyone to be heard, not for everyone to avoid being offended.

The ascendancy of liberalism has led liberals to forget, then, that there is absolutely no such thing as neutrality. If you believe that there is no God, your world view is valid, but it isn't neutral. Every human being has a world view. You will acquire that world view in different ways and from different sources. Maybe you get it fully or in part from a book that you consider to be holy, or from your parents, from your peer group, your teachers, the media or the culture in which you are immersed.

We can't, on the one hand, believe that the election of Donald Trump or the decision of the British electorate to vote to leave the EU were manipulated by fake news and troll factories, and then, on the other hand, believe that we have total control and critical independence over every notion or viewpoint that we hold – not without being conceited in the extreme.

Absence of faith is a valid world view, but it has no right to supremacy. If you believe that the absence of faith has the right to supremacy, or if you believe that the holding of a faith has the right to supremacy, then you are not a liberal.

I have often been encouraged – by well-meaning people – to make sure that my faith doesn't influence my decisions or actions as a politician. I was asked many times during the leadership election: 'When it comes to the crunch, will your religion influence how you decide what to do more than your politics?' The more I think about it, the dafter that sounds (apologies to all those very nice people who asked the question). But, seriously, who leaves their world view at the door before they enter a room? Who enters every situation empty-headed and value-free? Not you and not me, and neither should we.

I believe in pluralism, a society which permits many

voices. I am not a secularist but I believe in a secular society where there is no 'state faith'.

In the UK we have a church trapped as part of the furniture of the state – that is a waste of a church. A boat in the water is good. Water in the boat is bad. A church in the state is good. The state in the church is bad – really bad. It pollutes the message of that church. It compromises it and weakens its witness.

And let's be clear. It is just as illiberal, and just as silly, to make atheism the state religion.

As we seek to eradicate faith schools or rub out the teaching of Christianity in those schools, to marginalize and ridicule in the media those who hold to that teaching, then we are making atheism the state religion.

Letting go of the Christian belief in unshifting rights and wrongs, and in the grace and forgiveness that goes with them, means that we have lost our reference point and our moral certainty. We have also lost the source of motivation to show mercy or kindness to anyone who falls short.

With no unifying code, we make it up as we go along, and values are a relativistic mist that comes and goes. What is true for you may be true for me, or it may not. And it might all change tomorrow. There is such a thing as society, but it is like a ship with neither an anchor nor a rudder – just a lot of people running around on deck following a few loud voices that sound temporarily convincing. Meanwhile, the boat heads in any old direction.

But the problem is that the political and cultural leaders of our day have made the arrogant and fatal assumption that everyone shares these shifting 'liberal' values and have sought to enforce them via Mill's hated 'tyranny of opinion'. And the consequences are . . . well, Trump and Brexit, to name two.

During the 2016 US presidential campaign, Hillary Clinton famously dismissed some of the supporters of Donald Trump as 'a basket of deplorables'. She was surely referring to racists in the Ku Klux Klan and other white-supremacist groups who were supporting Trump. Nevertheless, many Americans who were neither liberals on the one hand nor racists on the other thought that she was referring to them. Indeed, many of Hillary's supporters considered that the 'basket of deplorables' basically contained anyone who didn't sign up to the liberal values that they believed Hillary personified. The result was that Trump grew in the estimation of those who felt that 'the liberal establishment' sneered at them, disliked them and considered their ways and views to be backward. As a result, the USA's two parties have never been more bitterly opposed to each other, and neither of them appears particularly liberal in reality.

Liberalism is at a crossroads here too. In the UK, the rise of the far left in the Labour Party seems to have grown in correlation with the rise of the nationalist movement in England that led to the Brexit vote, and the nationalist movement in Scotland that continues to keep independence on the agenda.

These three groups have two things in common: first, they offer simplistic solutions to complex problems. Second, they share an apparent belief in the moral inferiority of the other. Of course, they wouldn't use such a term but, nevertheless, it characterizes their discourse. If you are not part of the Corbyn left, then you are a reactionary. If you are not a supporter of Brexit, then you are not a patriot. If you are not a supporter of independence, then you are not a genuine Scot. There is a common narrative of betrayal and an inbuilt aversion to compromise, common ground and tolerance. The same can be said of the Trumpians and some of those on the so-called liberal wing of US politics.

Those movements make our political discourse harsh, unforgiving and unpleasant – but it's far worse than that. If we demonize the other, then it's a short step before we begin to deprive those others of some key freedoms. In addition, of course, extreme political dogmas or slogan-eering populism tend to lead to disastrous economic policies, creating greater poverty and inequality.

Liberalism is the rational and inclusive antidote to simplistic and divisive populism. That is why liberalism is needed more than ever. So we can't afford to cast out those who ought really to be welcome in our movement. Many in the USA who considered themselves lumped into the basket of deplorables need instead to be welcomed into the liberal fold. Many in Scotland who favour independence need to be welcomed into the liberal fold. Many across the UK who voted for Brexit need to be welcomed into the liberal fold. The liberal fold needs also to welcome people who hold a religious faith, but who have grown increasingly suspicious of liberals' patronizing and even aggressive views about their beliefs.

We have come to make foolish assumptions about packages of beliefs. For instance, it is considered strange to be a liberal *and* a Christian or a liberal *and* in favour of Scottish independence or Brexit.

It takes me back to my first NUS conference in 1986. A woman went to the podium and opened her speech with 'As an out lesbian . . .' The audience burst into applause and cheered; many rose to their feet. She paused for breath, then added: 'And a Tory . . .' You could almost see people's heads exploding with confusion! What? Surely you can't be gay *and* a Conservative? Well, yes you can. Our lazy assumptions about packages of values are far more pervasive now than they were in in 1986. The liberal movement is against that kind of simplistic thinking and empty-headed labelling.

The crisis in Western liberalism is therefore a crisis of confidence in the project on the part of liberals themselves. We cannot deny that there is growing inequality and social decline, that biting poverty is real and advancing in our communities. Rather than seriously address these problems and admit, perhaps, that there is nothing especially liberal about poorly regulated markets and that we should intervene more, liberals have ducked the economic question. Liberalism has chosen to pivot on to something more comfortable. Identity politics, then, is the solution for liberals who are anxious that their economic project may be failing. Liberalism's social aspect is the trench into which many have dug themselves in order to claim a moral superiority over the 'deplorables'. However, this is more than just a tactic to divert attention away from economic failure, it is a natural consequence of liberalism's ascendancy. It is as if we have reached a point where too many liberals think that liberalism has won, so why listen to any other point of view? It is tied up in notions of 'enlightenment', that liberals and liberalism are intellectually superior.

The Oxford English Dictionary defines identity politics as 'a tendency for people of a particular religion, race, social background, etc., to form exclusive political alliances, moving away from traditional broad-based party politics'. In other words, my politics are less about what I think and are more about who I am.

In economics, it has long been said that 'when America sneezes, the world catches a cold'. What is true in economics is true for our culture. America has exported identity politics, but my feeling is that the right is at least as responsible as the liberal left for this. And I am afraid that the church in America bears huge responsibility too. By aligning itself so closely to the Republican Party, particularly in the campaigns to elect and re-elect President George W. Bush in 2000 and 2004, evangelical Christianity has succeeded in politicizing faith in the most unhelpful of ways. In so doing, millions of those whose self-identity is 'anything but Republican' – and especially 'anyone but Trump' – now have their fingers in their ears when it comes to the gospel. It has defined Christianity and churchgoing as conservative and intoler-ant, and secularism as liberal and tolerant. This definition has most certainly crossed the Atlantic. We liberals have found our creed sullied by identity politics, but we are not alone and we are not solely responsible for it either.

Living in this time of heightened identities, people don't think or believe something so much as they *are* something. So, to challenge my identity is to commit a personal assault against me. In the UK, the rise of nationalism is a case in point. We have, in an extremely short time, found ourselves in a situation where it is considered that causing offence is to commit violence.

What is at the heart of a liberal society? It is to uphold the position that we have a right to offend and a duty to tolerate offence. George Orwell said, 'If liberty means anything at all, it means the right to tell people what they do not want to hear.'

What too many of us liberals do not want to hear is that liberalism has eaten itself partly because it has been taken in by identity politics.

We will make an important step in the right direction if we remember that many of those in the UK dismissed as 'deplorables', 'gammon' or the 'Brexidiots' will have voted for New Labour in 1997 or for the Liberal Democrats in 2010. These are people who wanted the liberal project to succeed and have since gone looking for something else because they perceive it to have failed for them, their families and their communities.

We do not have to like Donald Trump or UKIP, the Brexit Party or the hard right of the Conservative Party to seek to understand and feel compassion for those who are drawn to them.

I regret that many of us liberals have instead chosen to insult those people and to alienate them even further and push them ever more into the arms of populists and nationalists of the left and right.

Whether the believer in Scottish independence and the unionist; the metropolitan millennial remainer and the mature suburban Brexiteer; the angry Rust-Belt Trumpian and the equally angry college liberal – a liberal society has a home for them all. In fact, a truly liberal society is the only place where they can co-exist. None of these people needs to compromise their world view, each must simply accept that the other has the right to a different standpoint and – if at all possible – behave respectfully and courteously towards all.

Yet five minutes on social media will give you a window into a society that condemns and judges, that leaps to take offence and pounces to cause it – liberals condemning those who don't conform as nasty and hateful, the right condemning liberals as fragile snowflakes. Christianity rebukes both sides: don't judge, show kindness, show gentleness, show patience – especially to those who don't deserve it. Shouldn't liberalism do the same?

I believe liberalism is better than conservativism because it doesn't accept the status quo, the loss of freedom for the sake of tradition and the convenience of the powerful. Instead, liberalism asks tough questions and doesn't accept glib answers. I think liberalism is better than socialism because liberalism dictates that we must all be free, but that we must not all be the same.

So liberalism has won, but it is now behaving like the established church of the Roman Empire in the fourth and fifth centuries. It has gained ascendancy and lost itself in the process. It isn't very liberal any more. So many who declare themselves to be liberals really aren't.

John Stuart Mill may be spinning in his grave.

I once led the British liberal movement. I have given my entire adult life to that cause. I am in no mood to walk away from it now. I am determined to challenge the tyranny of opinion and join those who seek to redeem liberalism.

In the UK, that liberal movement has a home in the Liberal Democrats. But as I indicate above, it might also include people whose home is currently another party or, indeed, who are currently politically homeless.

I am very proud that the Liberal Democrats doubled in size to a record high of more than 100,000 members during my leadership – although we are still dwarfed by the 500,000 Labour members. Nevertheless, could my party be the gathering point that could create a truly inclusive and effective alternative government? I increasingly think so, but our challenges are threefold.

First, we need to establish who and what we are for. We need a defining narrative to draw people to us beyond the fact that we oppose Brexit. Second, we have to overcome people's instinctive assumption that Liberal Democrats do not have the credibility to form or to lead a government. Third, we must counter the reality of tribalism.

How do we meet these challenges?

1 Clarity of *narrative*

The most useful thing I did as party leader was to make the decision that the Liberal Democrats would not simply shrug and accept Brexit as inevitable. Instead, I committed the party (against a large amount of internal opposition) to campaigning for a further referendum, establishing ourselves as the UK's pro-European party. I will go so far as to say that this approach saved the party from potential extinction because it gave us a purpose; it doubled our membership and it led to the huge gains made in the 2019 local and European elections. Being pro-Europe has been like Marmite for the Lib Dems; it has appalled some and attracted others – but when you are the leader of a party on 4 per cent in the polls as I was, 'nuance' is a dirty word. Marmite was the right choice!

The beauty of the Liberal Democrats' Brexit position is that it is clear and simple. We need to be about more than Brexit if we want to advance further, but we need to make sure that the next part of our narrative is just as simple. Having a raft of terribly worthy policy initiatives is not what I would like to see. I suggest that we add just two things to our pro-Europeanism. The first, as I have argued throughout this chapter, is a return to a true liberalism in which we defend the liberties of the awkward outsider, championing freedom of conscience and a truly diverse society, which includes tolerating world views that we really don't like. The second is that we embark on a British, Franklin D. Roosevelt-style New Deal to unite our country in a common endeavour while rekindling loyalty to the wider liberal project. Here's what I mean: there are huge challenges to be overcome, the growing catastrophe of climate change chief among them. We should face that challenge in a way that unifies us as a society and restores faith in the liberal project.

If the only people who care about climate change are *Guardian*-reading liberals, then we are well and truly stuffed. A truly liberal government would acknowledge the power of identities and the value of intervention by harnessing sentiment through a unifying patriotic endeavour to invest in and build the world's best infrastructure here in the UK. We should launch a fast-paced, wholehearted national project to build the world's best public transport, the greatest renewable energy schemes (after all, we have the second largest tidal range in the world after Canada, so let's use it) and, while we're at it, the most impressive expansion of social housing, the quickest broadband . . . Why not be energized and proud of tangible things built with Victorian-scale ambition that make us a richer, more environmentally sustainable country and therefore more able to afford the best social infrastructure, which includes the NHS, schools and police? I want to suggest that liberals should invoke the spirit of FDR's New Deal and embrace the concept of active, ambitious, liberal government.

In this age, elections and referendums seem more often to be won by those whose emotional appeal is strongest – but there is nothing to say that those whose politics is grounded in logic cannot be successful with their emotional appeal. Hitting people in the gut isn't the unique preserve of the extremes of left and right. Our identities are important and a reality, so why not use them to achieve great aims? If we were to embark on a vast project to transform the UK's infrastructure to make us entirely energy self-sufficient through renewables, we could use a message of national pride, unity of purpose and 'being first and best' to bring the country with us. Why can't patriotism be invoked in the name of progress?

253

Why must it only be brandished by those who wish to divide and discriminate? There is no good reason, apart from our own squeamishness.

This would involve accepting that state intervention can be a part of the liberal armoury. To me, that's a no-brainer; of course we should see the state as a tool to deliver greater freedom by protecting people from the climate catastrophe and creating hope and opportunity through economic success.

2 Credibility

There is no complex formula for overcoming this one. We just have to stick our chests out and claim the space. The Liberals have not formed a majority in the UK House of Commons since the 1906 Parliament. As I write, we have 12 MPs. But we also have Conservative and Labour parties that are extreme and unappealing to an unprecedented degree. On 23 May 2019, in the elections for the European Parliament, the Brexit Party came first and the Liberal Democrats came second. For the first time in the history of British democracy, there was a national election in which neither Labour nor the Conservatives were in the top two.

If all we want to do is return the Liberal Democrats to the days of being the go-to 'none of the above' option for voters and to being the undisputed third force, then we probably only need to stick to the strategy that I set for the party while I was leader. Namely to pick and stick to a clear and unequivocal position on Brexit and to invest in and inspire our members to build our strength in local government.

But shouldn't we aspire to more than that? Shouldn't the UK's liberal movement seek to provide a real alternative to increasingly nationalistic conservativism and increasingly far-left socialism? And when I say 'alternative' I mean 'alternative government'. If we think that the UK deserves better than the Labour/Tory duopoly, shouldn't we do all we can to give the UK the chance to *get* better?

I am assuming that Liberal Democrats want to do more than just recover, that we want to replace the current administration and govern.

In the past, we have always shied away from saying that we seek to be the leading party of government because it was simply not credible to suggest such a thing. But these are different times. The Scottish National Party went from just six MPs to winning all but three seats in Scotland because of an electoral turnaround during 2014 and 2015 that took a mere eight months. Nigel Farage's Brexit Party went from nothing to first in the polls just a few weeks after forming. We can also look overseas to see Emmanuel Macron's En Marche party going from nowhere to government in just a few months. I think we have to accept that a coalition with the current leadership of either the Labour or Conservative parties would be unacceptable to our party or the electorate. This means that we have only one option: namely, to develop the brass neck to say baldly that we aim to lead a government of our own.

3 Overcoming tribalism

So how do we achieve this? The fluid situation in other parties means that Liberal Democrats should surely take advantage of the opportunity to work with those who have come out of – or who may soon come out of – the Labour and Conservative parties. Tribal loyalties on the part of voters and politicians will have to be overcome if we are to succeed.

I see three possibilities here.

First, that we work publicly and positively with those who have recently left Labour and the Conservatives (eleven of whom formed the short-lived Independent Group aka Change UK, in February 2019). There may be more social democrats and liberal one-nation conservatives who leave their parties in the coming weeks and months.

The problem, though, is that the centre-ground in British politics is littered with generals without armies. Grand people with great CVs but no significant following. Say what you like about the Labour left or the nationalists, but they do have followers. They have armies.

Those MPs who bravely have left Labour or the Conservatives need to join a movement with an army. The Liberal Democrats' 100,000 members, 2,500 councillors and 120-plus parliamentarians (across the Commons, the Lords, the devolved parliaments and the European Parliament) provide an infrastructure that no defector, Labour or Conservative, could muster on their own or from scratch. So, option one is that those future defectors simply join the Liberal Democrats. Ingrained party tribalism might make it hard for some to do this, in which case option two would be for the Liberal Democrats to continue to welcome, and actively work with, the liberal defectors from other parties in an electoral alliance.

The alliance of the Liberal Party and the new Social Democratic Party from 1981 to 1988 provides a model. Indeed, the fact that the Independent Group/Change UK struggled to make an impact equivalent to that of the SDP is a reminder that the story of the SDP is far from being one of failure. I am about to digress now – predictably – but I would argue that the SDP is, so far, the most successful breakaway movement in the modern era. At one point, the Alliance was touching 50 per cent in opinion polls, winning parliamentary by-elections by the bucketload, gaining record-breaking numbers of councillors and, for most of its lifetime, ensured that the UK had a genuine three-party system. Although the project didn't ultimately succeed, it very nearly did. Arguably, its lasting impact was the end of Conservative rule in 1997, when Tony Blair's New Labour was elected; many consider that the New Labour project was a direct response to the strength of support gained by the Alliance. Without the SDP's formation and the establishment of the alliance with the Liberals, the Labour Party might never have been forced into a position where they needed to adopt a more liberal and moderate platform and thus have the broad-based appeal required to defeat the Conservatives in 1997.

Still, after an underwhelming result for the Alliance at the 1987 general election, the two parties merged. The merger was messy, costly and humiliating. We've all heard of rancorous divorces, but this was a rancorous wedding! The new Liberal Democrats were born out of that union and it took several years for us to regain credibility or any level of electoral success. End of digression!

Which brings me to the third option to consider when it comes to overcoming the challenge of tribalism: the Liberal Democrats could decide not to go into alliance with those who choose to leave their existing parties but, instead, choose to 'merge' with them without the defectors setting up a party of their own. We could collectively form a new entity. The Liberal–SDP merger happened after seven years of alliance. What I suggest is that, this time, the Liberal Democrats might cut out the seven years of alliance and instead go straight to the merger. My feeling is that such a move would attract many who would otherwise not risk defecting at all.

In those circumstances, then, the new party (might we be The Reformists, The Liberals or The Democrats?) could count on me as a founder member. Many Liberal Democrats will feel horrified by the prospect that we might merge ourselves into the new party. I understand those concerns. In the UK, most liberals are social democrats, but many social democrats are not liberals. New Labour's policies in support of ID cards, detention without trial and the limiting of religious freedoms are testament to that. Some will therefore be concerned that the Reformist Party might have less sharp liberal instincts than the current Liberal Democrats, and would be more inclined to desire and exercise power. However, this tension already exists within the Liberal Democrats and existed in the Liberal

Party before it. I don't have any doubts that the new party would clearly be a liberal party, and a worthy successor to previous incarnations of the great British liberal movement.

It would, however, only deserve to be considered liberal if it accepts the need for liberalism to be redeemed. That means that the economic failures of liberalism can no longer be overlooked. It will need to embrace the concept of active, ambitious liberal government, which intervenes directly to drive growth, new employment and great environmental and social infrastructure projects in energy, transport, housing and communications.

That kind of a liberal movement could appeal to those who have been attracted to the empty sloganeering engendered by nationalism and Trump, and seen during the Brexit campaign, by offering them something tangibly better to improve their lives and give all of us a sense of unifying endeavour. This would not be identity politics, but identity economics.

The Reformists would also only deserve to be considered liberal if they acknowledged that when it comes to the holding of world views, there is no such thing as neutrality. We can't be a liberal movement that champions diversity when we sneer at those who choose to be diverse.

I want to continue to serve but I am, as I said at the start of this chapter, 'post-ambitious'. I've got plenty to offer in terms of energy and zeal, but I don't crave any formal role. I have been President of a party in power and Leader of a party recovering from power. I don't need any more 'positions' to add to my CV. Been there, done that. But I am still passionate about my country and angry at the mendacity that has led to the appalling situation in which the UK and our people are heading for relative poverty and insignificance while our politics offers bitter, unpalatable extremes.

There has to be something better. In the absence of 'something better', we will have to build it.

Maybe in one single act, we could save the UK and redeem liberalism? That would be a project worth throwing our weight behind . . .

11

The wondrous loss

'I will stop drinking . . . in January', 'I will start running again . . . after the holidays', 'I will give a larger sum to charity . . . when I next get paid . . .'

We have all made decisions to do something . . . later. Not just yet, you understand. I couldn't do that just *now* of course, but I will get round to it . . .

I made a suchlike decision sitting at the back of the bus about four weeks from polling day. The Pardew Boudoir™ wasn't sealed off by anything more than a nice yellow Lib Dem curtain, but it gave me enough privacy for team discussions, writing, making calls and occasionally dozing off. I was regularly interrupted by the journalists (their editors had paid good money for access to me on the bus), and by my team, which was of course absolutely fine. On this particular journey between St Andrews and Edinburgh, though, I was left alone. I had time to think.

I pondered life beyond the election on 8 June.

Once the general election was over, the questions relating to my faith wouldn't stop. Two convictions crystallized in my mind: I wanted to be faithful to God, not to deny him again. At the same time, I was determined that the party I love would be led by someone who would not be a distraction from our messages. As we bumped along the

261

A92 road to Edinburgh, I calmly resolved that I would step down.

But not just yet.

As I got closer to Edinburgh, a further thought occurred to me: if I did step down after 8 June this, then, would be the only general election in which I would lead my party. In which case, I needed to throw everything I had at doing it well.

I couldn't undo the damage of the first week or two, but I could use the last four weeks to give the party nationally, and all our candidates, the best chance I could.

I chose to enjoy the last four weeks and to *look* like I was enjoying the last four weeks.

The TV debates, the rallies, the visits and the interviews were exhilarating. There were stressful times, times of distress as I missed my family, times of worry – fear even – of what the result might bring. But I tried to put my failures behind me and do the job I was elected to do – indeed, the job I felt that I had been born to do.

Earlier chapters tell you that story – the ups and downs of a general election from the perspective of a party leader. But once it was over and the spotlight shone less brightly upon me, I had time to think about what I would do next. I had given my post-election Leader's speech to members in central London, alongside the newly elected Layla Moran, and now it was time to go home. After I left that event at the National Liberal Club at lunchtime on Friday 9 June, I headed back north to Westmorland.

Would I now stick to my decision to step down?

No, I wouldn't. At least not yet – but this wasn't lazy

prevarication. There was a logic to staying in post, at least for now. I realized that if I stepped down straight away then people would read that as my throwing in the towel because I felt responsible for a poor result. But the Liberal Democrat result was anything but poor. Sensational it wasn't, but we had just made gains – the first time the party had done so since 2005. After a decent result, I wasn't going to give anyone an excuse to write up a false narrative of failure. In this way, my mind was made up to keep going for a few weeks and to step down following the Queen's Speech later in June.

After a weekend of sleeping, making and taking phone calls, and playing football and cricket with the children, I returned to London on the Monday. I spoke to all my parliamentary colleagues, and to colleagues at HQ and in the Lords. It became clear that the overwhelming sense was one of relief and moderate satisfaction at the result. It was an election that could have killed us off, but instead it had renewed us and seen us begin to climb the steep path back to the top.

The expectation among colleagues was mostly that I would continue. In my head I was still planning to keep going until later in June or July and not to step down immediately, but I decided I would announce my intention in June rather than July for two reasons.

First, at a meeting with the party's Chief Executive, Tim Gordon, we talked about the party's plans for the future in terms of funding, reforms and political message. Afterwards, I felt that it was unfair of me to allow Tim or anyone else to assume that I would continue and to make plans on the basis that I would carry on as Leader, when I had it in mind to step down in a few weeks' time.

Second, I had two separate conversations with senior members of the House of Lords. One with Brian Paddick and the other with Dick Newby. Brian was our spokesperson on home affairs but had just announced that he was stepping down from the post, largely due to his concerns about how my faith had affected my leadership. He made it clear on the phone that for my own good I should step down. Brian had always understood me better than most. He had been a strong supporter and a good friend, even if he had a habit of sometimes wearing his heart on his sleeve and writing about it. I didn't give Brian much indication of my state of mind, but I listened carefully to him and we had a good chat. I then sat down with Dick Newby, our Leader in the Lords. Dick made it clear to me that there were a number of peers who thought I needed to go. When names were mentioned, there seemed a stark correlation. Many were those who had stoutly defended Chris Rennard, ironically making his position all the more difficult, who were oblivious to the consequences to the party and to our work at rooting out harassment and discrimination, and fighting for genuine equality. Those people had been opposed to me since my time as Party President and they now spied their opportunity. On hearing this I was, for a moment, extremely tempted to keep going anyway out of bloody-mindedness.

Pride and vanity are dangerous sins – but I was then, and I now remain, very confident that if I had wanted to, then I would have continued as Leader and seen off any challenges.

I woke on the morning of Wednesday 14 June to the horrific news of the Grenfell Tower disaster in which up to a hundred people had been killed in a senseless inferno. I felt numb at the colossal loss of life, the scenes of devastation and the unspeakable suffering of the victims.

If I'd been planning carefully, I would have avoided stepping down that day.

I headed in to work that morning praying silently for the Grenfell victims and with no intention of resigning.

But over the course of the day my mind was made up.

I owe many people an apology, but I ought to single out just one. At lunchtime on Wednesday 14 June I had a phone interview with Sara Royle of the *Westmorland Gazette* during which I told her I was planning to continue as Leader for the time being at least. My promise to Sara is that at the point that I gave the interview, that was still my intention. She wrote it up in time for the paper's deadline that afternoon ready for publication the following day. In the couple of hours that followed, though, it dawned on me that there were two weeks or more until the Queen's Speech and that this was a long time to keep people assuming I was continuing if I was secretly planning not to. That struck me as not right. It would be wrong and unfair of me to do that.

I also considered the likelihood of some people in the party going public and calling for me to step down. Because I wasn't planning to continue, any pushing back required of me would have been less than half-hearted. After two short but pretty successful years as Leader, I didn't want to leave the post on anyone else's terms but my own.

So, while I stood in the queue to take the oath and be re-sworn in as a Member of Parliament, I silently reached a conclusion. I drafted a resignation speech in my head.

I emerged from the Chamber with quiet resolution. I rang Rosie and the kids. I rang my dad. Jo Swinson came to my office to say that she wanted me to continue and I had to tell her thanks, but no thanks. Jo's decency and loyalty match her determination and talent. So I was grateful to her but I'd made up my mind. I spoke to my team in Kendal, to my close team in London, to my parliamentary colleagues and then to the staff at HQ. Then we made my statement to the media via a BBC-pooled camera. In my statement I talked about the successes we had achieved over the previous two years and the progress we had made in the election. But I felt that I should be direct and honest about why I was stepping down.

I was stepping down because to continue seemed to mean, either that I'd compromise my faith, or else remain faithful only to have my party damaged by the incessant focus on my beliefs. I wasn't prepared to tolerate either situation. Stepping down was the right choice.

I ended my speech, with lots of slightly bemused and uncomfortable Liberal Democrats standing behind me, by saying:

> I want to say one more thing. I joined our party when I was 16. It is in my blood. I love our history, our people. I thoroughly love my party. Imagine how proud I am to lead this party. And then imagine what would lead me to voluntarily relinquish that honour. In the words of Isaac Watts, it would have to be something 'so amazing, so divine, it demands my heart, my life, my all'.

That was it. I went into Tim Gordon's glass office – affectionately known as the Tim Tank – feeling really calm and at peace. Then I got a text from my daughter Gracie saying that she was proud of me and I wept.

Within a few minutes I was standing having a smoke outside at the back of HQ with a Lib Dem staff member, Christine Longworth – she swore at me lovingly (I assume it was lovingly . . .) and apologized. We hugged as I got into the car to go north.

The next day, after a short night's sleep, I went to Langdale Primary School at Chapel Stile. The school has around thirty children and serves a vast and sparsely populated area across one of the most stunning parts of the Lake District. I did a question-and-answer session with the whole school and was asked some great and pretty tough questions. There were two seven-year-old girls sitting right in front of me in the first row. They both had their hands up.

The girl on the left went first: 'When will we know whether there are fairies?'

This is an awesome question. It is not, 'Are there fairies?' but rather '*When* will we know *whether* there are fairies?' It was almost like, 'When will the select committee inquiry into the existence or otherwise of fairies conclude?'

I managed an answer that went something like 'the jury's out', citing the Cottingley Fairies mystery as evidence. I concluded that the time had now come for 'fun' questions, rather than political ones.

The seven-year-old girl to the right was next to speak. 'Do you help people with their passports?' she asked.

That was a bit random, I thought, but I searched my memory banks for a decent answer. Something came to mind. 'Actually, I do sometimes. I remember a couple whose son went to live in Brazil where he met a lovely woman and they got married and had a baby. But the sad thing was that they couldn't get permission to come back to Britain because the baby wasn't allowed a British passport. Anyhow, I fought very hard and we got that baby a passport and it all ended happily.'

The little girl beamed back at me and said, 'That was me!'

The rest of the class giggled at my stunned reaction. They already knew the story.

That was the point when I remembered what gets me up in the morning. I was through with being Leader, but I wasn't giving up. Not when there are things to do, people to serve and a difference to make.

And so began a distinct fourth 'chapter' of my time as an MP. I count myself lucky to have these rather distinct stages of my time in Parliament, each providing an insight into a different period of UK government and politics – from Blair to Brexit.

The first from 2005 to 2010 saw me sitting on a majority of 267, having gained my seat from the Conservatives against the trend, as they reduced Tony Blair's parliamentary majority.

Just as it had been in the early hours of 9 June 2017, I was sitting with Rosie at 3 a.m. on 6 May 2005, waiting in a deserted Asda car park in Kendal as my agent, Paul Trollope, kept telling me to hold off arriving at the count at the Leisure Centre down the road. He wanted to be sure of the result before I turned up. In the end, our national Deputy Director of Campaigns, Hilary Stephenson (who had now arrived from being at the successful counts further south in Hazel Grove and Cheadle), rang me to say that she couldn't predict either way but that I should now come along to the count, look relaxed and be ready for anything. 'I think you've narrowly lost, but I can't be sure,' she added. Great. Hilary had also instructed all the Liberal Democrat volunteers not to applaud or appear in any way triumphalist on my arrival – not least because we didn't know whether we had won.

Rosie and I walked into the count and were greeted by huge cheers from all our activists who had chosen to ignore Hilary's advice. Next, veteran Conservative councillor and all-round 'character' Roger Bingham bounded over to me to shake me by the hand enthusiastically and tell me that I had won. Really? It was some time before the count produced a result. I was ahead by a couple of hundred votes. The Conservatives, quite rightly, asked for a recount. For the first time in the election, I became nervous. I was prepared for defeat, but not this way, not after having been so close to becoming an MP. I asked Hilary, 'Do majorities of this size get overturned in recounts?'

'It's been known,' she said.

I sat watching as votes for my opponent Tim Collins were checked one after the other. I saw a number of votes that had been counted for Tim which were actually votes for me. This was hugely encouraging, as it meant that I was gaining votes in the recount. What I didn't know was that on the other side of the room, votes were being transferred from me to Tim. I'm very glad that this didn't occur to me at the time. The majority was now 267 but the result was accepted by all sides. I texted my dad who was on holiday in Tenerife nervously watching the results. I wept quietly in the corridor outside as I thought how proud my mum would have been – she had died just nine months earlier. I also had a sober moment when it occurred to me that despite this nail-bitingly tiny majority I was – in theory – more likely to win at the next general election than I had been to win at this one. Why? Well, because next time I would be the incumbent and I was determined that I was going to throw myself at my new vocation with a passion for serving my constituents hitherto unknown.

Mark Twain said, 'Nothing so disillusions the voter than backing the winning candidate.' It's a rather jaded but mostly fair observation – if the candidate you vote for wins, then almost inevitably he or she will disappoint you. I was determined to confound that maxim.

The 2005 to 2010 Parliament began as it went on, with me investing my time in loving my constituency to death. I did this by giving my time wholeheartedly to the people and the places that I served. I was in London from Monday afternoon until Wednesday evening – but spent Thursday to Monday lunchtime in Westmorland, immersing myself in our communities, throwing myself into every issue and campaign as I sought to serve the people I now represented.

The village of Witherslack had lost its post office, the only shop the residents had, and so they gathered together to explore the possibility of setting up their own community store. I went to numerous meetings at the village hall, wrote off for grants and helped to publicize the new venture. I did that kind of work in villages throughout my area, and I couldn't have done half of it had I not kept to my decision to rush to Euston almost every Wednesday night to get the last train north.

Jesus says that where your treasure is, there your heart will be also. Well, my treasure is being Westmorland's man, not a denizen of Westminster.

My time in Westminster was focused almost exclusively on making an impact back home. I would seek out opportunities to speak in debates, to ask questions and put down motions to Parliament. All of these demonstrated real action and were enthusiastically reported back to constituents either through the local media representatives (whom I would ring every week with a list of stories I was keen for them to run) or through our own local Liberal Democrat literature.

One such publication came to national attention on BBC Radio 4's *The News Quiz*. Quoting from the Liberal Democrat *Focus* newsletter from the village of Arnside in Westmorland, they read out the exciting revelation that 'local MP Tim Farron is angry at the closure of local public toilets and has therefore presented a motion to Parliament . . .'

Who proofreads these things?

I developed a style of frenetic activism. I would throw myself at every local campaign, provide energetic support and – where required – leadership.

The local hospital trust proposed to close down the adult mental health ward at the Westmorland General

Hospital in 2006. The campaign against closure was loud, persistent and personal as we engaged thousands of local people in adding pressure upon the trust management to reconsider. In the end, we won that campaign and the ward was protected. The high point of the campaign was a Saturday in the autumn of 2006 when I led a march of over 4,000 people through Kendal, up the main streets of Kirkland, Highgate and Stricklandgate. The weather was appalling, but somehow this added to our determination. At the end of the march, I went into the Liberal Club on Stricklandgate and out on to its rickety old balcony with a microphone and rallied the crowd. The *Westmorland Gazette* captured the moment as I stood on the balcony, soaked to the skin and with a sea of umbrellas down below stretching further than the eye could see. This felt like an iconic and transformative moment. I went from being the local MP to being *their* local MP.

Although I didn't realize it, that first Parliament for me was (for now at least) the high point of the Liberal Democrats' parliamentary strength. In total, 62 of us had been returned in May 2005 (a net increase of 10), and then Willie Rennie's success in the Dunfermline by-election in February 2006 took that number up to 63. By way of contrast, the Lib Dem Parliamentary Party of recent years (between 8 and 12 in number) feels so tiny. Sometimes I let my mind drift back to the packed Committee Room 10 in the Commons, few of us, if any, realizing at the time that our fortunes would wane and wax so spectacularly in the years ahead.

One thing I miss, now that our numbers have been so reduced, is that I no longer have much of a social life.

Don't get me wrong, that suits. I have always aimed to fill every hour of my days in London, away from Rosie and the children, with work in order to have good family time when I return north. However, in my first two terms, I developed something of a routine on a Tuesday. I would work at my desk until about 10 p.m. and then Greg Mulholland would persuade me to go to the Strangers' Bar at Westminster for a pint. Then we would go for a curry . . . only Greg would often know of an excellent little pub nearby with great real ales and so we'd go there on the way, finally apologizing to the curry house staff as we rushed in at just gone 11 to claim our table. More often than not we would go to the Top Curry Centre in Pimlico, a curry house that traded more on its name, history and longevity than anything – but the staff were nice and tolerant and never sent us away when we turned up late. In the Top Curry Centre's window was a blown-up black-and-white picture of Diana, Princess of Wales as the 19-year-old Lady Diana Spencer being snapped by the paparazzi as she walked past the curry house window. The photo revealed that the restaurant hadn't changed its sign or its frontage for 30 years!

Over time, this Tuesday night ritual began to attract a few more of us – notably Lembit Öpik (MP for Montgomeryshire), John Leech (Manchester Withington) and, after 2010, Ian Swales (Redcar). We became the TNCC or Tuesday Night Curry Club. There were a few highlights over the years, including being joined by both of the Cheeky Girls (one of whom was Lembit's girlfriend for a while – I can't remember which one), bumping into Kevin Spacey in the Three Stags at Kennington where I went up to him and told him that he looked a lot like Bob Mortimer, and having Lembit's phone passed to me so that I could speak to Steadman from 1980s British soul-pop combo Five Star whose career Lembit was apparently 'managing'. I didn't ask . . .

Come to think of it, Lembit was at the heart of quite a few of the more memorable moments.

Tuesday nights aside, I was about as diligent as it was possible to be. I established a reputation for being hard-working, attentive, down to earth and sympathetic in my constituency. I probably also established a reputation for being a bit dismissive of the grandness of Parliament.

I love being an MP, but I'm not a massive fan of the institution that is Parliament. I see MPs 'going native' when they seem to enjoy their MP status, or being part of the 'Westminster club', just a bit too much. I look at them and think to myself, 'I don't want to be like that!' Then I see the obsequious climbers of the greasy pole, those for whom seeking promotion, holding office and career advancement are all that matters. I look at them and I think to myself, 'I don't want to be like that!' And then I see the arch-tribalists whose every utterance seems to be a partisan point, or a jibe against the other side. I look at them and I think to myself, 'I don't want to be like that!'

But I recognize that, while having this frame of mind might be healthy up to a point, it is also a bit self-righteous and judgemental. Maybe I was right to identify compla-cency, selfishness and narrow-mindedness as traits that I should fear and avoid, but I also had to keep an eye on my own failings – perhaps I had a creeping Pharisee spirit, sneering at others' failings without considering my own serious weaknesses.

I had my own ambitions of course, but they were slightly different. While I didn't seek the approval of my parliamentary colleagues or my party's leadership, I did seek the approval of the people, especially the people of Westmorland. There is a huge temptation to be a people-pleaser. Some would argue that my resignation from the party's front bench over the Lisbon treaty in 2008 and my rebellion against tuition fees in 2010 were driven by my seeking popularity, to signal my virtue and so on. My besetting sin is vanity – I know, it's hard to believe, right?

Yet, in the end, the greatest tension of my political career has been between doing what I think is right, and keeping my head down and toeing the line. It does not take much imagination to realize that this is not always consistent with being a 'team player' or pursuing conventional political ambitions.

This was demonstrated as the second phase of my time in Parliament began in 2010. I gained promotion not by winning the leadership's approval, but by going over their heads and appealing to the party's members. It is worth adding to my earlier account of the coalition that, from the moment it was formed, I found myself in a place where I was the one rallying the Liberal Democrat troops to believe in our greater mission even if they didn't agree with everything that the party was doing in government.

As party President during most of those years, I relied not on the support of my colleagues in Parliament but on the support of the members across the party. I didn't use my position irresponsibly, but I was able to speak out about tuition fees, the NHS, the Social Care Act and the Bedroom Tax knowing that I couldn't be sacked. The President is not appointed by the Leader nor easily disciplined by the Chief Whip, but is appointed by and accountable to the card-carrying, rank-and-file Liberal Democrats.

I needed to be around the Commons far more during the 2010 to 2015 Parliament, simply because a government's MPs are needed to vote through legislation. I continued to work hard as a constituency MP although I would now return north more often on a Thursday rather than a Wednesday. Being away from home for longer most weeks undoubtedly put more pressure on the family. My absence from the children or from sharing the running of our household during this time, and later when I was Leader, always felt uncomfortable. This is something I'm now enjoying putting right.

The Tuesday Night Curry Club continued through the coalition years. On a social level, at least, little had changed. With 57 seats after the 2010 election, we were still a decent-sized group in Parliament. The dynamic had changed though. We hardly ever saw the 18 who were ministers or the 5 who were parliamentary private secretaries. That left about 30 of us on the 'backbenches', but with me as a strange hybrid of a backbencher who was a member of the party's leadership. So I would naturally be the one whom people came to if they were disgruntled. I like to think that, informally, I prevented as many rebellions as the coalition's Whips.

The coalition began as an exercise in presenting unity between two very different parties in order to demonstrate to the watching world that coalition government can work and provide a stable administration. The coalition ended with the Conservatives ruthlessly calculating to devour the Liberal Democrats seat by seat in their bid to win a parliamentary majority. It worked.

The 2015 election saw the Liberal Democrat Parliamentary Party all but wiped out – down from 57 to 8. The two years I spent as Leader were frenetic and I was away from Parliament far more than I was in attendance. I toured the country while insisting on having no fewer than four nights a week at home so that I might continue to be a good dad, husband and local MP. I dashed around the country seeking to rebuild the devastated Liberal Democrats, planning our recovery in local council by-election after local council by-election, winning new donors, working in the media to do all I could to make us relevant and gain coverage for our messages. As a result, I didn't really have time to feel lonely. I had lost most of my friends in the 2015 wipe-out. The shape of Parliament had changed – the SNP had 56 members, had taken our place as Westminster's third force, and we were relegated to minor-party status fighting for spaces on the third bench back . . . but I was so busy, so surrounded by advisors and consumed by the excitement and novelty of having become Leader, that I didn't really feel the loss.

I observed David Cameron and George Osborne striking out to govern on their own without the Liberal Democrats. I saw the deeper cuts to public services, the U-turn on renewable energy investment, the hardening of immigration policy and the preparation for the EU referendum.

Meanwhile, I saw the Labour Party transformed into one where over 90 per cent of its MPs would sit behind Jeremy Corbyn, their new Leader, shaking their heads in sadness and anger rather than cheering him on.

In December 2015 David Cameron proposed that RAF manoeuvres in Iraq should be extended to Syria. At that time, the so-called Islamic State, or IS, covered a significant area of land that straddled the two countries. While US and other forces were deploying their air forces to degrade the capabilities of the terrorists across this zone, the UK alone was limiting itself only to the IS-held areas within Iraq. RAF fighters were literally turning back at the Syrian border even if they were in close pursuit of the terrorists. IS had murdered countless people, most of them Muslims, many of them in barbaric style. Their actions contributed to the fleeing of hundreds of thousands of refugees, some of whom I had met in the camps in Greece and France.

I was convinced that the Government was right to seek Parliament's approval for British planes to pursue this evil regime across a border they did not recognize. David Cameron rang me on a Sunday evening while I was out running with my sons. I breathlessly apologized and asked if he could call back a little later. To his credit, he was happy to do so – even with just eight votes at my disposal, I suspect that he feared that he might need them. I said that I would support the extended action on condition that there would be more support for refugees in the region, a greater involvement of other Islamic countries in the fight against IS and an investigation into the UK sources of funding for IS terrorism.

When the matter came to the Commons, the atmosphere was at times electric. Jeremy Corbyn had signalled that he would vote against the proposal. His standard approach to all difficult international issues, it seems, is always to do the easy thing, that is, nothing at all. I have often voted against military action, but knee-jerk anti-militarism is little better than knee-jerk militarism. They both entail weakness and lack of wisdom.

However, Jeremy Corbyn's front bench took a largely different view. Hilary Benn, then Labour's shadow foreign secretary, spoke in defence of action – spelling out that IS were murderous fascists, that democratic socialists should stand up to fascists, and that Labour is an internationalist party and must therefore intervene to defend the defenceless against such an evil force. It was one of the best speeches I have ever heard in the Commons, and it was a privilege to witness it.

Later, in the lobby, there were around 60 Labour MPs who voted with the Liberal Democrats and with the Government in favour of action. Many Labour MPs were in tears, embracing one another as they lingered in the voting lobby together. Some told me that they had received a barrage of personal abuse from local Labour Party members for choosing to vote for action. That night it felt as though moderate Labour MPs had begun to come to terms with the probability that they had now lost their party to the hard left. At the time of writing, most of those Labour MPs continue to sit on Labour's backbenches. As our country experiences the awful combination of an incompetent government and an extremist opposition, I cannot deny that I long for them to leave and join with the Liberal Democrats to provide the country some hope.

The fourth phase of my time in Parliament is the phase following the 2017 election. Since then, I have become more acutely aware of the reduced size of the Liberal Democrat Parliamentary Party compared to its size during my first two terms, when we had between 56 and 63 MPs. Of course, matters were marginally better than they had been, the party having grown from 8 to 12. Each one of the Lib Dem MPs elected on 8 June 2017 showed every sign of actually wanting to be there, rather than belonging to a bedraggled posse of shell-shocked survivors, as the eight of us seemed in 2015. Nevertheless, a return to the 'backbenches' after being President and then Leader meant that I somehow felt the losses from two years earlier in a more real and personal way.

After I stood down as Leader, some people were not quite sure how to relate to me, even though most were very supportive. After a summer spent rebuilding my constituency team and having a much-needed family holiday in the mountains of Andalusia, I attended the party conference in Bournemouth in September 2017. Some at first regarded me with both the wariness and sadness one might show to someone who had been bereaved. However, I was able to speak from the stage early in the conference and received a lovely standing ovation. That changed the mood completely, with members realizing that I genuinely was fine about not being Leader and was in good spirits. As I did my stint DJ-ing at the Lib Dem disco (playing a solid set, including The Clash, Buzzcocks, The Smiths and

The Strokes), it became clear to all present that the former Leader was not exactly in mourning.

In Autumn 2017 I focused on developing my new team in Westmorland. With five new staff I invested my time heavily in building relationships and re-immersing myself in what I love the most: being a campaigning constituency MP who serves everyone with compassion, effectiveness and energy.

After the most peaceful Farron family Christmas for years, I returned to London in January 2018. A few days into the New Year, I went along to do an interview with Premier Christian Radio one Wednesday morning. The presenters covered a range of issues but at one point they asked about my statement during the 2017 election that 'gay sex is not a sin'. Did I regret saying that? My answer was careful, I said I regretted giving such a simplistic response to a question that is *asked* in one language yet *understood* in another. In the two or three hours following the interview there was little pick up on this, which seemed natural; it was, after all, a nuanced thoughtful interview. Then, at around 11 a.m., there appeared what can only be described as a sensationalist clickbait tweet implying that I had now stated that I considered same-sex sexual relations to be an abomination (I exaggerate only slightly). I had said no such thing of course.

I think I count this as one of the most horrible times of my life. I am pretty good at turning the other cheek and laughing off a Twitter storm but, this time, I was plunged into an appalling darkness. People who listened to the interview could hear that I had made a nuanced and open reflection on the intense questioning I had had through the election. However, 99.9 per cent of those who commented online made no effort to listen to what was actually said but instead enjoyed believing the worst of me.

What affected me most was that some in the party were among those queuing up to condemn me. Rather than taking the time to understand what I had actually said, many impulsively threw me under the bus, putting out official statements condemning my 'personal view'. Many of my colleagues resisted that temptation and defended me – Nick Clegg stands out as one in that category, I am grateful to all who followed his example.

The experience of the social media storm, and the grief and personal ridicule that resulted, the loss of friendships that were decades-old in some cases, affected me deeply – far more than anything that had happened before.

In that interview, I felt I should acknowledge that while I had never sought to comment on the issue, it was nevertheless not right for any of us to say that we know better than God what counts as sin.

A basic Christian belief is expressed in the Bible through the words: 'it is by grace you have been saved, through faith . . . not by works, so that no one can boast' (Ephesians 2.8). That is to say, I didn't need to earn forgiveness by publicly clarifying what I thought. Nothing can earn forgiveness apart from Jesus' death on the cross, and since that had already happened, my receiving forgiveness was a done deal. So that was not the point of saying what I did on Premier Christian Radio. The point was about being honest. I had had quite enough of saying things I didn't mean or of being evasive, so I wanted to give a carefully worded but truthful answer. I made the mistake of holding up a Christian radio station to a higher standard than its secular rivals and felt well and truly stitched up by the way in which my comments were clipped and tweeted. But I don't hold it against the radio station; the experience has made me wiser and more careful.

Nothing in what I said, or believe, condemns or judges. My voting record, my relationships, and the evidence of my entire life tells you that to draw such a conclusion is simply bogus, whether that conclusion be mistaken or deliberate.

So I was extremely saddened by those who felt that a good use of their time was to tweet condemnation about what I hadn't said, just because it was easier to do that than to seek to understand.

To issue a statement publicly condemning a colleague for their 'private beliefs' is reprehensible on two levels. First, it makes one a pretty dreadful colleague and a fair-weather friend. Second, it undermines any claims of being a liberal. What dystopian gloom have we entered when a person's private beliefs (that they seek not to impose on anyone) can be grounds for condemnation? I was essentially pounced on for a thoughtcrime by people who I had assumed were my friends, or at the very least were my fellow liberals.

This made a difficult situation ten times worse for me and my family because this was then marshalled as evidence that I really had become a terrible bigot. That's when the messages of hurt and betrayal from those I had known for years began piling in.

For me personally, that was when the darkness began. I haven't fully come out of it.

Since then, I have had other times of being subjected to torrents of condemnation. I was due to speak at a Christian event in May 2018 but the person who had written the publicity for this added some peculiar, gratuitous and unacceptable things to the literature about immigration and the 'gay lobby' – including things that I, personally, strongly and passionately disagree with. I pulled out of the event as soon as I saw this literature – which was sad because it turns out to have been a really good day of discussion and conversation in a church in Manchester with hundreds of people in attendance.

The day after, *The Spectator*'s Isabel Hardman wrote that 'Tim Farron just can't escape gay sex' which I confess made me chuckle – it conjures up certain images . . . but I guess that's why she wrote it. Ridicule is more powerful than appraisal.

My response following the Premier Christian Radio interview has been to turn the other cheek and endure the media battering whenever it comes. I do this consciously because clarifications or rebuttals do not help my mental health and tend only to pour petrol on the flames. As time goes on, I feel God helping me to be less concerned about my pride and my image. The consequence is that I don't care quite so much about what people write or think about me.

I don't want to attract unwanted attention to the party, upset or distress my colleagues and friends, so when the next cartload of poop gets poured over me I tend to just struggle my way out of the dungheap, wipe myself clean of most of it, and carry on.

I'm much happier as I come to the end of writing this book than I was when I began. I love what I do, and I am still a very positive person. I love my family, love my constituency, and love my God. But I do feel wounded. It is hard to describe the dark times – they can be triggered by something that someone says or they can come from nowhere. It is a sense of being broken, hopeless and useless, that I have let everyone down, especially my family, not for any particularly logical reasons.

Increasingly, though, I don't feel the need to justify myself. To be a Christian, in these circumstances, means trusting God completely for my identity and my standing – and being at peace with that. It also means that I feel more concerned about the state of those who are confused or upset by my faith than I am about what they think of me. I know I'm saved, so I have nothing to worry about. I want to be sure that others don't miss out because they have misunderstood the gospel because of something that they wrongly attribute to me.

I do understand why some think less of me on account of my accepting what the Bible teaches. Some feel that because I didn't bang on about judgement and forgiveness while President or Leader means that I misled them. Some will feel a more personal hurt because of an assumption that I judge them, think less of them, and think that their love and relationships are less worthy than mine. I promise you, however, that none of this is in the slightest bit true. Nevertheless, it hurts me that I have hurt people.

When you believe that the God who made the entire universe claims you as his own, loves you and died to redeem you, it helps you through difficult times like this. It helps a great deal. It moves me to tears and it can motivate me, but the partially inexplicable darkness lingers at times. I've broken or sprained my ankle a number of times. Running is a risky pastime! I recover and heal, and I get out running again, but I have to be careful because my ankle is now more susceptible to pressure. The pain and weakness can be just one slight twist away. That's how my heart is now – but God uses all things for good. I am a less selfish person now, more reliant on him, and less proud about what people think of me.

The Book of Psalms includes many psalms written by David, who spent so much of his life being pursued, rejected and ridiculed. Most famously in Psalm 23.4, he writes, 'Yea, though I walk through the valley of the shadow of death, I will fear no evil; for You are with me' (NKJV). To follow Christ is to know that God will not always deliver you from difficult situations, but he will most certainly deliver you *through* them. That has been my experience and it continues to be so.

As soon as I stepped down as Leader, I ceased to have any personal ambition politically other than to continue to serve the communities that I love in Cumbria. But some thought that I might be persuaded back into the leadership at a later date. Former advisors and colleagues in Parliament had raised this with me especially after my valedictory speech to the 2017 conference. The fallout from the Premier Christian Radio interview in January

2018 ended all that. My ambition has gone, but so has the ambition that people in the party had for me.

So what now? Well, it turns out, whether I like it or not, that I am one of the UK's best-known Christian politicians. Christians who are political animals, and indeed Christians who aren't, have overwhelmed me with their support and commitment. I now speak regularly to Christian and 'mixed' audiences on the need to bring liberalism back from the dead in a Western society that seems to have become a dangerous mono-culture, as well as on liberalism and Christianity, on my experiences, and – most importantly – on the gospel. I am not a trained preacher and I have not been to Bible college, but I love speaking about the gospel. The best speeches I have given in my life are the ones where I am driven by emotion, where I can feel the tears behind my eyes as I speak – speaking on the plight of refugees comes to mind. The gospel brings me close to tears. Grace brings me close to tears. The character of Jesus brings me close to tears. More than close actually. The opportunity to speak and write about these themes is hugely exciting to me.

My ambition is to serve my constituents and to serve God by using the space he has given me to speak out on the need for real liberalism, for rational politics, for a politics that is genuinely kinder and gentler, and for the duty of a free society to understand that faith is an essential part of a liberal and decent country.

I want to challenge the lazy consensus that has grown up in the West that atheism is neutral and that faith is eccentric; that society should be constructed on the assumption that people don't believe in anything super-natural; that those who do probably only do so because of cultural reasons or family heritage; and that the ones who seem to really mean it are to be marginalized, ridiculed or worse.

A genuinely liberal society would have no truck with such nonsense.

More importantly, though, I want to use the opportunity that I now have to challenge people to take at least one open-minded look at the gospel.

When I gave my resignation statement on 16 June 2017, I implied that I was making a sacrifice; that I was giving up the leadership because I had got myself into a situation where I had to choose between continuing in that role and being faithful to Christ.

I didn't realize that the true cost was to come later. I felt the loss of the leadership but, at the time, it was compensated for by my sense of freedom and of having done the right thing. The loss that I have experienced since then was the loss of reputation, standing and even dignity. A loss that costs is a loss that counts, and I value and appreciate that loss all the more now that I have had the opportunity to endure it, even to enjoy it.

We began this book in the air over England as the general election began in April 2017. Let's finish it in what we now call (rather absurdly) the Middle East, around 900 BC.

The Old Testament Book of Kings tells the story of the series of kings who ruled over ancient Israel and Judah. It's a miserable read. Most of the kings are dealt with by the author in a chapter or two. The account of each king's reign begins with a statement of how God viewed him – 'He did evil in the eyes of the LORD . . .' – before then giving us some details of that evil, normally involving idol-worship, greed or violence. In some rare cases we read that 'he did right in the eyes of the LORD'. Either way, at the end of the account of the king's reign, we read something very similar to this about King Manasseh of Judah in 2 Kings 21.17: 'As for the other events of Manasseh's reign, and all he did, including the sin he committed, are they not written in the book of the annals of the kings of Judah?'

Manasseh was king for no fewer than 55 years. He fought wars, built towns, fortifications, roads and bridges, made countless decrees, sacked and appointed prime ministers, and presided over every aspect of society for over half a century. And yet all of this is dismissed in one short sentence. The rest of the preceding chapter focuses on Manasseh's relationship with God. Was Manasseh faithful to God, did he treat God as God, or did he put himself in God's place? Was he just and compassionate, or not? How was his character?

Manasseh scored disastrously on all of these by the way, but that's not my point. The point is that what human beings consider to be important (activities, ambitions and achievements) are of secondary importance – while the things that we tend to neglect and consider less important (character, integrity and our relationship with God) are of ultimate importance.

That is not to say that ambition and earthly achievements are to be viewed with contempt, but they are to be put into a broader and wiser perspective. And that is why I do not grieve for my loss of the leadership – which is the very definition of a footnote.

I am much more interested in my main story. How's yours looking?

Tyler's Story

A little story about learning to read in prison

It's probably my drinking that got me into prison. That and not having a proper job.

I wasn't bothered about school, but in prison I had a chance to join a reading group. The books are interesting but not too hard to read.

In one book, *Forty-six Quid and a Bag of Dirty Washing*, we read about Barry, a guy who got mixed up with a drug dealer, but has now just left prison. I saw how he had to make good choices every day – and fill in lots of forms – to stay out of prison. I don't want to end up back inside again, so I've decided that I'm not going to drink on my way home. I won't get home drunk before the evening's even started – that just makes me drink more. And I'm going to get better at reading so I can fill in forms when I get out.

Inspired by a true story. Names have been changed.

Help us to tell more stories like Tyler's. Support the Diffusion Fiction Project. Just £4.99 puts an easy-to-read book in prisoners' hands, to help them to improve their reading confidence while encouraging them to think about life's big questions. Visit www.spck.org.uk to make a donation or, to volunteer to run a reading group in a prison, please contact prisonfiction@spck.org.uk.